THE GREEK GODS AMONG US

By Michael Mahana

To Hermes, my constant companion

The Greek Gods Among Us

Table of Contents

NOTES ON THE TEXT

I will be alternating 'he' and 'she' throughout the text because the gods are not limited by gender. Women like Elizabeth 1, Margaret Thatcher, and Hillary Clinton are close to Zeus and men like Paris, Montgomery Clift, and Paul Newman are close to Aphrodite.

Italics represent phrases and words taken from the Greek. Capitals indicate specific and original Greek names of the gods.

INTRODUCTION

All good things come from the gods.
Ancient Greek saying

The ancient Greeks used to say that when two people are in love, there are four people in the room: the two humans and the two gods acting through them. They called anyone drunk *Another Dionysus,* after the God of Intoxication, because in that state you are not the same person you are when you are sober.

You are always possessed by a god or gods, even if it's just the normal waking self--the one we call Ego and the Greeks called Athena the Waking Goddess.

The advantage of personifying instead of conceptualizing mental states is that it lets you relate to them like people, rather than trying to figure them out, own them, or let them go. Humans have highly evolved social skills: the brain got bigger in order to help us manage our relationships, not to do mathematics. Those same social skills can be used to relate to our mental states in a way that concepts can never match, because concepts always refer back to a single, conceptualizing Self—a self that does not exist.

There is no Self. There are only selves. You can't take an MRI of the Self, only of various simulated behaviors. These selves are not part of some overarching Self. They are independent selves that appear singly or in various groupings, in response to various situations in life, like when you're at home, at the office, or with a lover, a neighbor, or a friend.

Consciousness evolved with the brain, adding selves with each adaptation instead of appearing all at once in humans. Our emotions have parallels in other animals, something that anyone with a pet has known all

1

Introduction

along. The difference between us and other animals is that we have *more* instincts, not *fewer* instincts—or selves.

As the Greeks said, *nothing happens without the gods*. They are the very shape of experience.

The Greeks were on to something. Evolutionary Psychology states that our multiple selves compete, form alliances, deceive each other, and manipulate us to shape our behavior—just like the gods. These 'evolved responses' are predisposed in the brain like apps in a cell phone, but they are always shaped outwardly by culture. The gods of a culture define the personas and behaviors used by the people in that culture. They provide the invisible frameworks that act like windows onto the world, showing how to process experience and how to behave in different situations.

Western culture rests on two pillars: the Judeo-Christian tradition and the Classical tradition of Greece and Rome. The Judeo-Christian tradition is monotheist--meaning, somwhat paradoxically, that it has two gods—God and Satan—one god to worship and another to battle. This duo reconfigures today as Ego/Id and Self/Unconscious. In the monotheist tradition, there is always some superior single Self, floating on a hostile sea of unconsciousness or negativity. There is always a built-in longing to resolve this conflict, rather than to refine it, usually through some horrible conflagration like Armageddon.

Greek mythology has long been recognized as an ancient psychology, yet even Archetypal Psychology, which is completely based upon the Greek myths, retains the single Self. James Hillman, the founder of the Archetypal school, insisted on the independence of the gods but never recognized them as ideal selves, preferring a more mystical relationship between them and the supposed 'Self' he inherited from Carl Jung. However, when freed from the encumbrance of the single self, the Greek gods offer a perfect match to the operations of the mind. The Greek gods provide a remarkable behavioral repertoire that we can adapt to make the most of any situation in life.

Everything is behavior. Inner speech is behavior, thinking is behavior, meditating is behavior. It all happens in the brain and it can all be observed in MRIs. The answer does not lie within, because there is no 'within'. Everything is 'outside'. You will never meet a 'Self' on the sidewalk, but you will always interact with multiple selves. It's time to set aside the single Self with its neuroses, its bottomless need for attention, and its longing for a final resolution. The Greek gods offer ideal selves that are both traditional and flexible, with no requirement for belief, confession, or humiliation. All they require is desire—or Eros.

You already live this way. When you go to the office, you perform a vestment ceremony of putting on your business clothes so you can don the professional persona for the office. You put on workout clothes for another persona at the gym. You shower, dress, and have a cocktail before a date because you know that no one wants to date the person you were at the office. Tiny adjustments in your smile, posture, and tone of voice indicate the subtle changes of persona you adopt to greet a neighbor, a family member, or a lover. You use screen names to adopt new personas online. The sense of self changes whenever you become absorbed in a book, movie, or television show.

These selves seem invisible because you're so busy looking through them at the world. The many selves conspire to present a seamless reality, the same way you never stop to ask what your left eye is looking at. According to Daniel Dennett, our consciousness is "gappy" and contains a lot less than people think is there. No bell rings when you fall asleep, drive without thinking about it, or become impassioned during sex. There are no outlines in experience like in a painting by Manet--and that's the point. We confuse the smoothness of consciousness with the idea of a single Self, a self that does not exist.

Introduction

The Greek gods offer a way to recognize the various selves coming and going, which helps to organize experience in the most adaptive way possible. Learning to recognize the various selves is like learning to hear the under- and overtones of a plucked guitar string—tones that may have been 'silent' before they were pointed out to you. The gods provide a better set of metaphors for finding your way through the world than Self, Ego/Id, Unconscious, and all the host of complexes and neuroses. Seen as interpersonal selves, the Greek gods are perfectly consistent with Evolutionary Psychology, for they unite the 'inside' with the 'outside' by describing shared, culturally defined motivations and behaviors.

Look at your lover sleeping next to you sometime. Do you know that person? Does she even know that person? Or is the self you know and love a million miles away? Where has Aphrodite gone, and who is lying next to you?

You don't fall asleep: MRI's show that upon falling asleep, the waking self (Athena) simply dissolves, only to reappear upon waking. The reason dreams are hard to remember is that *you* didn't have them. The dream self (Hades) had the dreams, and you can usually only remember the ones that were going on when it walked past the waking self (Athena) on its way out the door. *You* may forget your dreams, but every detail remains intact when that dream comes back to you, sometimes years later.

We've all had the experience of being able to do something the first time and then not being able to repeat the performance because we became too 'self-conscious'. That's because the wrong self took credit for the action and the self who actually did it went away unnoticed and unappreciated--and perhaps offended at the slight. We've all had a word 'on the tip of the tongue' only to have that word present itself while we're in the middle of doing something else. That's because another self went to work while our attention was diverted.

The Greeks would try to befriend that other self, to thank him and encourage him to do it again. If they didn't know which god was involved,

4

they'd address *One of the Stronger Ones.* They constantly sought to befriend the gods in order to share in their gifts and to attain *Arete,* or Excellence, which was a religious virtue among the Greeks. Excellence can apply to any sphere of human activity, whether in art, business, parenting, or cooking. The Greeks considered Excellence to be the principle joy and meaning of life, for it allows us to *know what it is like to be a god for a time.* Without the gods, we are just *disgusting bellies,* for *only the gifts of the gods make life worthwhile.*

Excellence is easy to recognize when athletes and performers take to the field or stage. It's as if they become someone else. Pianists spin their fingers faster than anyone consciously could, as if listening to the score instead of playing it. Baseball players pass the ball as quickly as thought. An Olympic diver pauses at the end of the diving board as if praying—his face changes, and it is as though someone else performs the jump. And a good actor seems to become the character he is playing, leaving his 'real' self far behind.

Performers and athletes fascinate us because they show what it means to have multiple selves. We instinctively recognize in them our own uncanny potential. Immersed in what they are doing, they seem strangely removed at the same time. Their perfect actions embody the Zen idea of 'flow'. They are like the Greek statues: in the midst of throwing the discus, the athlete appears to be in a state of contemplation, as if observing the experience rather than controlling it. Tests show that Michael Phelps is completely relaxed while he competes, swimming efficiently and without any wasted movement. As James Hillman would say, he is "conscious and unconscious at the same time", or as the Greeks would simply say, *he has befriended a god.*

When you go on a diet, just who is telling whom not to eat? The reason diets don't work is that the fat self has become hard-wired into the brain as another *me.* It is *One of the Stronger Ones,* like being 'an alcoholic' even after years of sobriety. Neuronal assemblages—the

Introduction

patterns of brain activity that resemble road-kill on MRIs—don't ever go away, but they can be countered by new patterns of behavior. in this way, one god modifies another by providing a counter-balance, rather than eliminating it altogether.

Our monotheism and its single self make us seek answers in singularity and binary choices. We create our own demons and neuroses by denying selves who simply want our attention, saying, 'I mustn't even think that' or fighting a mood so much that it gets angry with us and exaggerates its worst aspects, like a friend we are constantly belittling. Our presumption of a single self makes us overlook the uncanny independence of the selves by treating them as 'parts of me', which is a selfish idea of friendship.

The Greeks said to *honor all the gods*. Trying to eliminate contradictions or let go of hang-ups is not only misguided—it's positively rude. Every point of view, mood, and image has a place in the psyche, and it is far easier to cultivate new personas and capacities than to fight whoever is already *me*.

You can counter the fat self by cultivating a friendship with Artemis, who is your health and independence, by doing things she likes—like running or being out of doors--and getting into her mindset while you do it. If you have problems with food, you don't help yourself by hating food, eating fake food, or counting calories. That offends Demeter, the beloved goddess of shared meals partaken with gratitude. Food should be a source of pleasure, not anxiety. You can cultivate a friendship with Demeter by eating healthy, delicious food, eating it slowly, and enjoying it alongside other people, so that eating is a shared experience instead of something stolen, furtive, and hurried.

The Greek gods give you images to hang onto so that you have a slim self waiting for you when you stop spending so much time with the fat self. The gods provide a cultural template for experience that helps you complement selves that need a little help and counter those who threaten to

6

take over your life, like an addiction. Each god balances out the others by adding his own virtues and curbing the others' excesses. In the Greek view, balance is achieved not by standing still as in the Eastern traditions but by going in all directions at once like a dancer in arabesque.

The many selves are *gods* and *immortal* because they reside in everybody. Even the mortal self—the one the Greeks personified as Psyche—is a god because we all have one. Psyche is the human being that things happen to and the one who suffers, like Jesus or Mary. James Hillman called her "the *me-ness* of *me*." Psyche provides a good home base, but she is still just one self among many and not all-encompassing. The other gods see her, too, 'from the outside'.

Each god rules his or her own province of the psyche and each desires to live through your experience. The gods are selfish and don't care about the consequences to you, just like Richard Dawkins' selfish genes . Aphrodite would have you sleep with one person after another and Hestia the Homebody would have you play the old maid. Psyche--the mortal human being—pays the price. If a man killed another in ancient Greece, the question of insanity would never arise. Of course he was insane, because Mars Insanus or Ares the Killer possessed him at the time. The man is not responsible for what the gods made him do. He retains his dignity--but he has to pay the penalty.

The gods can take any shape, according to the ancient maxim. You can recognize the gods in anything you can personify-- in yourself, in others, and in events. The gods reside in the meaning of the experience. For instance, Aphrodite is sex and love personified, and your relationship to her is your love life and your idea of beauty. She is the love story in novels, she is all the lovers in your life, and she is *maklozenae*--the wanton atmosphere of New Year's Eve and Valentine's Day. Above all, Aphrodite is an individual in her own right, and not just a concept or category. The Greek gods were people first, just like Jesus, and they were knowable within experience.

Introduction

The gods are often keyed to location: the office, the highway, the gym, or the beach. Our multiple selves evolved during the Pleistocene in response to various environmental challenges, such as male competition, female mating choice, the upholding of group norms, and self-sacrifice for the sake of shared genes. You might think nothing of wearing a bathing suit at the shore but you would be mortified to wear one at the bank, because there are different gods there. However, if you're at the beach when you get a phone call telling you that you have just won the lottery, the gods of the good luck and the news stand front and center while the gods of the beach are only 'in the room', because the gods dwell in the meaning of the experience.

They lurk in conflicts and desires. If you get an enticing job offer overseas, Athena the Professional, Hera the Social Climber, and Hermes the Opportunist might be all for it, but Hestia the Homebody and Demeter the Family may not want you to move, so you might work out a deal where you take the job and sublet your home for a couple of years to try to keep everybody happy. The Greeks were always making deals with their gods. In fact, they would more admire someone who smoked one cigarette a week than someone who quit them altogether. Nevertheless, the gods act freely and cannot be forced, just like people.

Whenever you say, *I*, you are speaking for a specific group of selves, including the roles other people play in each situation. We bring ever-changing configurations of selves to the meeting of *you* and *me*, depending on which behavior is needed. We also share selves, for instance, when we listen to music or get caught up in stock market bubbles, fads, and war fever. Instead of a never-ending story about *me*, the Greek gods frame experience as an archipelago of selves like the map of Greece, which is why it seems like 'it's been no time at all' since you were at the gym, or at the office, or with that friend you haven't seen for years.

This is a radically different way of framing experience than the way to which we are accustomed. The single Self requires us to think in terms of concepts--concepts like guilt, stress, or responsibility. These formless Titans are difficult to imagine clearly because *they are unlike men or gods in shape.* The Classical tradition uses personification rather than concepts as a mode of thought, like when we say 'this job is killing me', 'my heart goes out to you', or 'it was a cruel winter'. Concepts arose when the names of the gods were forgotten, so that Athena Judgment or Athena Wisdom became simply 'judgment' and 'wisdom'.

The Greeks considered even gods with conceptual names like Peace or Justice as individuals first, as in 'Justice had a bad day.' The gods are like characters in a novel or a movie that you can see from the outside and feel from the inside at the same time. The gods are knowable within experience, and this knowledge brings joy, help and meaning.

The monotheist god does not want to be known. He resents images because he wants to be nowhere in particular but everywhere at once. The monotheist god requires its followers to turn a blind eye to reality and to the world in which we evolved in favor of some imaginary, future world where nothing ever happens. Monotheist religions are careful not to discuss how you'll spend all that time up there because they know how ridiculous it all is. Besides, if you want to fly around bathing in white light you should've been born a fruit fly, not a human being.

The Greeks spoke about the Beautiful and the Ugly, not about Good and Evil—a word with no parallel in their language. To the Greeks, every mood and behavior needed a statue—an ideal shape to give it form and beauty. Impulses were not to be fought but to be shaped and then related to, preferably as a friend. Their viewpoint is deeply conservative in the original sense of the word, for it works with what is already there.

Greek religion was not a religion as we are accustomed to thinking about them. There was no dogma, no caste of priests, and no requirement for belief. Even the Greeks did not so much believe in their gods as they wanted to be like them: to be alluring like Aphrodite, a leader like Zeus, or pragmatic like Athena. The Greeks knew they were dealing with

Introduction

metaphors, for *the realms of the gods and of men must remain separate*. Saying that you 'believe in Aphrodite' is as silly as saying you 'believe in sexuality'. No one cared about conflicting stories about the gods, because everyone is different in Paris than in Kansas.

The Greeks lived in reality—just look at their statues. They saw the gods in actual moods and capacities and in the press of real circumstances. And they sought to attain Excellence as the best way to know the gods in the here and now, not in some fantastic, endless future life. *Use it well* was the only advice they gave about life, for we each have our own particular relationships to the gods. That is the nature of our individuality.

Thinking of Aphrodite as a person instead of as a concept allows you to relate to her rather than be responsible for her—and Aphrodite is notoriously irresponsible. You do not choose whom you are attracted to: Aphrodite does the choosing for you, just as she pulls Helen by the hair and forces her to run off with Paris, starting that terrible war at Troy.

If your love life is disappointing and all you do is complain about it like Hera the Nagging Spouse, you are not bound for a night of passion. The person complaining is not the person your lover once found so appealing, and you would do better to try to become that other person again. Rather than staring in the mirror and saying, 'my love life is terrible,' you can say, 'Aphrodite has been giving me a hard time,' or even 'Aphrodite's been a bitch lately'. Then you can go do something about it. You can go to the hairstylist--not for the sake of your self-esteem but to practice feeling pretty like Aphrodite and to do things she likes in the way she likes to do them. Befriending Aphrodite can be as simple as picking up an apple at the grocery store the way Aphrodite would do, not to search for its imperfections like Apollo but to admire its beauty. By acting like Aphrodite you attract her attention and soon enough, that mental state takes on a life of its own—if it so desires. The gods can't be forced, just like people, but they can be enticed.

10

The Greek Gods Among Us

They don't want you to kneel before them and plead like a sorry wretch, blurting out your problems and begging for mercy. You would avoid a neighbor who acted like that. The gods like people who act like them and display their own god-like dignity and virtues. The key is to stop trying to fix your self—a self that does not exist. Instead of changing your self you can change selves, like when Hera borrows Aphrodite's negligee in order to seduce Zeus, or when couples rediscover each other by going to the Caribbean and leaving their home selves behind, because the home self is Hestia and she's a virgin.

The disintegration of the single Self and its terrible shadows is upon us. Like the multiverse, the Greek gods beckon with a complexity and beauty suitable to our wondrous brain, by far the most complex object ever discovered. You can see the unformed fractured selves bubbling up in the culture: in screen names, in multi-tasking and alternate endings, in advertisements depicting your Las Vegas self, your depressed self, or your constipated self, in the voices and memes that express multiple feelings, and in roles assumed with irony.

The Greeks lived in a media age analogous to our own. In Ephesus, there were more statues than people, each setting the tone for behavior in a particular setting: the market, the home, or the academy. But the Greek statues had names, so you always knew whom you were dealing with. Any Greek shown the sexy blond model draped over the new Jaguar would instantly recognize Aphrodite helping Hermes to close a sale.

We are like the people in Plato's cave who stare at images projected from behind them by unseen agents, an image that uncannily foreshadowed television. Greek mythology is a map that shows the way out of the personal narratives that hem us in and provides a vast repertoire of other people to be.

This is a unique joy, because the greatest pleasure is to see your self as someone else. That is the way to be 'someone else' in the other

Introduction

sense, and to achieve Excellence. And the way to be someone else is to let someone else be *me*.

Friendship with the gods begins by recognizing them in ordinary experience, like a neighbor you pass on the sidewalk every day. Recognizing the gods requires thinking metaphorically and being willing to ask yourself at any moment, 'who would say or do this', 'which god(s) is acting in this moment,' or 'which self feels this way?'

During the war at Troy, Athena grants to her favorite soldier, Diomedes, the ability to tell a man from a god so that he won't engage a god in battle, because fighting a man possessed by Ares' bloodlust is insane: 'I have taken from your eyes the mist which before was upon them, so that you may well recognize god and man' (v. 127-128). Athena helps Diomedes recognize the gods in the shapes of ordinary people and events while other heroes recognize only mortals and particularities, unable to see through the fog of war that is the present moment.

The gods reside in the meaning of the experience. Who was Zeus to you in your past and who or what is Zeus to you today? When you stopped to chat with a neighbor was there a seductive whiff of Aphrodite, a nosy hint of Hera the Neighbor, or the practical concern of Athena the Citizen? Once you become familiar with the gods they're as easy to recognize as picking familiar voices out of a crowd or instruments out of an orchestra.

And so we turn to that Goddess of Culture, who presides over the treasure house of the Classical tradition, for the metaphorical vision that articulates our multiplicity and offers an escape from the tyranny of monotheism's Titanic self, with its perverse trajectory towards Armageddon. Once you become acquainted with the gods and their personas, you will see them in the mood that sweeps over you unannounced, in the facility with which you perform a certain task, in the breeze that moves your hair as you stand on the sidewalk thinking about a decision, and in the events of the day.

12

The Greek Gods Among Us

The gods like to be recognized, just like people. Their friendship makes life worthwhile. Our interpersonal selves are already here, watching and wondering what you're going to do next. Seek Excellence through them and *know, for a time, what it is like to be a god.*

Imagine what life would be like if you really used your brain.
Ancient Greek proverb

PART ONE: PSYCHE

Psyche provides the needed home base among our multiple selves. She is the mortal human, the person things happen to—the person the gods happen to. Without the gifts of the gods—which include *all good things*—you are Psyche, the human being. We all share this self so, paradoxically, Psyche is also a god and only one self among many. Some animals like elephants have a sense of mortality as well, so this is an evolved response that probably includes a number of cognitive adaptations.

Psyche is one of several gods that unify experience. Other gods that do this include Hera, who is your personal history, Athena, who is the normal waking self, Zeus, who is reality, and Apollo, who is your intellect. Gods that disrupt experience include Ares, who is violence, Poseidon, who is emotional turmoil, and Dionysus, who is intoxication. The gods weave into experience without announcing their presence, so the very gappiness of our consciousness is itself a unifying factor.

In Homer, *psyche* is discussed without reference to the character in the tale, but the meaning is the same: she is the fact of our mortality and the meeting point of the gods. Without the gods, there's not much to 'psyche', because without your brains, your health, your personality and all the rest, what's left anyway? Just the capacity to suffer. When you are stuck in a wheelchair with tubes sticking out and no idea who you are, you are still Psyche, the person things happen to—the person the gods happen to.

The tale of Eros and Psyche was a sacred text in the ancient world and merits a re-telling, for it is full of insights into this crucial self.

The Tale of Eros and Psyche

There once was a king with three lovely daughters, two of whom were pretty and married well, while the third was so amazingly beautiful that no one dared to ask for her hand. People came from all over to stare at her beauty, even calling her A Second Venus and forgetting that she was human like the rest of us.

The adoring crowds didn't make Psyche happy, but she

looked in the mirror and didn't contradict them.

This made the real Venus furious because people started neglecting her altars. She told her son, Eros, or Love, to make Psyche fall in love with the most horrible creature he could find. And then she kissed him--but in a very un-motherly way.

When Eros saw Psyche, one of the arrows in his quiver pricked him and it was love at first sight. He had the Oracle tell her family to leave her in a wedding dress on a high cliff where she would meet the monster destined to devour her.

Psyche resigned herself to her fate, telling the weeping crowd that they should have despaired when they were calling her a goddess. With that, she leaped off the cliff--but a gentle wind caught her and landed her in a hidden valley before a palace. There, unseen voices spoke and sang to her all day and invisible helpers tended to her every need while she awaited her dreaded bridegroom that night.

Eros came in with the darkness and transformed Psyche's life into a dream of perfect love, although she didn't know what her lover looked like or even his name.

Psyche longed to reassure her family that she was all right, but Eros warned her to forget about them. When she insisted, her two sisters were transported by the same gentle breeze down to the palace.

At first they were glad to see their sister alive, but they quickly grew jealous and suspected that Psyche had married a god, who might even make her immortal, too.

By the second visit, they learned she was pregnant and hatched a plot against her. They told Psyche that her lover was a dragon who took his real shape at night while he slept beside her and advised her to check him out with the oil lamp, but to keep a dagger ready in case he attacked her.

When Psyche held up the lamp she was transfixed by Eros' beauty--his sweet face, his downy cheeks, his divine young body with lovely white wings folded behind his back. As she stared, the hot oil betrayed her by dripping onto Eros' shoulder and waking him in pain, only to see Psyche crouching over him with a knife. He flew off while she clung to him past the high cliff, where she lost hold and fell to the grass.

Distraught, Psyche wandered to her sisters' homes. She told each of them that Eros wanted to marry her instead, so they both threw themselves off the cliff to their deaths, because there was no gentle breeze waiting this time.

Psyche went to the temples of Ceres (the Roman Demeter) and Hera, but the priestesses there told her she had to deal with Venus, since she was the one she had offended.

Venus received her in her temple like the Wicked Witch, berating Psyche and having her slaves, Habit, Worry and Sadness, beat her mercilessly. Then she gave her a series of impossible tasks.

The first was to sort a huge pile of seeds. Psyche despaired at the size of the pile, but the ants felt sorry for her and sorted the seeds for her. Next, she had to fetch the golden wool off of a flock of man-eating sheep. She was suicidal until a reed in the stream told her to wait for the sheep to take their noonday nap and to collect the wool from the brush nearby.

Her third task was to collect a flask of water from the Styx, the terrible river which surrounds the Underworld. When Psyche saw the high, craggy gorge and the deadly waters, she prepared to jump to her death. But then the eagle of Jove (the Roman Zeus) came to her and carried the flask to the falls even as the waters themselves told him to turn back.

Venus was furious and suspected that some god was helping Psyche. She gave her a little box shaped like a coffin and told her to go see Hades' wife, Proserpina (the Roman Persephone) in the Underworld and get some of her magic cream of *Invisible Beauty*—or *the Beauty That Cannot Be Seen.* This is deeper than Venus' physical beauty, because Persephone is the Self Who Loves Death—she's married to him—who wants you to live an authentic life.

Psyche knew no human could go to Hades and come back alive, so she climbed a nearby tower and got ready to jump.

But then the tower spoke to her and gave her directions to

Hades via the back roads. It told her how to act in Hades--not to get distracted by any begging souls, not to presume or to accept any honors, and not to open the box of Invisible Beauty.

Psyche followed the instructions, refusing the fancy chair that was offered her in Hades and taking the lowest stool instead, and accepting only the humblest of refreshments. She listened patiently to the Underworld gods speaking around her—the selves that seek your attention—and she only answered when she was asked, and then fully and appropriately and without calling attention to herself or presuming any special status.

Proserpina gave her the box of Invisible Beauty and sent her on her way, but the temptation to win back Eros by putting on some of the Invisible Beauty cream was too great—and Psyche fainted into a deathlike swoon.

Meanwhile, Eros was at his mother's house recuperating from the burn on his shoulder and missing Psyche.

With permission from both Zeus and Venus, he swooped down to Hades, wiped the deadly cream from Psyche's face and brought her up to Olympus, where he made her his Queen and himself King of the Gods forever. When their child was born, they named it Voluptas, or Pleasure.

Eros and Psyche

Eros is the god in any experience and Psyche is the mortal human being, the *me* that things happen to. *The gifts of the gods include all good things,* including your health, your mind, your body, your memory and sentience your feelings and sentience, your personal history—it's all on loan from the gods. As the Greeks said, *your life can be altered within a day, even within an hour,* such as through a car accident. Without the gods, Psyche is just a mortal body, *a disgusting belly.* Eros and Psyche are present whenever you hold both the actual and the metaphorical meaning in an experience—in other words, when you know what you are doing and who you are while you're doing it.

Not all experience requires Psyche. Not every moment

Part One: Psyche

requires you to bear your mortality in mind. You can read, have sex, or thread a needle without feeling mortal or having a clear idea which god is in charge. The gods can run the show. Psyche does not constitute another monotheism, nor is she anything more than another self among other selves. She is simply the sense of the person things happen to.

Psyche begins the tale without any sense of metaphor, without any detachment from herself or capacity to see beyond the pretty face in the mirror. She comes to believe the multitudes that proclaim her a second Venus, thinking things will go on this way forever. Yet she is sad and filled with emptiness. Other forces impinge on her literalistic reality because she is more than her physical beauty. She longs for meaning in life, as we have all evolved to do. This same longing draws the young Kore to pluck the strange, one hundred-petal crocus she marvels at in the field that is so strange, so otherworldly, and so uncanny in its beauty.

Eros is Spirit, while Psyche is *Soul*. Spirit seeks perfection. Eros tells Psyche to forget her family, because the Spirit urges you to leave the mess behind—the old neighborhood, the extra weight, or the guilt trip—and to be free like a god. He is the immortal life of our instincts, unchecked by Psyche's knowledge of human limitations.

Psyche is the Greek answer to Jesus and Mary. When we weep for them, we weep for our mortality. Personifying the mortal individual as Psyche allows you to separate from it and to see it as another self among selves, common to us all. Psyche is the self who dies. That is the paradox of her divine mortality, just like Jesus.

Psyche means Soul. The Soul wants you to be loyal to needs, symptoms, places, and people because they have meaning. She would have you stick with the mess of your life and to make something out of it, like people who write about the Holocaust or the AIDS epidemic rather than putting it behind them.

In the story, the Soul and the Spirit are lovers. The Greeks depict Eros bending down through the celestial spheres from his comfortable home of guarantees in order to be with his mortal Psyche. You do this when you get involved in life instead of rising above it, daring to love

18

and to be hurt, or to venture out and possibly fail rather than staying safe and apart from others.

Voluptas

Voluptas, or Pleasure, is the child of Eros and Psyche. She is the pleasure of human existence. The Greeks imagined the gods coming down from Olympus and visiting the Earth to experience human pleasures, not out of pity for wretched humans like Jesus. The Modernist Greek poet, Cavafy, depicted the gods coming down looking for sex.

Pleasure has a bad reputation in monotheism. Most religions long for some otherworldly pleasure, because human pleasures remind us that we are mortal animals. Hera lurks behind this attitude, because she is uneasy with the animalism of sex and imagines a self that is not contained by the body—a person that God/Zeus loves more than anyone else.

But whoever thinks that pleasure is piggish has a piggish idea of pleasure--and probably underestimates pigs as well. Pleasure can be artistic and spiritual, and it can include all the joys and suffering of life--and the fact that you'd do it all again if you could. Pleasure is deeper than personal happiness. It is greater than the good health and lack of stress that define happiness today. Taking care of someone you love who is dying is a pleasure if you really love her, despite the sorrow. Looking back at the years of caring for my dying loved ones, I feel grateful for having had the opportunity to serve the gods through them and to let them know they are truly loved.

Phanes Eros

Phanes Eros or Eros of the White Light is the inspiration that sets the heart on fire. The Athenians held a torch race in his honor every year, just as you may carry a torch for someone or for something in your life.

The old Orphic myths say that at the beginning of the world there was Chaos, followed by broad bosomed Earth, *Gaia*, and then *Phanes Eros*, Eros the White Light, imagined as a Cosmic Egg that hatches

19

Part One: Psyche

the world and all the gods. This Eros is the son of the mysterious goddess Night, *Nyx,* who is Mystery and the Unconscious and everything that you cannot know. Her brothers are Sleep and Death.

Eros is *Him of a Double Nature,* because he is the oldest and the youngest of the gods.

In the tale, Eros hides his identity from Psyche at first. There is a joy in not knowing everything about someone or even about yourself, for it allows you the freedom to change and to be other people. Eros flies off every night to be with Night and Chaos just as you dream and imagine freely, wandering with other selves in lands beyond your waking life.

The White Light of Eros shines in the darkness without illuminating it. His kind of love requires accepting people with all their faults instead of trying to change them. At the end of the tale, he wipes the poison from Psyche's face, overlooking her mortal vanity and accepting her as she is—flawed and human.

Eros the Deeply Desired

The *most beautiful of the gods* is shown in the artwork as a handsome and athletic young man wearing a crown of leaves and leaning against a tree like Adonis.

Eros the Golden Winged makes things mingle. His flowers announce the season of love. You are under his influence when you get entangled in life or go looking for adventure. Eros makes the world young again and keeps you young at heart when you're old. He is the wisdom of keeping a dirty mind into old age.

Identify too closely with him and you can become trapped in an adolescent dream of finding the One True Love or of being rich and famous for nothing in particular.

At the end of the story, Eros stands up to his mother in order to love Psyche. You do this when you give up the easy life of comfort and guarantees and take risks for the things you love, whether it's a passion, a political cause, or a dream.

The oldest depictions of Eros are raw, un-sculpted stones,

because love involves a good deal of projection and can take any shape. Eros has many genealogies because there are so many kinds of love.

When his father is Uranus the Sky, he is intellectual and homosexual love, like Plato's Academy and British schoolboys. When it is Hephaestus, Eros is the love of art and beauty. When it is Ares, he is the friend you would die for, like soldier comrades and blood brothers. And when it is Hermes, Eros Lord of the Gymnasia embodies the sheer pleasure of exercise and the beauty of the human form.

The Greek idea of love is darker than the Christian or Hollywood variety. To the ancients, love is not all positive and optimistic. Falling in love is a fall, not a promotion, because you realize that you and your lover will die one day and that the Fates delimit your time together.

Gravestones show Eros of Death flying downwards towards the dead soul. The Greeks said that to die is *to embrace Eros*. Eros Life After Death is everyone you have loved and lost, while Eros Joy of the Blessed Dead is your memory of them and your gratitude for their lives, which are engraved upon your soul and in your dreams as gods.

Cupid

The mischievous angel of Valentine's Day is romance, personified.

Cupid carries a bow and two kinds of arrows--golden arrows that inspire love and leaden ones that inspire disgust. His brothers are *Himeros.* Physical Desire, and *Anteros,* Unrequited Love. The latter is also a son of Ares the God of War, because he can cause you to seek revenge when you are rejected for another.

Artwork shows Eros playing with his friends *Pothos,* Longing, and *Penia,* Poverty/Neediness. These two often show up when Love is around. They may make you repeat that you love someone over and over again as if one self is trying to convince another self of the truth. Neediness is unquenchable because it comes from a god.

Cupid can heal the sick heart, but he is also a Holy Terror and a Dragon who crazes people with desires and obsessions. Cupid

21

bewitches the heart he would destroy, wrecking homes and wreaking havoc wherever he goes. An ancient Greek prayer begged Love *never to come by with murderous intent.*

He is the third force in a love affair--the force of attraction--and he can leave lovers behind wondering what happened, as in so many love songs. Blind Love fools even the wise, especially those who think they are past love and its insanity or worse--those who mock it.

The son of Iris the Rainbow and Zephyrus the West Wind naturally has a fickle nature. This boy decides the fate of lovers with a careless toss of the dice. He refuses to share his toys with his friend, Ganymede, because his love makes you want someone all to yourself. Cupid is playful and creative but also heedless and dangerous, because love can eat your heart away or turn you into a stalker.

Anima

Psyche is a two-sided god like Eros and Cronus and like some people. Anima is her young woman self, the one who stares in the mirror at the beginning of the tale identifying with her physical image. She is consciousness that doesn't know what it is.

The vague self is all potential and no substance. You're like her when you sit passively in front of the television, eating absentmindedly. Anima makes you feel like life is drifting and you're at the mercy of moods and unknown external forces. She resides in statements that begin with 'they say', and the passive acceptance of cliché behaviors like up-speak. Possession by Anima gives you the feeling that something is missing from your life, so you fill the void with food, shopping, or promiscuity—anything at all.

She is the soul as a fairy with butterfly wings flitting to harps and trembling Celtic voices—a picturesque, asexual creature like Tinker Bell without power or passion. Anima makes you prefer magic, ghost stories, and pipe dreams to real life with its gravity and consequences. She makes you feel mushy, half asleep, fearful or passive, as if life hasn't begun yet and nothing really matters. She brings apathy, boredom and indifference so that you find yourself in a television trance or hesitating like a deer peeking out from the edge of the woods. This passive self is dangerously vulnerable to cults and crazes like psychics, seducers, and spiritual or reactionary leaders who dominate their followers. Anima can drown you in food, fat, and addictions that make you self-absorbed and lower your awareness of the world.

In the beginning of the story, Psyche does not realize her effect upon others. They fall all over her while she stares in the mirror, feeling sad. Her fantasies and lack of connection to the real world lead her to believe the others when they tell her she is Another Venus, as if being young and pretty was her unchanging birthright.

Anima makes you like Psyche in that unreal palace surrounded by invisible voices. She robs you of irony and self-awareness by making you forget that the clock is ticking and that you are a human not a god. Anima prevents you from separating from your mental states and makes you relate to others as if they were gods and not merely humans presenting various roles in your life.

Psyche finally comes to know reality through the treachery of her sisters, who seek to destroy her. These wicked stepsisters are 'frenemies' who conduct friendships while wishing the worst for you. Psyche learns that love is not mere familiarity and habit. Love depends upon real actions based in compassion and good will towards the mortal person or animal or building or ancient tree that has a right to exist for its own sake. Psyche comes to the realization that love is not everything and cannot solve everything, especially love that hides manipulation.

Echo

Echo is a variation of Anima, in this case, a nymph who couldn't stop talking. Zeus set her to distract Hera with conversation while he carried on an affair behind her back. Hera punished Echo by allowing her only to repeat the last words spoken to her.

Some say she lost her body after Narcissus scoffed at her and she faded with yearning, or that she refused to have sex with Pan, who crazed his shepherds into tearing her apart, leaving only her voice.

Echo is emptiness. You can see Echo in people who get their behavior and speech from television sitcoms or who follow fads and think they are acting authentically. The empty self is an extreme extrovert who lives the kind of un-reflected life that Socrates said was not worth living--but then, he was another Apollo and above it all.

You are like Echo when you cling to people like an over eager mother, a celebrity follower, or a fag hag, trying to live through someone else's identity.

Narcissus

This child of a river god and a nymph was so handsome that his mother took him to Teiresias the Seer to ask whether he would live to old age.

He answered, *only if he never knows himself.*

By the time he turned sixteen, lovelorn men and women were following him everywhere. Narcissus spurned them all. When Echo professed her love he told her he'd rather die than love her.

One neighbor, Ameinias, annoyed him so much that he sent him a dagger, with which Ameinias dutifully stabbed himself, saying *may he be consumed by love and be denied the one he wants.*

One day, Narcissus stopped by a beautiful spring in the woods and leaned over to drink when he saw the image of a beautiful boy looking back at him and fell in love. He couldn't turn away. Narcissus wasted away staring into the pool until all that was left was the waterside flower that bears his name.

The medieval Church said that Narcissus was punished for vanity and psychology has presumed the same, but that is not how the Greeks understood it. When the gods turn someone into a flower, a tree or a stream, it means that person is a lasting image of an experience common to all of us.

The story of Narcissus is not about the dangers of self-love. After all, he thought he was looking at someone else, not at his reflection.

He was not self-absorbed--he was absorbed in an image like any dreamer or artist. He was not narcissistic in the way it is commonly understood.

Narcissus is the lover of images. He is the love of dreams and images that takes you out of the world.

You are like him when you prefer images to real life. He is who you are when you are absorbed in books and movies and live so much in images that you seem self-contained and cut off from others. He is the artist who is completely absorbed in his work.

Psyche

Psyche is the Mortal Self.

Several times she contemplates suicide, for she lives close to death. Only by accepting that death is final do humans have a real reason to be kind to one another and to respect the world. Religions that promise immortality pose as loving but act with cruelty, laying waste to the world and always seeking to punish those who are different, whom they consider to be 'the animals'.

Psyche lives in an enchanted world where people matter, the old and the poor matter, animals matter, old trees matter, and meaningful places matter. It's the Arcadian world of the Minoans or Henri Rousseau where humans belong, not one that they dominate. Psyche talks to the ants, to the tower, to the rushing waters because Psyche gives us the sense that things have a right to exist even if they can't be turned to profit.

Paradoxically, a life lived close to the soul doesn't feel like contentment. There's too much suffering and sorrow in the world for that and too much cruelty and indifference. Psyche makes you feel incomplete, inferior, and full of loss for all the people and things that die, including yourself. And she fills you with love, for Eros loves Psyche as a mortal being, and not only for her virtues and gifts.

In the tale, she changes from an unknowing thing to a mortal goddess through a series of tasks. First, she must sort the seeds, which is a lesson in sifting through what is important in life and not acting on every impulse. Second, she must gather fleece from man-eating sheep, which means she must learn not to take things personally. Instead of confronting the sheep directly, she gathers their wool from the reeds, which you do when you learn to befriend someone without having to like everything about him or leaving yourself vulnerable to his worst traits.

Third, she must fill a flask with the deadly water of the *Styx*, the dreaded river of Hades, whose name means Hate. Her helper, the eagle, flies over the river teaching her the objectivity that comes when you see things in the context of death, an ever present peril that awaits in the treacherous waters below.

Psyche learns the importance of hate and is no longer fooled by her sisters' appeal to personal love. In Hades, she listens carefully to the people around her, who are the gods and instincts that tell her what they want. You are like her when you pay attention to dreams and impulses and let them speak for themselves instead of fighting them or trying to control them, just like people.

Psyche the Night Moth

Psyche is also the name of a strange moth that flies at night. This may seem unusual to us because we think of the soul as human and ending at the body. The problem with thinking that way is that it turns the rest of the universe into a meaningless void. If animals, places, trees and buildings have no soul, we might as well tear them down or use them up. Thinking of the soul as only human makes us act like Psyche's wicked stepsisters.

In the Classical view, *you* don't have a soul. The soul has *you*. The soul may choose things for you that you would never choose, like cancer, suffering, or a broken heart. Psyche the Moth includes the vast areas of the brain that precede the human reaches.

The Greek spoke about the psyche as if he was talking about a friend, telling a lover that *you are the master of my psyche* and going drinking *to give my psyche a good time.*

And yet it is a strange and inhuman thing--a giant moth and not a pretty butterfly.

26

Just look at your hands and feet. How strange they are. How uncannily they move with their own intelligence like insects or as if someone possessed them. The Greek idea places the Soul before or beneath human identity. The soul demands you fall to sleep every night to dream and nourish on the images in the Underworld and thereby escape the tyranny of your waking human identity.

Queen Psyche

Psyche's last task is to go to the Underworld to fetch a jar of the mysterious Invisible Beauty cream from Persephone, Hades' Queen. There she acts humbly, *not assuming any honors, sitting on the lowest stool and answering in fullness and sincerity whatever is asked of her*, as instructed by the talking tower.

This shows us how to behave around the gods, which are our own instincts: be humble, completely mortal, and pay attention. There's no time for self-importance or identification, only for listening and obeying politely and fully. You can either cooperate with the gods and 'make it look good' or you can refuse and suffer the consequences. That is our freedom and only that.

The meaning of the cream of Invisible Beauty was fiercely debated in ancient times. Hillman calls it "psychological beauty", because it belongs to Psyche and is a gift from Persephone, the wife of Hades and the Self Who Loves Death, so it is somehow tied to knowing you are mortal. As you are dying and in full Persephone mode, you will look back at your life as if at a stranger's, for you are leaving that person forever. The cream goes on your face, which is your *eidelon*, the image of you that remains in other people's memories when you die.

Ignoring the warnings, Psyche opens the jar and applies a daub hoping it will make her irresistible to Eros. Then she swoons into a deathlike sleep.

At this point, Eros comes to the rescue and wipes the cream off her face, accepting her faults and loving her despite her imperfections. Then he brings Psyche up to Olympus as his bride to reign over all the

Part One: Psyche

gods.

The meaning of Psyche's swoon was a subject of fierce debate in ancient times. Queen Psyche is the personified self. You are like her when you see your mortal self from the 'outside'--as someone else in the psyche, the self who happens to be mortal. Seeing life this way puts you in the position of Eros loving Psyche, and it is the ultimate act of personification. This makes your soul steadfast and ready for anything, including your own death. It is like switching to the third person singular even when you are saying, *I*.

It's as close as paganism gets to immortality. When '*I*' become an image like the rest of the gods, then "*I* am not real", as Hillman said. Invisible Beauty is a kind of non-recognition that sees life as a strange and poignant dream about someone else, like a character in fiction or a friend you remember from long ago.

You may be a proud athlete and that person feels like *me*. But when you are old and unable to walk, you will look back at old photographs as if you were looking back at someone else, someone gifted with athleticism--a friend of Ares and Artemis and other sporting gods who forgot about you long ago. Looking at photos of your younger self has the same effect. When I was a teenager, I had photos taken in which I was addressing my older self from my youth.

After years of war and death, the key characters in Homer see life as a dream that happened to someone else. Priam says of Hector, *Now take my son—or was he all a dream?* Helen of Troy says, *There was a world…or was it all a dream?* She talks about herself as though she was talking about someone else: *shameless whore that I was.*

Odysseus does the same thing: *Odysseus. There was a man, or was he all a dream?* And old Nestor looks back at his youth: *So, such was I in the ranks of men, or was it all a dream?* Some characters even say, *or was I all a dream?*

He does and he does not. I am and I am not. This is uncanny speech.

As the poet Theognis wrote:

The Greek Gods Among Us

Acting, I did not act.
Completing, I did not complete.
Achieving, I did not achieve.
Doing, I didn't.

It is startling to read this in an ancient text. It doesn't mean that 'nothing matters', as in Eastern spirituality. 'Life is a dream' does not mean that 'life is an illusion', because that is a judgment.

This is the dreamy world of *The Odyssey*, *The Tempest*, and Botticelli's *Primavera*. All is numinous and animated, real and yet imaginary, like the terrible but comforting world of fairy tales. Selves come and go, grouping to form alliances and coalitions but also fighting and deceiving each other, just like people.

They are people. There is no ghost in the machine. There is no theater where some overarching Self resides, watching the show. There is only the drama of the many selves--- the stories about the gods.

Reality is Zeus, but reality is not a prison. It is just that god's point of view. As the Greeks said, *you do not have only one fate.* If you get brain cancer or die alone on the highway, that's not all you are nor what your life was all about.

Death is not a summing up but a falling apart, as one by one the gods walk away from you. There is no life flashing before your eyes, only a void, as if the film just ran out of the reel. The sexual self, the married self and the teen self may die before you actually die as you lose those capacities and become a remnant of the people you once were. The last thing left is your mortality--and that is what it means to be human. When Psyche swoons, Eros comes to her side as the tearful, parting embrace in death of all you have loved and the person you were—as if it were all a dream about someone else.

Moving On

Psyche personifies and lives in a world full of subjective others. She personifies the ants, the tower, and the water, and they all come to her aid. You can befriend any mood or talent by treating it like a person, because that's exactly what it is.

To love Psyche, you have to personify yourself as well. Accept yourself with all your faults the way Eros accepts Psyche despite her vanity. You don't have to change because Psyche doesn't have to change. Stop 'working on' yourself and learn how to change selves instead.

If you want to be confident like Ares, let Ares be confident for you. Get a clear image of the god and find instances in your past when you acted like him, however faintly. Then begin to befriend Ares by giving him symbolic gifts and doing things he likes to do as if he was the one doing them. Once your friendship is established, you can ask Ares to act on your behalf. Confidence resides in the psyche and that person is in there somewhere.

Maybe you are afraid of success. There's no need to get over it. Let Psyche have her fears and learn to call upon Athena *Nikephoros*, Athena Who Leads to Victory. Let her be the successful one, not you. Leave Psyche out of it and love her with all her fears. This is easy to imagine. If you can't imagine it, imagine Athena imagining it for you.

Psyche leads to all of the gods because she is the self who personifies. You can visit any god by seeing yourself as a mortal first and accepting that self with love, for that is Psyche and she is loved by Eros. Then pay attention to that other self, the god you are visiting. See traces of that god in your experience, or if you're starting from scratch, make ritual gestures to that god and begin an acquaintance. Slowly a basis for friendship can develop. Admire that god in others. Encourage it and you can be a friend of a friend. Then you can eventually ask that god for favors—namely, the favor of possessing you and living through you for a time.

PART TWO: GODS OF ACTION

These gods help you to bring things into reality and to act in the present moment.

Athena is the normal self and the common idea of the Ego. The God called *Mind and Thought* is the rational self--the voice in your head urging self-restraint and telling you what to do. Her variations include the professional self, the citizen, the colleague, and the co-worker. Athena is the ability to plan, strategize, and judge wisely.

Zeus is Reality and the World, personified. Zeus *Cosmetas* is the Order of the World. You honor Zeus when you focus on reality and seize the opportunity to change it. Zeus grants courage, the greatest of virtues because it enhances all other virtues. Zeus is especially pleased when you stand up for human dignity and improve the world in some way.

Herakles is the Hero and the sense of having a mission in life. The adopted son of Hera shares her feeling of being special, but he is so competitive he resents the success of others. Herakles wants you to act first and think later, but his effort and ambition can be put to good use when directed by Athena's reason and strategy.

ATHENA

The Bright-Eyed Goddess is the normal waking self. She is the Ego, as it is commonly understood.

She is not Apollo's intellect. Athena is bright-eyed wakefulness, and her priestesses are Lustrous, *Auge,* and Bright, *Aithra,* because brightness is as much a question of attitude as it is of intelligence. If you dress well, sit up straight, and pay attention you will come across as bright. The cult of Athena Head Born, *Tritogeneia,* centered on the Akropolis—the rock, *athene,* which is the geologic head of Athens, where the markets and the main temples were situated.

Statues show a fine, well-built woman in flowing robes or a simple dress with a severe, masculine hair-do and broad, strong features— but she is anyone who looks reliable and trustworthy and is not overtly sexual. Athena's nose and eyes display a famous, noble symmetry. She looks thoughtful and stately as she leans on one foot or rests her weight on a spear or shield. Her eyes were inlaid gems. In many images, the helmet makes the head take up nearly half her height, showing that Mind and Thought *(Nous kai Dianoia)* are the concerns here.

Athena is never drunk, sexual, carried away, or asleep because those states take you out of your normal mind. She is the soul of sobriety and self-restraint. Athena helps you create an image at the office and in the neighborhood that inspires people to take you seriously. The Goddess of the Golden Mean is the law of averages and common sense applied to everyday life. She is ordinariness, which is really quite extraordinary considering the constant bombardment of the senses from all directions.

There is an advantage to thinking of your ego as a person rather than as a concept. Concepts refer back to a single, understanding self—the self of monotheism. Thinking of the Ego as a person instead of as a concept or 'a part of me'—a *me* that does not exist-- frees you to relate to it without identifying with it or feeling responsible for it. Personification spreads the *me* around and is the hallmark of Greek thought. It is a tactful and diplomatic way to relate to the other selves in the psyche. So let

Athena carry the Ego's load. You don't have to be responsible for it—you only need to relate to it. And for Athena, it's as light as a feather.

Athena Polymetis

Athena *of Many Minds* has you consult with friends and experts before making a final decision on anything. The Goddess of Counsel and Conscience is your inner narrator, telling you what to do and what not to do. When you are thinking, Athena *Noos kai Dianoia* is doing the thinking.

Zeus fathers her on the Titaness, *Metis,* or Craft/Bold Action. It makes sense that the Goddess of Wisdom and Strategy is the child of Reality and Craft/Bold Action. She is the self that helps you make your way through the world. This affair takes a bad turn when Zeus learns that Metis' son will exceed his father. Luring her to the couch during sex, he tells her it would be hot if she turned into a fly, and when she does so he swallows her. Now she gives him advice from his belly, like a gut reaction. The Greek reference to the stomach is telling: there are so many nerve endings around the abdomen that it is nicknamed *the second brain.* That's why a sudden bit of bad news can send you right to the bathroom.

Nine months later, Zeus rages and howls as he walks along the shores of Lake Tritonis with a horrible migraine. Hermes fetches Hephaestus to split open his skull with an ax. Out jumps Athena with a mighty shout, dressed in armor and shaking her spear. The Earth shakes at her war dance and then all is calm.

A precocious child like many of the gods, Athena never asks about her mother--but she does inherit her smarts. She is *Poly-Metis*, or Many-Minded, the inclination to consider all the angles before you act. This self is too complex to ever be simple and trusting. Athena knows the world is full of risks and secret agendas, and that it is not an ideal world of justice or love. Athena casts a suspicious eye on everyone and doesn't take events literally.

Her festival, the Panathenaea, celebrated her birthday with athletic, equestrian, and musical contests, along with readings of Homer.

33

Athena

While the more famous Olympic Games offered mere laurel wreaths of glory and free meals in one's home town forever, this festival paid serious money, like 60 jugs of olive oil for the first prize in the men's footrace— because Athena wants material proof and results more than glory.

Every year, the women of Athens wove a birthday robe, or *peplos,* embroidered with images of the War of the Gods against the Giants, because Athena emblemizes the triumph of reason over monstrosity. Eventually, the robe grew to the size of a sail and was fastened to a ship as a tribute to Athens' navy.

Athena of Civilization

Athena is your inner grown up. In the Greek model, you don't need to get rid of your Inner Child to be grown up. You only need to change channels to the ready-made adult within, for Athena is born into the world fully armed and with a mighty shout.

When Achilles readies his hand on his sword to strike Agamemnon in revenge for stealing his captive bride, Athena pulls him by the hair from behind. When he turns to look into the eyes of the goddess, she says, "Follow me if you will," and he relents.

Athena is self-control imagined as obedience to someone else. Mighty enough to make the axle of her chariot creak and light enough to stand on a cloud, Athena is in charge when you show your strength by restraining yourself.

Athena doesn't want you to be overwhelmed by anything, especially by base instincts and emotions. You can see her battling Poseidon the Emotions whenever someone in an interview tries not to cry while describing some personal tragedy. You obey Athena when your head rules your heart.

Pericles, one of her champions, was a blueblood and bound by Athena's civic honor to act with distinction and humility. His gravity and justice earned him widespread admiration. One time, an enraged citizen followed him around town hurling insults all day. Pericles never answered

34

him but when darkness fell he sent his servant with a torch to light the man's way home.

The One Who Marshals the Troops doesn't enjoy fighting like Ares the God of War, but when she does have to fight she does so with strategy and decision. She bests the God of War twice in battle, for Ares is the fighting spirit while Athena is the battle plan and its execution. The One Who Gives Commands prevails because she doesn't lose her head in rage like he does.

Nevertheless, Athena admires Ares' courage and daring and tries to mold him into a good citizen and soldier. She promotes his manliness in her followers. At her festival, there was a contest for *manly excellence*, which weighed size, strength, and deportment in movement, voice, and gesture, like a butch contest in a leather bar.

What Athena doesn't like about Ares is his unreflecting rush to judgment and action. Athena would rather harness wildness than give in to it. This is why it is very Athenian to get young people involved in physical disciplines like marching bands and sports, channeling the lust for battle productively, as in the 'do sports not drugs' campaign.

A goddess, Athena Areia, combines the two. She gives the ability to make sense of events as they unfold, like thinking on your feet on the battlefield, during a corporate shakeup, or during a car crash. She is presence of mind, uniting Athena's judgment with Ares the Soldier's attention to the moment.

The Near Goddess

Athena is the Goddess of the Golden Mean--the law of averages applied to everyday life. She is ordinariness and the tendency to see a predictable pattern in events. She is the Normal Self, including its common sense and pragmatism. Distinct from Apollo the True Self and Hera the Personal Self, Athena knows it is wise to conceal one's thoughts and normal to tell white lies for the sake of politeness.

She is the balancing act of ordinary consciousness. We function best when we don't have too much information--just enough to glide along the rails--because you don't really need to see the hallway at night when you get up to go to the bathroom. You only see what is relevant and can glide along by force of habit.

One of the great paradoxes of Greek chauvinism is that their Ego is a woman. Perhaps the proud heroes would not yield so easily to a man. Athena is masculine for a woman and also a virgin, so she stands outside of sexual competition. She wants you to relate to others as a citizen, friend, neighbor or colleague—and to keep things 'normal' and not sexual. Athena gives a realistic self-assessment and brings awareness of your effect on others.

The Near Goddess is like the twin, transparent images of the nose in front of your face which no artist in all of history has ever thought of painting, yet everyone sees. She is perseveration: the ditties, repetitions, and martial counting in your head as you work through a task, as though the Master Weaver was numbering stitches in her work. The Greeks imagined her standing a little behind the individual and to the right, whispering in his ear and narrating events while planning the next action.

If you are unaware of this, that is precisely the meaning of her nearness. You wear the mask of normal consciousness so closely that you forget that it, too, is a god or distinct self. That's an advantage because it would be distracting to always be aware of normalcy as possession by a god.

The Greeks typically offered Athena shallow clay bowls as ritual gifts because hers is a horizontal kind of knowledge—general knowledge that gives you perspective and helps you set priorities. Athena champions the liberal arts and the many sided Athenian life, so to keep her happy you need to keep learning into old age.

This self knows it is healthy to change personas, because the Goddess of the Golden Mean wants proportion in life, analogous to Apollo's *nothing in excess*. She tells you, 'enough of that, now try this.' If you are brilliant like Apollo, don't be brilliant all the time. If you are an artist like Hephaestus, don't be an artist all the time. Athena the Many-Counseled wants you to find room for all the selves in your portfolio.

36

This doesn't mean you have to spend an equal amount of time visiting each god because everybody specializes in one or two friendships with specific gods. Athena only asks that you visit other gods in the city of the soul. If you work all day as Athena the Professional, she wants you to go to the gym or walk through nature or take a nap to get some distance from the self you are all day. If you have a fight with your spouse, change the subject: not everything needs to be worked out, especially if it's just Zeus and Hera's eternal bickering. If you're stuck on a problem, do something else, because the agents in your mind will keep working on the problem while you get out of the way. Doing something completely unrelated to the issue at hand helps you deal with the issue at hand.

Bright Eyed Athena

Glaukopis, or *Bright Eyes,* comes from *glaux,* the owl, Athena's animal form.

Her eyes glint with understanding. They are gray and they glow in the dark like the eyes of an owl. Athena's consciousness is as bright as day. She is sober wakefulness and she goes away when you fall into daydreams, reflections, or fantasies.

Athena never sleeps. MRIs show that upon falling asleep, the waking self simply dissolves and other selves take its place, only to reappear in the morning when Athena springs from her father, Zeus', head fully armed and fully grown. You summon Athena the Waking Self with the daily ritual of coffee and newspaper to chase away the dream self and Hades' realm of images. It is a paradox that watching television about faraway events and reading about people you will never meet brings you into the collective Athenian reality.

She is a very visual self, for most of us get the majority of our information visually. Athena is the reason that you don't really *see* someone until you make momentary eye contact.

She is mindfulness and awareness of the world around you. Mindfulness recognizes that there are real dangers out there, like a car zooming through the intersection or a symptom that just showed up.

37

Athena

Athena brings a touch of wariness and suspicion to experience, because she wants to understand motivations, to know what is really happening, and to anticipate its implications.

She grants Diomedes, one of her favorites, the ability to tell men from gods so that he will never challenge a god in combat. The Greeks in battle were often taken up by Ares' blood madness, so a soldier in that condition is as dangerous and unstoppable as a suicide bomber.

This ability lets you spot talent and notice enthusiasm. The Goddess of Culture helps you recognize the gods in symptoms, compulsions, dreams, and ideas by thinking metaphorically and availing yourself of the culture's rich storehouse of imagery. This is the patron god of this book, which seeks to show you how to recognize the gods in everyday experience. The advantage of Diomedes is to not waste your time resolving 'your' contradictions or fighting 'your' impulses, but to see them as someone else acting in the psyche.

Virgin Athena

The virginity of Athena *Parthenon* (*Virgin*) is the ability to avoid a prejudice towards beauty and to relate to others objectively. This virginity doesn't need to hide at home like Hestia the Center or in the forests of single-hood like Artemis.

Athena Parthenon is the professional persona. She is the ability to be personable without being personal and friendly without being intimate. She is the persona of the corporate careerist, the small business owner, and the neighbor with a reputation to uphold.

This self wants others to take her seriously, because professionalism in business is as much about attitude and behavior as it is about qualifications. Athena's friends are successful people, not idle dreamers or people whose feelings are hurt easily.

She claims she has no mother but the truth is that Athena doesn't accept any traditionally *feminine* feelings or vanity. Her virginity banishes Aphrodite the Goddess of Sex from the office—a taboo upheld by laws barring sexual harassment. You experience Athena fighting Aphrodite when the head overrules the loins.

In artwork, she holds a giant shield that covers her body. A helmet takes up more room than her head, so it is clear that the public persona conceals more personal selves. This is the persona you put on every morning through vestment rituals of dressing for work, because putting on a suit changes the way you act and speak and even your posture. At her most majestic, Virgin Athena is the Great Lady, *Potnia,* like Elizabeth or the ideal of America that people are willing to die for. Her virtue is unassailable.

She is also a god of friendship, along with Hermes and other gods. Athenian friends share mutual respect and self-interest, like colleagues, co-workers, or alumni. There is some healthy competition in Athenian friendships. This kind of friend is obliged to share your enemies, in accordance with Greek tradition, which seldom granted forgiveness. Once your boss senses you are not on his side, you are finished in his book.

Pallas Athena

Athena is not only your Mind. She is how you manage your mind. You honor her when you can leave the office at the office, although she can also be the terrible truth that calls out when you wake at 3 a.m. like the hoot of an owl in the dark.

Athena Who Doesn't Look Back doesn't want you to waste your life gazing at your navel or blaming your parents. What's done is done and what matters is what you can do now. She is never naïve or automatically optimistic but she is always constructive with a can-do attitude. The Greeks used to say that *a happy thought comes from Athena.*

Pallas can mean either *Maiden* or *Armed*—both are true of Athena. Accenting the word differently changes the sex, so it can mean the Strong Virgin or the Strong Young Soldier—which also describes her perfectly.

Athena

She takes the name from the daughter of the river Triton who took charge of her education. The two girls were best friends and played war games together. But one day, they had a falling out, and as Pallas was about to strike Athena with her javelin, Zeus stunned her with a blow and Athena went in for the kill. She immediately regretted her action and took full responsibility for her friend's death. In contrition, she added Pallas' name to her own and made a little wooden statue of her, the *palladion*, which she dropped from the skies in the midst of Athens, where it was brought to the temple. Pallas Athena knows the danger of the competitive type-A personality: when winning becomes all-important, people get hurt. Athena's conscience directs you to do something to pay off your guilt rather than deny it, resolve it or let it go.

Pallas Athena is your conscience as a lifelong friend. She is there when you console or make amends. If you cause a car accident and someone gets killed, you honor Athena by offering some kind of service to the people you have hurt, something substantial enough to show that you care about what you have done, however accidentally.

Odysseus

The main character of Homer's *Odyssey* combines virtues of Hermes and Athena, mixing resourcefulness with practicality. He is the survivor, who adapts to ever new situations. While Achilles, Homer's other great hero, stands for living intensely for the glory of today, Odysseus shows how to make it into old age.

The Greeks called Odysseus *Polytropos*, Of Many Twists and Turns, because this self always has something up its sleeve. This is his Hermes aspect, which he combines with Athena's wariness and strategy. His name alternately means *the one who gives/receives pain* or *the one who hates/is hated*, which sounds like a reasonable self-assessment for just about anybody.

Odysseus invents new identities for each situation in his adventures, creating a tremendous advantage, like a salesman who can tailor his style to each client's personality. Athena admires his effectiveness and prudence. You are like Odysseus when you know how to turn it on, turn it down, or change the subject. Having a repertoire of personas for each situation is what Athena's culture is all about.

When I was a stockbroker, I tailored my personality to fit each client. I acted innocent for the old ladies and told dirty jokes for the fashion executives. This didn't make me dishonest or inauthentic. It just made me adaptable and widened my client base. We all play Odysseus to survive, even if we don't think of it that way.

Odysseus is a master of diplomacy and tact—useful tools for relating to our multiple selves. When the sorceress Circe offers him eternal life by her side, he tactfully declines without insulting her, carefully saying that he belongs to his beloved home with his wife, who is nowhere near as beautiful as she is.

It's significant that Homer doesn't choose a virile young hero for his story. Odysseus is already getting on in years when he appears in *The Odyssey*. The point is that force of personality is more important than youth or physical strength. When he needs to appear younger and more virile, Athena pours strength of character over him like a blacksmith pouring liquid silver over a mold, making him seem taller and nobler to impress the royals he meets during his journeys. She also makes him seem older and weaker for the angry suitors vying to replace him so that they underestimate him, although one of them notices a muscular leg showing through the rags.

You are like Odysseus when you only reveal as much of yourself as you need to in any situation, instead of letting it all hang out and 'being yourself' as our confessional Hera-soaked culture encourages us to do. You are like him when you assume whatever identity is needed to be most effective in a given situation. It's easy to imagine any god's traits being poured over you or filling you like a glass by focusing on that god's image as clearly as possible and seeing his/her aspects in yourself.

Athena Champion

Athena Champion, *Promachos,* is the leader whose civic values make the world a better place. The true Athenian hero achieves

Athena

glory for the city—meaning, for everybody—like the sports team that wins the tournament, the politician who gets wise laws passed, or the entrepreneur whose company provides the next great source of jobs like Athena the Driver of Booty.

Athena Champion has no use for the superiority of the tragic artist or idle dreamer. She wants you to choose one thing above all others and to pursue that thing to Excellence, so that you can change the world in some small way. She is the deed well done, from the brilliant strategic move to the positive adjustment of your attitude to a given situation.

She is fond of Herakles the Hero despite his selfishness, because his kind of strength can make the world a better place when directed by her wisdom. Athena guided America's military when it liberated Europe in the World Wars but it was ignored when we pushed aside France's advice and invaded Iraq.

You are Athena Champion when you make something out of your life or engage in any struggle that possesses greatness, whether it's starting a business, innovating in the arts, or living with cancer. Athena doesn't want you to accept your fate passively. She wants you to show everyone the stuff you are made of. But her help is never direct or miraculous. During battle, Athena directs the arrow of Diomedes to his opponent but Diomedes pulls the string. Athena only helps or hinders at crucial moments to increase your natural talents, and she only helps those who help themselves.

Athena Victory, *Nike,* is the spirit of the Olympics and of the Super Bowl, but she is also present in any moment of completion and triumph like when you meet a deadline, finish a degree, or get a Christmas bonus. Many people have trouble finishing things because they make the completion of something about them rather than about the thing being completed. If you imagine Athena Victory finishing that thing then you don't have to turn it into an existential issue born of Hera's personal crises. And when you do finish something, it honors Athena Nike to perform some ritual to help it sink in—perhaps a celebratory drink, a cake, or some indulgent purchase--instead of moving on immediately to the next thing without pausing to thank the god and realize what's happened.

Greek soldiers prayed to Athena Leads to Victory, *Nikephoros,* for the courage to seize the victory that lies within reach. The Greeks never took success personally and no Greek general would claim victory in battle until Alexander, who claimed to be a son of Zeus Ammon. When a Greek accomplished something significant, he would say he did it *with Athena's help* or with the help of some other god, so that success was never personal. That would be considered arrogant, impious, and ungrateful and a formula for future failure, because whatever god helps to make something happen can always change his mind or resent ingratitude.

Athena has no time for jealousy because even losing in a worthy contest means you are in the presence of a god. Being jealous only makes the victor's success personal and forgets that Athena can be friends with both of you—but only on her terms. Instead of being jealous, admire the god's manifestation in your rival and try to emulate it, so that the god might pay more attention to you the next time. This is not a heroic 'every setback is an opportunity' model, because the focus is on the god, not you or your rival.

Athena the Knowing One

Athena the Knowing One, *Ideia,* is a goddess of attitude and hidden intentions. She is the consciously chosen public persona imagined as a person separate from you—someone you wish to promote. This is not Hera's social self, who wants to point out to others how special you are and to glory in their admiration. This is a self with a program.

Actors and rock stars manage their images like a brand, although some like Madonna cannot separate themselves from it and suffer accordingly. Corporations, politicians, and the Federal Reserve cultivate gravity and credibility, which matter immensely to Athena. Her heroes are glorified in statues throughout Greece, forming a second population of silent, idealized men and women, many of them doubles of a god. Alexander used personification masterfully, standing like a statue of Ares and shining the same unfaltering movie star gaze as his chariot paraded down the long line of soldiers.

To project an image it must first be clearly imagined. Then the god can pour its virtues into you like water or gold. Or you can imagine the god standing in the room, or perhaps behind your shoulder, giving you advice. Or you can do any ritual, but you must do so sincerely like a friend.

The light in your eyes, the expression on your face, your bearing, and the tone of your voice—all of these the gods can change, but the gods are not dispensers of miracles. They can only help you become the person you need to be for a particular situation. And of course they choose their own friends and cannot be forced, just like people.

Goddess of Wisdom

Athena *Sophia*, is Wisdom personified.

The Greeks would never say that a man is wise. Instead they would say that he 'knows wisdom'. They would never say that he is fair or has good judgment, but that he 'knows fairness' and 'knows good judgment'. In this way, they avoided implying a self that 'has' these virtues, speaking instead in terms of knowing the right people. Personal failings have little bearing on wisdom, for they belong to other selves. But it is wise to know how to relate to them with Athenian reserve and tact, so that they don't sabotage your life.

Wisdom has nothing to do with knowing everything. Leave that to Apollo the Brilliant. Wisdom does not require fulfilling some list of 'things to do before I die' because that list belongs to Herakles the Hero, who has to experience everything. Athena Wisdom wants you to participate meaningfully and strategically in the world, and she leaves you when you hide at home. The only advice a Greek was given about life was to *use it well*.

You are like Athena Wisdom when you focus on what you can do that is productive and uniquely contributes to the world, which is Zeus.

Athena the Worker

Athena Worker, *Ergane,* is the God of Workers.

She engages in many trades but is most famous for weaving and knitting, literally and metaphorically. Athena Ergane draws you to work that requires intricacy and skill rather than simple tasks that require brute force, which belong to Herakles. Athena wants you to have a good job within the community.

Arachne challenged Athena to a weaving contest and when she lost, Athena turned her into a spider. This sounds like punishment, but punishment by a god also signals election. Arachne is a double of Athena, for skilled work is its own person and it isn't even human. We spend a lot of our workdays going into automatic, performing tasks in a way that has nothing to do with our personal feelings, busy like spiders spinning their webs.

"What do you do?" is the Athenian question par excellence, meaning, "Where in the community do you fit in and how do you contribute?"

Athena Techne

Athena Techne is Skill, personified. She is your field of work and the fine points of your trade. Techne is also tactics on the battlefield and in the corporate boardroom.

Athena and Hephaestus the Artist were closely associated in ancient Greece, but she is more interested in professional skills than in artistic virtuosity. Athena thinks Hephaestus is strange ever since the embarrassing incident at his workshop. She prefers acting normal to acting like an artist.

She sees technology and science as social progress. She is the democratic and very Athenian fondness for new media and devices.

Athena of the City

The Goddess of the City, *Polias,* is the citizen and taxpayer. You are like her when you vote and when you respect other people,

Athena

property, and the law. You are especially like her when you engage civically.

My father built a small bus shelter for the local kids. He enlisted in a number of town committees and served as a Selectman in Mansfield for years, and derived great pleasure from his friendship with Athena Polias.

She is the patron of civil society, whether you are a regular Joe on the street or a refined gentleman or lady. Athena of the City embraces group identities and affiliations: ethnic, gay, religious, unions, sports clubs, and so on. The Goddess of Weaving works everyone into the tapestry of city life.

The worldliness of a city is not determined by the sum of its population, because Paris is not less important than Mexico City. Athena Citadel is a city's uniqueness including its institutions, culture, and sophistication.

Every city or political entity has its reigning deities. Athena Polias combines with different gods in New York and Cleveland. New York has Hermes running all over Wall Street, Madison Avenue, fashion and the media--and many other gods--so Athena is more complex there. In Cleveland, she's closer to Hephaestus and Ares and other working class gods, so citizenship there has a different style. Boston belongs to Apollo, with its medicine and universities, while South Beach goes to Aphrodite and Poseidon with its fashions and the beach. But Athena is in all of them as the city that brings out refined qualities that people lack in the country.

She is the Statue of Liberty standing for freedom and self-determination. You feel Athena's breastplate when your chest swells to a corny march at a parade. Athena Patria and Zeus Patrios are gods of the fatherland--but not of the earth, which is Gaia. They are civic spirit and patriotism, but not nationalism, which brings in Poseidon's resentment and border issues.

In Athens, young men sacrificed to Athena Patria upon completing their military service, offering vows and prayers to the goddess along with public resolutions.

46

Athena of the Council, *Boulaia,* is the government and its institutions. In the city council, a lamp burned day and night to protect the city's immortal life. Officials who broke their oaths or neglected their duties were routinely fined and the money offered to Athena of the Council. You honor Athena of the Council and Athena of the City when you engage in political discussion while listening and respecting the *rest of the council.*

Athena Mother

Athena Mother is not your mother and she was never shown with a child. She is the Alma Mater, the mentor, or the coach who sent you after your dream. She is the Queen of England and America imagined as an ideal.

Athena the Mother, *Meter,* promotes family life through public policy and institutions like night school, daycare, and affordable housing. In Europe, she is the socialist state, occupying the same space once occupied by the Church.

The Boy Nursing Goddess, *Athena Kourotrophos,* shares that nickname with other goddesses, each with her own style of nursing. In Athena's case, Kourotrophos means raising children without mothering them in order to prepare the next generation of citizens, like the tough coach, boss, or teacher who gets the best out of you.

Athena Health

Athena *Hygieia,* has no stories because the Greeks didn't want to distract from her literal meaning. She is good health personified and the steps you take to promote it, whether it's brushing your teeth, washing your hands, or getting proper exercise. The government honors her by providing clean water, requiring vaccinations, and distributing condoms. She is OSHA, safety on the job, lunch breaks and weekends off and benefits like disability insurance.

The Greeks considered hygiene a social virtue and not something you do only for yourself, for they lived in an age of contagion armed with few medicines. They believed that soundness of body and mind come from good sense and sound proportions in life. They recognized that we create a lot of our own health problems through bad habits, making our lives more difficult than they need to be. To them, ignoring symptoms like a cough from smoking was a kind of stubbornness that defied the gods. Doctors honor Athena Health through a holistic approach, examining lifestyle, habits and support network and not only test results.

Athena Health was worshiped by the sick as well as the healthy, either through supplication or gratitude. The snake of Athena sheds its old skin, renewing itself the way people can do when they take care of themselves.

Pericles, the leader of Athens, built a temple and statue for Athena Hygieia and Asclepius the God of Doctors on the Acropolis after a workman fell off the scaffolding surrounding the Parthenon, claiming that Athena appeared to him in a dream and gave him a course of treatment that saved the man's life.

Athena Pronoia

Athena Who Stands Before, *Pranoia,* has a statue before the entrance to Apollo's oracle. She is a goddess of omens and intuition.

Your brain sifts through millions of stimuli, so if you are open to omens you may perceive a message from some other self who is trying to get your attention. You can ask for an omen and notice coincidences, puns, or anything to do with animals, etc. This is a psychological phenomenon like the I Ching and has nothing to do with magic.

Athena Pronoia is wariness. She keeps you on the lookout for hidden intentions and meanings so that you do not interpret events only literally and naively. A slip of the tongue does not escape her notice.

You can take this too far, as with any god. Athena *Pronoia* becomes *paranoia* in the artwork as an armed goddess almost entirely covered by her shield. It is paranoid to see meaning in everything, like refusing to go out because you saw a black cat on television. Even Odysseus, who perceives the gods frequently, never realizes that it is

Poseidon, not Zeus, who is angry with him, even as he floats on the *ocean*, the meaning of *Poseidon*—an ironic detail not lost on Greek audiences.

The gods often send misleading omens and dreams, because some self may be out to deceive you—perhaps an addiction or a secret which doesn't want discovery, or a longing that is only momentary. The Iliad shows many betrayals by the gods, so omens and intuitions need to be pondered and weighed carefully.

An old Greek proverb sums it up:
I come in quest of you
And so create an omen.

Daughter of the Mighty Father

Athena the Daughter of the Mighty Father, *Obrimopatre,* identifies completely with her father because he bears her with no female help. She has no interest in sentiment or vulnerability or any 'feminine' virtues.

She is credibility and gravity. Hers is the power of reputation. Obrimopatre is one of several gods called *chryse,* or *golden*, but this is not the golden of Aphrodite's charm or Apollo's brilliance. It is closer to the *sterling* of a sterling character or reputation. In statues she holds a shield high to show her discretion, because this self cares very much what others think about her.

While Zeus is Reality, Athena is the Reality Principle. She is his closest advisor and the only god to whom he entrusts the thunderbolt. You are like Zeus' right hand man when you take action in society, politics, or business with credibility, honor, and justice. You stray from her when you show off or indulge in grandiosity or personalism.

Athena Commerce, *Stathmia,* is why most business dealings are genuinely honest and you don't generally have to worry that the grocer is going to overcharge you on purpose. Athena Marketplace, *Agoraia* is the mall and the stores downtown and the peaceful order of exchange that reigns there. Athena Peace, *Eirene*, holds the child Wealth, *Ploutos,* while Athena Prosperity holds the *cornucopia*—the horn of plenty—representing

49

the good times when wealth grows in a broad and Athenian way, like the Sixties and the Nineties.

Like numerous other gods, Athena is called *Soter,* the Savior. In her case, salvation comes through education, common sense, and practical measures. It has nothing to do with magic, because Athena the Normal Self serves reality, which is Zeus, and tolerates no magical thinking. When Greek citizens were acquitted in court, they thanked Athena by giving to her temple or to the Kindly Ones--formerly the Furies, demons of vengeance.

The Furies

The Furies, *Erinyes,* are ancient gods who live in caves and in the deepest recesses of the Underworld. They are basic human instincts of justice and revenge for ancient laws that cannot be violated, like matricide and the burial of family members. The Furies have bronze claws and many hands and feet. They were universally hated.

They are blood-guilt. The Furies punish those who commit crimes against family or strangers, including lying about neighbors and breaking vows. The Greeks called on the Furies by striking the ground while pronouncing a curse.

They know no pity. The Furies care only about avenging the crime committed and not the circumstances. In ancient Greece, anyone who killed a relative--even accidentally--was sent into exile or locked in a tomb and starved to death.

They were imagined as horseflies, pestering relentlessly, snoring as they breathe and dribbling foul mucus from their eyes, because guilt makes it impossible to breathe or see clearly. Some call them beautiful but stern goddesses, carrying snakes, torches and instruments of torture. Their beauty is our innate sense of justice that demands placating. The Furies can send temporary blindness, *Ate,* so that you look back in regret at your own stubbornness in bad habits, bad decisions, or procrastination. Get rid of one Fury and another takes its place, as anyone ridden with guilt can attest. There are many Furies, for there is no limit to the variety of neuroses. The Furies chase away all joy.

They pursue Orestes after he avenges his father's death by killing his own mother, even though Apollo commands him to do so. Orestes clings to the statue at Athena's temple, begging for mercy. A court is set up in the temple and when the jury announces a tie, Athena casts the deciding vote for innocence, setting a precedent in Greece.

This angers the Furies, but Athena quells them with praise---— something they aren't used to—and then grants them a cave in her Acropolis. To the Greeks, guilt is not a 'negative' feeling to get rid of as in Christianity or New Age religions. Trying to do so infuriates the Furies by questioning their very right to exist. After all, guilt helps to preserve the social order. The Furies keep a healthy watch over people's minds. Only psychopaths are guilt-free. Instead, guilt requires its own place in the city of the soul—a cave in the Acropolis itself, so that conscience has a home.

Thus, Athena the Rational Mind finds a place for all gaps in reason--like neuroses, compulsions and crutches. She weaves every self into the fabric of our consciousness. Athena does not want you to let go, deny, or get rid of your hang-ups or neuroses, because they have a right to exist and are their own persons. Instead, she would have us honor and respect them, just as she praises the Furies. It is perfectly normal for the Normal Self to have a neurosis or two, so there's a cave for that.

The Furies are so pleased with Athena's gestures that they turn into the white Kindly Ones, the *Eumenides.*

Medusa

Medusa is the cold and terrifying shadow of Athena's daytime persona, the Ego. She is Athena's objectivity taken to the extreme. The Goddess Who Petrifies has a look that turns people to stone.

Medusa is merciless honesty or scorn. Her look is damning. She is the experience of disapproval by someone whose esteem matters greatly to you. She is also the facts that are too terrible to face.

Her name means *Guardian* and her image on stoves kept

51

Athena

children from the hot flame. Greek parents told their children to eat their vegetables or Medusa would come get them like the Bogey Man.

She once was a beautiful woman, born in the sea and chosen to serve Athena in her temple as one of her virgin guardians. But Poseidon rapes her in the temple—an unforgivable offence to a Virgin goddess, despite Medusa's innocent victimhood. Athena makes horns grown on Medusa's head, gives her a protruding tongue and snakes for hair—and a look that turns people to stone. This may seem unfair to our sensibility but the Greeks knew that life is unfair and never imagined their gods righting all wrongs like a concerned parent.

Medusa is a double of Athena because the boundaries of the normal self are not maintained through kindness, but through terror and hatred. Medusa freezes your attention with her merciless glare, just as the River *Styx* (or Hate) sets the boundaries of the Underworld--so you don't mistake dreams for reality. The gods must remain distinct and they jealously defend their boundaries.

Medusa's merciless stare keeps people from acting sexual at church, crying at the grocery store, or picking their noses on the street. These actions violate the discretion of Athena the Normal Self and are frozen in their tracks by her terrible scorn.

You can see Medusa behind the smile of the neighbor you wish you didn't run into, or in the customer service rep or waiter who treats you with professional distance. This look holds you at arm's length even while Hera the Personal Self or Hermes the Friend carries on cordially, 'because you don't really know me'. Medusa can help you stick to a diet or a budget because she is so brutally honest. She is a good antidote to a life overloaded with self esteem, personal indulgence, and procrastination.

When she later loses her head to the sword of Perseus, Athena attaches it to her shield as a weapon.

Aglauros

Aglauros is the Dweller on Tilled Land, perhaps because she marries well, but she is a shadow of Athena's rational self. Aglauros gets terrified and suicidal when she confronts a challenge instead of keeping her head like Athena on the battlefield.

Aglauros is the neurotic self.

She shares a house on the Akropolis with her sisters, Dewfall, *Herse,* and All Bedewed, *Pandrosos.* To the Greeks, dew is a precious gift from the moon to their arid land that can affect your moods just as it covers every leaf of grass.

Hermes falls in love with Aglauros' pretty sister, Herse, after noticing her in a procession and asks Aglauros to arrange a meeting. She asks for gold. When he pays her, she sabotages his plan out of jealousy and when he finds out, he touches her with his staff and turns her to stone. Aglauros is the stone heart of jealousy.

Athena entrusts Aglauros with the basket holding the baby that results from her unfortunate incident with Hephaestus at his workshop. She tells her not to open the basket, but curiosity gets the better of Aglauros. When she opens the chest and discovers a child with snake's feet, she and her sisters leap in terror to their deaths off the high rock of the Acropolis. In their memory, the women of Attica wear the same clothes for a year in ritual mourning like Lent.

In artwork, Aglauros holds the pomegranate—the Underworld fruit with its seeds arranged like a graveyard—in the same attitude as Persephone, Queen of the Underworld. She is the Strong Fate and the Athenian Persephone, because Athena's daylight consciousness casts a lot of shadows. Thinking that you are reasonable means that someone else must be crazy, including other selves.

Aglauros is self-loathing and suicidal impulses as if they belong to someone else. She can show up as exaggerated self-deprecation because she was overlooked for Herse. This self just cannot handle life. Personifying this part of you as Aglauros finds a place for those dark feelings and gives you a little distance from them as well, because they belong to Aglauros, not you.

Moving On

53

Athena

You know you've been around Athena too much when your routine becomes a rut and you can't remember the last time you let yourself go. Athena can make life so normal and predictable it gets boring.

But she has vast resources. She is the Goddess of the City in your mind and the Goddess of the Golden Mean who likes you to try a smattering of each persona.

You can counter Athena's self-restraint by turning to Dionysus with his intoxication and passion, or to Aphrodite's pleasures, or to Pan and his laziness.

Ares the Soldier is another option. Athena likes to direct his fighting spirit into the martial arts or the discipline of any sport or work, because that makes his passion productive. She also admires Herakles, who gets things done on a grand scale even if he is an egomaniac—because some people are over-achievers and serve Athena well.

Hephaestus fascinates her, as do all the arts, for Athena is the Goddess of Culture. Getting out to the theater or to an art opening brings Athena some needed glamour and chic, for it invites Hermes the Cosmopolitan, Aphrodite the Gorgeous, and Hera the Glamorous Socialite into the picture.

Hades brings a complete change of persona because he brings you out of the world of action and into images, which you can do by seeing a lot of movies or plunging into some good fiction. Athena knows how to distinguish images from reality and to keep them from overwhelming you. You can even escape her routine by simply taking a nap in the middle of the day and visiting Hades' world of dreams—a practice being adopted by forward thinking companies today.

ZEUS

The Greeks used the words *Zeus, God,* and *the gods* interchangeably. Where we say 'life is against me' or 'the world is against me', the Greeks said *Zeus is against me* or *the gods are against me.*

The Greeks said *there is nothing that is not Zeus.* He is Reality and he is the Universe in all its complexity. Zeus is What Happens, including your destiny. He is there when you make things happen and when you realize your impact on others.

He is also a person you can relate to. Zeus is the god to call on when you need to face reality and stop spending so much time with his brothers Hades as fantasy, Poseidon as emotional turmoil, or with his sometimes brother, Dionysus, as addiction or passion.

Zeus the Highest

Zeus the Highest is authority. He is who you are when you have authority or obey authority, because most bosses have bosses, too.

Zeus Olympios is the popular image of a divine and benevolent father watching over the world from a mountaintop in the clouds. He embodies all the sublime ideas about a monotheist god like the Roman Jove or Jupiter and the Christian God the Father.

Zeus keeps the other gods in line with the threat of his thunderbolt. Mostly, he keeps them from invading each other's space like when an addiction from Dionysus threatens your life or Athena has you working so much you don't have any personal life.

But the King of the Gods is not all-powerful like the monotheist gods. He is the strongest among the gods but not stronger than all of them together. Mostly he rules through benign neglect, letting each god pursue his own interests and only intervening when one god infringes upon another. You are like him when you don't try to control life but let it play out instead, ready to seize any opportunity to bring your heart's desire into reality.

Zeus' style of rule is dominion not domination. He gives you the ability to thrive with the contradictions born of our multiple selves and their

55

Zeus

competing desires. Homer shows him most pleased when all of the gods are at war with each other, each exerting his utmost against the others to get his way, like when you live a many-sided and demanding life.

His statue at the Parthenon sat with half negligent but noble freedom, his eyebrows gleaming under thick locks of hair and his lips parted in a slight expression, looking mild and reserved. His noble brow shows majesty without ostentation. Zeus has a quiet and easy strength that makes you confident but not over-bearing, although later artwork shows him looking troubled and more introverted. His authority comes not only from force, for Zeus inspires the highest ethical and intellectual speculation from philosophy to cosmology.

Like all gods, however, Zeus is subject to Necessity and the Fates and swearing by the Styx. Even he cannot rescue his son, Sarpedon, from death at Troy. You cannot expect Zeus to grant you personal miracles because he is Reality itself, containing you. He is not there to save the planet from an asteroid or to spare humankind the fruits of their folly. The Greeks thought of Zeus as a person and not only as a concept--someone with very human faults and passions, who can be distracted just like anyone else like when you let things slide in one area of your life and then discover that everything has changed.

Brightness of Day

Zeus means *brightness of day* or *daylight.* He is the daylight of intelligence and civilization. Zeus is the reason you generally trust your neighbors and feel safe at the supermarket. His police are Force, *Kratos* and Violence, *Bias.*

He is civilization. The God of Order brings prosperity, peace and dignity. You honor him when you have a positive attitude and you offend him when you are cynical, selfish, or get in other people's way. The Greeks knew that Life/Zeus can be cruel, but they nevertheless drew some comfort from the image of a planning father who decides things.

He is the fact that you pay your bills, show up at work, generally obey the speed limit, and refrain from robbing people when you have the chance. You also obey Zeus when you break the law in deference to a higher authority like civil rights.

The Greeks spoke of the mind of Zeus in the world and saw his nod as the very occurrence of events. Zeus's mind has *noos,* or *the ability to plan,* and is *stronger than the planning mind of humans.* It is close knit, *pykinos*—and *a mirror that takes in everything without distortion.* Even when Zeus is deceived, it is because he secretly allows it, usually for the greater good, like when he allows Prometheus to steal fire and give it to mankind, even while he punishes him for the theft.

Themis

Zeus' double and first wife is *Themis,* the laws of nature imagined as a person. Themis is also your particular taste, sexuality, and way of living. She is your genetic makeup and abilities. It offends Themis to judge anyone for his nature, like being gay, of another race, or crippled. She demands that you be kind to others, especially strangers, as the basis of civilized behavior.

She is the Public Order and her daughter, *Eunomia,* is Good Order. Themis is the orderliness of public gatherings and the right of each individual to speak freely and in turn. She would have been deeply offended by Tea Partiers who shouted down politicians at town meetings. Themis is our innate sense of justice. She is the reason that audience members never walk on stage to interact with the actors and why doing so would offend everybody.

Themis maintains the natural order of things and resists magical thinking. It offends her to wish to stay young forever or to talk about the gods as if you know them personally and can speak for them. Themis demands that we live in reality and speak about the gods only metaphorically, as interpersonal selves defined by culture, rather than as historical people, space aliens, or helpful stuffed animals. No Greek would ever say 'I love Zeus' or 'Aphrodite made me buy this dress'. That would sound fatuous to them.

Saying 'I feel like a goddess' or that someone is 'like a god' or

57

Zeus

is 'a goddess among women' is more Greek than New Age, because those statements are meant metaphorically and uphold the *separation of gods and men*, as Themis demands.

Zeus Ares

Zeus leads the gods in revolt against the Titans, monstrous creatures *not like gods or humans in shape.* he defeats them establishes order in the cosmos, ruling from Olympus.

Ares, his son with quarrelsome Hera, is the God of War. Zeus Ares, *Zeus Areios,* combines Zeus' wisdom with Ares' fighting spirit as a god of prosperity and peace through strength. His female double is *Eirene,* or the Peace.

Zeus Ares is courage and innovation, personified. You are like him when you do something new, take a stand, or improve the world in some way. Zeus doesn't act rashly like his son, who is always up for a fight. He listens to many opinions before he makes a final decision and then he puts resolve into that decision, setting aside hesitation (if not doubts) and taking action.

Zeus is *polymetis,* or *many counseled.* You are like him when you run your major decisions by a few trusted friends or experts before making up your mind. He lets you make a decision with resolution while suppressing all other possibilities. Zeus' dignified nod expresses his essential nature. This resolve is an aspect of courage, which can lead you to victory or abandon you to defeat.

The snake, the eagle, and the bull are his fierce creatures. Zeus' tree is the oak, tall and majestic, and the tree most struck by his lightning. You are like Zeus when you stick your head out like the oak tree in the forest. He is the daring to do something before everyone else.

Zeus' ally is Briareus, one of the Hundred Handed Ones, gods of violent storms and hurricanes who help you get things done in no time, like when you brainstorm or work like a hurricane to make something happen. When the gods revolt against Zeus and tie him up, Briareus frees him by undoing all the knots at once. He is the all-out effort.

58

Zeus of the Rout is the god of losing, because to be a good loser is also to know Zeus, for it lets you show your courage and dignity and the stuff you are made of when confronted by reality.

Courage is a habit of mind. As the Roman Emperor and philosopher, Marcus Aurelius, noted: *Such as are thy habitual thoughts, such also will be the character of thy mind, for the soul is dyed by the thoughts.* Zeus' courage helps you change the things you can and accept the things you can't, as in the old Yankee prayer.

Courage requires rejecting the easy life, the one your mother might want for you. Zeus's mother, Rhea, forbids him to marry because she knows he can never be monogamous, which infuriates him. When she then turns into a snake to escape him, he does the same and rapes her just to prove the point.

This doesn't mean you have to rape your mother to be like Zeus. Rape happens when one self forces another, so to be like Zeus you have to be true to your nature even if it means going against what everyone else wants you to do. It means you have to be in the world and not hide from it by choosing what is safe and predictable but unfulfilling.

You might experience courage as simply forgetting to hesitate, like everyday heroes on the news who did something brave and then say, 'I don't know what got into me' or 'I didn't have time to think about it'. That is because Zeus Ares took over and guided their actions.

Zeus of Freedom

Zeus Eleutherios, Zeus of Freedom and *Zeus Polieus,* Zeus of Politics, are dignity. You are like them when you stand up for the dignity of the individual and of humanity. Zeus gives you the courage to be who you are; he inspires nations, religions, and ethnicities to celebrate their differences with pride and not shame.

The greatest crime against this god is intolerance and prejudice, which denies people and ideas the very right to exist. Swastikas, burning books, harassing abortion clinics, and similar barbarous acts are the antithesis of this basic ideal of civilization.

59

Zeus

Zeus *Phratrios* is the God of Alliances and Brotherhoods—the civic spirit of leagues, clubs, and unions. Zeus *Philios* embodies your ties with groups and your desire to connect with others. Zeus the Stranger, *Zeus Xenios,* treats strangers with respect and honor, for the stranger may be a *god in disguise,* as depicted in Greek myths.

Zeus stands for human welfare and dignity. You're like him when you promote respect, kindness, and trust in the system—or when you change the system for the better. Zeus wants you to leave the world better off than you found it, including by cultivating your own prosperity.

Dike

Another of Zeus' solemn female doubles is *Dike,* or *the Way.* She is the freedom of things to follow their own nature. Dike is the way the stars move across the sky, the way old men take a nap after eating, and the natural acceptance of aging as a part of life.

She is Justice. This is not our vast and personal sense of justice, but only correctness. Our identification with Hera the Spouse makes us automatically connect justice with retribution, because she gets angry at Zeus for straying and punishes his lovers. Hera makes us feel that God owes us an explanation and an apology.

That's not Dike. The Greek idea of justice is simply to right wrongs the way a ship rights itself in the water, the way an architect justifies a line, or a debater justifies an argument. Once a criminal paid his dues to society, the Greeks considered him a full member of society once again and helped him get back on his feet. Nothing could be further from our idea of crime and punishment.

Zeus and Hera

The conflict between these two is the conflict between the Personal Self and Reality. Hera's obedience to Zeus epitomizes the Greek priority of reality over the desire for permanence.

You are like Zeus when you get what you want without making a show of it, rubbing it in, or having to make someone else wrong.

60

You are like Hera when you are mostly interested in justifying yourself and proving how special you are.

Zeus relies on Hera for advice—because her sense of 'my life' does indeed matter--but he doesn't really trust Hera. He knows she is always trying to figure out his next move and to control the future, as the personal self always does. Zeus rules the gods with a loose hand and lets each act according to his nature, including Hera. He doesn't try to change Hera but he always gets the last word.

You are like Zeus when you focus on reality instead of on yourself.

Hera is in charge when you host a wonderful dinner and then later find fault with everything, filling the experience with doubt--wondering whether people had as good a time as they appeared to have, questioning how you acted or pondering some careless words. Hera wants you to dwell on doubts about the reality of what happened.

This is the shadow of her self-esteem, because Hera aims to steal the experience back from Zeus and make it 'all about me'—looking for problems where they don't exist in order to focus attention away from events on her Personal Self. Hera's feeling of being special and chosen makes people need to be the center of attention, whether by lording over others or by playing the martyr, because Hera makes all events bow down to self-importance.

Zeus the Acquirer

Zeus the Acquirer, *Zeus Ktesios*, is property—your own or that of others-- another source of dignity for the individual. He is shown in artwork as a garden snake protecting the storehouse from mice and other would-be thieves.

Zeus of the Fence, *Herkeios,* is private property, including your home where you reign like Zeus. In Athens, people didn't ask for your address. They would ask the location of your Zeus of the Fence, *Herkeios,* because the property lines like the house will be there long after you're gone. They are immortal—at least compared to you.

61

Zeus

Private property isn't only a question of material things. It is a mindset. When you own something, you are Zeus to that thing and in charge of its destiny. You can exclude others from it by saying *no* or you can share it freely. Your *nod of Zeus* decides.

Zeus Giver of Fruits, *Oporeus,* is your profession or business and the fruits of your labor. The falling rain spreads the wealth in the same way a successful company rains jobs and salaries on workers. Donald Trump is like Poseidon, Zeus' jealous brother, showing off his wealth and power, while Steve Jobs was Another Zeus. You have Zeus' majesty when you don't identify with your success or feel superior to others, but share your success with the world.

Zeus of the Storm

When it was raining, the Greeks would say that *Zeus is raining.* Rain comes from Zeus and is one of his physical forms like daylight. There is also a Zeus of the Storm and a Zeus of Good Weather because he is the sky god.

He is majesty, a mixture of greatness and dignity. It is dominion without domination. Majesty doesn't need to impress others, because it is impressive by its own nature, like clouds, mountain views, and mighty trees. People who have majesty make you feel that when you're with them you are at the center of the world.

Majesty does not try to change others, only to encourage them. This applies to how you relate to your emotions, moods, and talents as well, for they are other selves. Instead of trying to iron out your problems or get over your hang-ups, Zeus would have you remember your own contradictions and variety just as he reigns among the gods rather than over them.

Curetes

The sons of Rhea the Earth Mother are fine young men who love sports and fighting. They were associated with the ancient bull cults of Zeus and Poseidon. Rhea set the Curetes to guard the baby Zeus in the cave where she hid him from his devouring father, Cronus. They coated themselves with white gypsum powder, clashed their shields, and shouted and danced to a disco beat to mask the baby's cries from Cronus.

The Curetes are doubles of young Zeus, and there are many of them because there are many ways to be like him. The key to his persona is to focus on the result you want rather than on your self, because the Curetes are coated in white powder and their individuality is muted.

They are normalcy, like having all the right parts and being an integral part of the group. This is not the same thing as Athena the Normal Self, who is your Ego and not your normalcy, and it is the opposite of gods like Hera the Personal Self and Apollo the Brilliant Self, who always stand out from others and require special attention.

The Curetes make you want to fit in and keep things running smoothly, because it's not about you, it's about the matter at hand. They are the reason that people dress and act the same at the office and at the gym, places where results are prized more than specialness or individuality.

The Curetes are around when you chalk over differences for the sake of the group or goal, whether it's a sports team, a sales team, or a line at the movies. They are the desire to be a regular guy, whatever your sex, and to facilitate cooperation and quiet strength. They are the reason that the man who doesn't talk about himself is often the hero in cowboy movies and romance novels, for it is boorish to insist on your specialness all the time.

Zeus of Honey

Zeus of Honey, *Meilichios,* appears in the artwork as a bearded snake, but these days he is the Burning Man.

He is forgiveness and the self who forgives, like Jesus.

Zeus Savior, *Sotor,* was prayed to for just about everything, because there is always a chance that God will relieve you of your frustration, your cancer, or your poverty.

When Zeus forgives, it is final and there is no guilt trip or debt to pay, because Zeus is the very fact of your forgiveness. Zeus Catharsis

Zeus

heals guilt, purifies the murderer, and takes up his cause. One way to befriend Zeus is to help others. As the Greek poet said, *there's nothing stronger than a kindly act.* You can be like him by doing one simple act of kindness a day, however small.

Zeus of the Underworld, *Zeus Cthonios,* has a deeper sense of forgiving, which is simply forgetting because, to paraphrase the Greeks, *in a hundred years, you and everyone who knows you will be forgotten and dead.*

As Marcus Aurelius advised, "*Do not act as if you were going to live ten thousand years. Death hangs over thee. While thou livest, while it is in thy power, be good.*"

Zagreus

Zagreus is the ancient Cretan Zeus, a god of the bull cult dubbed A Second Zeus.

His story is a variation of the tale of Zeus' upbringing in a cave. In this version, the jealous Titans, egged on by jealous Hera, actually catch the baby. Coating themselves in the same white gypsum powder as Zeus' protectors, they lure the baby out of his nursery with various toys.

He changes shapes to try to escape them but the Titans tear him apart and cook and eat his flesh, leaving only his heart. For this, Zeus blasts them with his lightning. Athena puts his heart into a new body made of chalk—the same chalk of normalcy as the Curetes--and breathes new life into him.

Zagreus means the Wild Hunter, and yet he is the prey. He is recovery and the self whose heart must be saved. This victim of bullying, compulsions, or addictions needs to create a new understanding of reality and to rebuild himself in order to save himself.   He is the ability to recover from a situation and to respond to setbacks with alacrity and effectiveness.

That's where Athena comes in. She is reason, strategy, and therapy. Athena the Normal Self saves Zagreus' heart, like when you seek therapy to stop being a victim and become a patient.

Zagreus is a god of psychological pain and depths. He is an

64

Underworld Zeus with connections to Hades and Underworld Dionysus. The three were imagined as brothers, for you can know death through Hades, passion through Dionysus, and reality and the world through Zeus.

Part of therapy is seeing that your problems aren't personal or unique, because everyone else is covered in the same white gypsum dust. The talking cures of psychotherapy and 12-step programs help loosen the identification with your problems, lessening their power by letting you see them from the outside. Seeing your victimhood as Zagreus instead of identifying with it makes it his movie, not yours, so you are free to focus on other things.

The Greek way is to forgive but not to forget.   The wound heals into a scar but doesn't disappear entirely. Your problems are a part of who you are and your destiny, which is also Zeus. It was Odysseus' scar that revealed who he was to his old nurse just as it is what happens to you that makes your life unique. Closure is not the goal, only the ability to move on to other things. Closure belongs to Herakles the Hero, who wants to fix things once and for all.

Ananke

Zeus has a number of female doubles with conceptual names, because concepts are Zeus' way of thinking, but these goddesses were always thought of as individuals first.

Ananke is Necessity. She is doing what you have to do. You are with her when you obey necessity like working at a job you don't like or keeping appointments you'd rather not, because Zeus is the reality of the situation.

Ananke shares a temple in Corinth with *Bia,* who is Force or Violence. Her name is related to the Greek for *strangle* and has etymological connections to *anxiety* and terms for iron rings, collars, choking, binding, and enslavement. Necessity is the opposite of Freedom-- and it is stronger than you so it is a god.

All gods are subject to Ananke, just like people. Like Hades, the Great Lady of the Underworld has few altars because she always gets what she wants.

Your *moira* is your *portion* or *lot* in life. Zeus *Moiragetus, Leader of the Fates,* is shown in the artwork arbitrarily scooping out good and bad fortune to mortals with his bare hands from two large jars outside his door. The Greeks recognized the unfairness of life but found meaning in the image of a kindly father in charge.

Sometimes life sends limitations and permanent life changes like disability or illness, but by personifying necessity you soften it, because then you can relate to it as a person—a difficult one, perhaps, but one that doesn't define you. As the Greeks said, *you do not have only one Fate.* You are many other things besides whatever is imposed by Ananke, and by seeing her as someone else, you become separate from her and more than your limitations.

Ate

Ate is Blindness. This dread daughter of Zeus appears in the ancient artwork as a mist around the head and shoulders, for she hides your view of reality which is Zeus.

Any god can send Ate in order to mislead you or to get you to do something. Few can escape her. Ate is your blind spot and the thing you keep doing that you're going to regret later. In artwork she appears alongside her beautiful girlfriend, *Nemesis*, Ruin or Doom, especially the kind you cause yourself by denying a problem, ignoring a talent, or judging someone else.

You're like Ate when you pretend not to see or know something, like a friend's addiction or your own secret behavior. Ate is the one to blame when you are carried away by rage, obsession, or recklessness—but you are still the one who has to pay the price. The gods are the reasons for our actions but the human being must suffer or benefit from them. The question of sanity would never arise in Greek courts because the Greeks thought that anyone who kills would have to be insane and under the control of some god, but that individual is still punished for his crime. The gods hold us accountable for things we do even

66

unintentionally like vehicular manslaughter and for things they make us do through momentary blindness like drinking too much or having an affair.

It's always easier to see other people's blindness than your own because that particular Ate sits on their shoulders, not yours. Anyone can tell a friend how he makes his life worse than necessary, addictions look unnecessary to everyone but the addict, and many know someone whose gayness is obvious to everyone but himself.

Sometimes a god will lift the fog of blindness, like people who manage to quit smoking before it's too late. Sometimes all you can do is to ask for mercy and hope for the best. Most Greek prayers simply read, *Please do not be angry with me*, as in 'Artemis Goddess of Purity, I have smoked cigarettes, please do not be angry with me.'

What is fatal is when a god or part of life is completely overlooked. At first, Aphrodite Goddess of Love doesn't mind that Hippolytus, a gym fanatic, feels uniquely close to Artemis' physical perfection and refuses to have sex with anyone, but when he isn't even willing to greet anyone less beautiful than himself she kills him in a chariot accident--and Artemis does not try to save him.

That is how the gods are. None is angry if you are closer to one god than another and none is ready to fight the eager will of another. If you have a drug problem, your professional life can't save you.

Cronus

Zeus' father, Cronus, is a Titan who swallows the gods in order to prevent a successor. He is an extreme form of Zeus that seeks order and power for their own sake rather than for the common good. Cronus is Zeus on steroids: a control freak who resents change and resists anything new.

He is Old Age, personified. Cronus fears he will become irrelevant or lose his faculties or position due to age. You are like him when you become psychologically old, ignoring desires, feelings and symptoms or getting stuck in one part of the personality. Cronus makes you presume that things will go on the same way forever and that change cannot and must not happen.

Outraged, Mother Earth outwits Cronus by giving him a stone instead of the baby Zeus. When Zeus grows into manhood she advises him to lull Cronus to sleep on a honey binge, then bind and castrate him just as he had done to his father, Uranus. Zeus gives Cronus an emetic that makes him disgorge the other gods and then banishes him to Tartarus, the part of Hades that is like the Christian Hell.

Banishment to the Underworld means something can be imagined without being enacted. In the Underworld, Cronus cannot carry out his heinous acts in the real world.

Zeus later pardons and releases Cronus and sends him to rule the Isles of the Blessed at the farthest end of the Underworld, islands where the few lucky humans chosen by the gods live forever in unending pleasure: hunting, feasting, and telling old tales with the actual heroes from the stories.

Cronus is a contradictory god, like some people. He is a harvest god with sickle or shears and he is the Grim Reaper: white haired or bald, veiled, and dressed in black.

But he is also the wise king of the Golden Age and Elysium, another heroes' paradise. This Cronus is tradition, the old order, and the good old days. He is Good King Wenceslas, Santa Claus, and the golden years.

When you personify old age you don't have to identify with it so much, because that old self is Cronus and doesn't define you completely. As a human you are subject to all of the gods, so when you are old you don't have to be *only* old all the time. Remembering this makes you like the Golden Cronus--wise with years and young at heart no matter your age. You can know Golden Cronus in any long enduring happiness, like a long marriage or friendship, a well-established business, or a happy family.

Chronos

Chronos, or the god Time, is distinct from Cronus, though their names are closely associated. Chronos is the Fulfiller and the

Accomplisher, for he marks the end of the year. He is the passage of time and what time can accomplish. You can see him when you look back at what the years have done, like remembering an old friend.

At his festivals, court was suspended and all work stopped. Slaves and masters exchanged roles like a company outing where the boss works the grill. During this ritual day, society was turned upside down in order to refresh and maintain the old order in an orderly way.

You honor Chronos when you treat people of all classes as equals rather than condescending to people less lucky than you, because that remembers that Time treats us all equally in the end.

Saturn

The Roman version of Cronus is Saturn. The Saturnalia was Rome's most important agricultural festival and the forerunner of our carnivals and circuses with their lurid atmosphere of perversion.

He is another god of paradoxes. He is repression and the one who represses--he is the entire equation. Saturn can make you act prudish in public but promiscuous in secret or make you care too much about what other people think and then act like an idiot in public.

He is the sense of separate selves who don't know or relate to each other the way the Greek gods do, for their gods were lovers, rivals, friends and family to each other. Saturn is a god of schizophrenia. He is pornography and sex without feelings. He is addiction, compulsion, or a terrible secret. Saturn is the obsession with being healthy or in shape as just another unhealthy compulsion, like people who think of food as only medicine and forget the fun of eating. He's a control freak run amok.

Saturn can make you cling to superficial parts of the personality while losing contact with your rich inner person, identifying with your looks, status, or success instead of thinking about your honest desires and remembering your humanity. He is around when people avoid topics or dismiss ideas in a peremptory fashion or when they repeat conversations habitually as if they don't know what they're doing. Saturn thrives in reactionary conservatism and nostalgia.

69

Zeus

This self wants you to choose safety over love or risk and call it duty, like staying at home with your folks rather than striking out on your own or agreeing to do more than you want to do for someone. Saturn is the part of you that chooses self-sacrifice over getting involved and risking getting hurt. For him, the solution to any problem is always more discipline and sacrifice, as if patience and self-control can save everything.

Images show him with hooves and horns like Capricorn the Goat; the Church turned him into Satan. Saturn's typical posture is sitting with his hands on his head, ruing the day like the damned in Michelangelo's *Last Judgment.* He is Christ on the cross and your inner martyr. The Romans called him the Lord of Karma because he is the self who suffers hopeless situations that you did not want or choose, like being handicapped or hooked up to a machine.

Saturn can make you depressed, narrow-minded, or resentful. He can make you act out by feeling the need to fix everything or nagging someone 'for her own good'. You are like Saturn when you feel disappointed by others, probably because you forget that they are only human, too. He hides out in people who call themselves idealists but who are really jealous or cynical.

His tree is the hemlock--dark, evergreen and poisonous.

Ironically, the Greeks called Saturn the Gateway to Freedom, perhaps because when you imagine your hopelessness as belonging to Saturn, it's no longer about you and you are free to be other people as well. The blessing of Saturn's stoicism is that you can live with a fatal disease or impossible situation without false hopes and then spend some time being someone else. He is the thing you don't want to admit about yourself and your point of greatest vulnerability. Saturn's freedom comes when you finally admit the truth, like coming out of the closet or admitting guilt like Raskolnikov in *Crime and Punishment.* Saturn is the exhilaration of confession.

Studies show that students who write down that they are nervous before an exam score higher than those who don't because admitting that fear frees them from having to worry about having it as well.

70

Saturn is the terrible truth and the truth that sets you free because then it is no longer a personal secret, dread, or burden.

Only Aphrodite can change Saturn. Only love can soften his heart of stone, because when someone else matters to you, it is hard to stay within his remoteness.

Moving On

Sometimes you need to spend less time with reality and more time with Zeus' brothers--feelings (Poseidon), fantasy and passion (Dionysus, his double), and dreams (Hades).

If Saturn is around and you are filled with duties and obligations, a detour to irresponsible fun with Hermes or Aphrodite might be in order with games and laughter and love chasing him away for a while. Artemis the Outdoorsman can bring a fresh breeze of authenticity and the outdoors because it's good to do something for its own sake. Apollo's art and music can enchant, as can Dionysus' passion and wild side.

Demeter and Hestia offer a softer and more personal side of life, which can warm your heart if you've spent enough time with Zeus' orderliness. Taking action is another idea. Turn to Athena, Zeus' right hand man, by doing something you've been putting off for a long time so you can check that off her list. This will also invigorate your friendship with Zeus, who is Reality personified.

An abrupt change can get the blood flowing again like Ares the Sudden, so doing something completely different gets you into another self.

HERAKLES

Herakles is the Hero. *Hera* is the feminine for *hero* and *Herakles* means *The Glory of Hera.*

Herakles is Hera on steroids. He isn't content for you to feel special like Hera. He wants you to feel better and more important than everybody else. Herakles makes you think you were put on earth for some grand purpose and that God is directing your actions. He is the purpose driven life. Herakles makes you prefer action to reflection and to see life and history as progress. His complete self-absorption causes a lot of collateral damage, for he can only see others as rivals and never as equals or even friendly competitors. His intention towards nature is complete domination. He is raw ambition that requires material proof of success because he is literal-minded and competitive. To him it's no good being a Hero unless everyone else envies you.

Herakles' cult is strong in America. People here increasingly think that their lives are indispensable to Planet Earth.   He is the economic Hero of Ayn Rand, the "purposeful instrumentalist" mentality Max Weber, and the indispensable individual of actions movies in which the fate of the world depends on one person, just like Jesus.

I once attended a talk by a retired U.S. diplomat who was making the rounds of the Catholic parish lecture circuit discussing his experience of faith and diplomacy. Someone asked the reasonable question of how to reconcile his duty to God as a Christian and his duty to America as an ambassador. His answer was that America is God's nation so there can never be a conflict, because what is right for America is right for God. That was Herakles talking with chilling conviction.

Herakles was born to Alcmene, a mortal woman Zeus seduces by taking on the appearance of her husband, pretending to return home from a business trip and feeling very horny. He tells the Sun to take the day off and Sleep to put mankind into a stupor to make the evening last for 36 hours. When Alcmene's real husband shows up later, she can't believe he still wants sex. Of course he doesn't know what she's talking about. The oracle tells them to keep away from each other because the lover was Zeus in disguise.

Most heroes have a goal and try to achieve it, like securing the Golden Fleece. Herakles is the need to win at everything. He makes it impossible not to measure your status against everyone else's at all times, no matter the context. His grandiosity makes you opt for easy morality with clear lines between good and evil: 'you're either with me or against me'. He wants you to judge everybody and everything as a matter of habit, like people who say they don't *believe in* homosexuality or prostitution, as if those are questions of belief. Herakles sees freaks everywhere. He hurts a lot of people on his upward climb, like the music teacher he murders for critiquing his playing by hitting him over the head with his lyre or the friend he pushes off a tower because he doesn't like the way he admires his cattle.

Herakles makes you hypersensitive to criticism to the point of paranoia, because he sees others as rivals, not friends. He always claims to be acting defensively even when he is the provoker, as in America's 'defensive' first strikes. He is the American resistance to learning from other countries, because to do so means 'you don't love America'. Identifying with him leads to religious crusades and jihads like bombing abortion clinics, invading Muslim countries, or planning terrorist attacks. The Hero leaves a trail of destruction behind him.

He does have a lot to brag about, including a top-notch education. Herakles embodies the ideal of the well-rounded individual, which is not the same thing as cultivating a specific talent or multiple selves, because getting close to a god is not the same thing as insisting on being the gods' one and only friend.

His godlike strength and courage come with a violent temper and misogyny. He murders one of his wives. You are like him when you think of life as endless progress, every new lover or job as a step up the ladder and every experience as a valuable lesson. Herakles convinces you that you are getting better and better—which is quite a challenge for us mere mortals.

73

Athena is one of his few allies because she sees his potential. Athena the Strategist can channel the heroic drive into a project that is ambitious and worthwhile. With Athena's guidance, Herakles is like America on the right side of a war or promoting the Marshall Plan.

The Glory of Hera

Herakles means the *Glory of Hera*, but Hera hated him at first because he was born to one of Zeus's lovers. She starts her long campaign against him while he is still in the cradle, sending two snakes that he strangles and throws at his nurse's feet, giggling and gurgling.

Athena sponsors him from the start. She invites herself over to Hera's mountain for a walk and then plays dumb when they come across an abandoned infant. Athena innocently suggests that Hera suckle the child, but the baby bites her so hard she flings it to the ground, calling it a *little monster*. Still, Athena is happy because Herakles has suckled on a goddess.

Most heroes in ancient Greece were local and identified with gravesites and memorials, like town leaders whose names adorn municipal wells and ball fields and statues of soldiers on the town common. Outstanding heroes like Theseus, Jason and Perseus were *friends of a god* the way some people are gifted with tremendous talent and success.

Herakles differs from other heroes because his goal is immortality itself. He is the Immortal Self—meaning, the self that wants to live forever. You are like him when you presume a glorious future after death as the same person you are today. He is the very wish to live forever and not to be a mere mortal.

He is the god of Christians and their longing to live forever as the same person. He is their fear and denial of death and science. He is the source of their anger and their need to punish, for he is just like his mother, Hera. He makes Christians see others, especially racial minorities, as 'animals' who die so that they can somehow not be animals, too. He is the secret belief in being one of the Elect.

When *Hera's Glory* possesses you, it seems the world can't go on without you and that Armageddon must be right around the corner. This dangerous belief was described in *On Christian Longing for Apocalypse* written by Porphyry in Alexandria during the third century A.D., so it's been around for a long time and it comes from a god. I have Christian cousins who believe we should set off all our nuclear devices so that Jesus will come and save the world from destruction.

Herakles's denial of reality (like evolution or global warming) makes him prone to madness. After all, if you can believe in Heaven then you can believe in anything. His first marriage ends when Hera makes him insane and he kills his six children and two guests. He then hands his grieving wife to his nephew and annuls the marriage, calling it *inauspicious*.

Herakles makes it easy to dismiss people and responsibility and move on, because 'it's all about me'. He is the belief that whatever doesn't kill you makes you stronger, even though some things that almost kill you make you weaker, like HIV or a broken hip. He is the source of America's compulsive optimism, eagerness for war, and need for 'closure' and 'healing'—often before proper reflection and grieving—code words for leaving the *inauspicious* mess behind.

The Death of Herakles

When Herakles asks the Oracle of Delphi to cleanse him from murder, Hera sends him to King Eurystheus to perform twelve labors in repentance. The prize is immortality. Herakles does not like serving Eurystheus, because the Hero makes you resent anyone who tells you what to do and makes you think you're smarter than the boss.
Next he marries Deianeira. When that relationship gets stale he moves his newest lover, Iole, into their home. Deianeira tries to save her marriage with a magic potion guaranteed to make Herakles love her forever—or so she thinks. Long ago, when she and Herakles came upon a river, Herakles swam easily across but Deianeira needed the help of Nessus the Centaur, a usually savage creature, who kindly offered to carry her on his back.

Midway across the river, Nessus tried to rape Deianeira and Herakles shot and killed him with an arrow. The dying centaur gave Deianeira a vial of his blood, calling it a magic love potion. With Iole now installed in her own house, Deianeira desperately wipes the liquid onto Herakles' shirt as he goes off on some pursuit.

But soon after he leaves, the drops spilt on the ground start smoldering like acid. In panic, she sends messengers to warn Herakles but they arrive too late. The shirt sticks to him as the liquid burns his flesh, which falls away as he frantically tears at his clothes.

Herakles tells his followers to burn him alive on a bier. When they do, his body disappears in a flash of lightning as his immortal soul flies up to Olympus and his mortal parts fall down to Hades to be among the normal dead. Hera then forgives Zeus for his affair and adopts Herakles as her own son, pretending to give birth to him from under the sheets.

The bloody shirt that sticks is identification. When Herakles is around, you believe in yourself instead of in a cause. When Herakles burns himself alive he demonstrates the amazing strength and egotism of martyrs.

Seeing him as someone else acting through you frees you to be friends with him instead of acting out his story blindly. Remembering that you are mortal puts Herakles in perspective, because he is only one self among many.

Herakles and Hades

Hades is the world of images while Herakles is literalism.

You can see Herakles in people who want to censor movies in order to fight crime or who take the Bible literally instead of recognizing it as an ancient document written for ancient peoples and full of metaphors.

Herakles prefers action over reflection. For him, a setback is not a chance to re-think an approach or consult with others but a reason to try harder or move on to something else. Rather than working out issues with a lover, he would have you take a new one. He is the impulse to leave problems behind and go somewhere else—which works fine until the baggage arrives. He is the bucket list of things to do before you die, because for the Hero it's not enough to watch a documentary or read about climbing Mount Everest. You have to do it yourself to prove you have really lived. Images don't count as experience to him. Only actions and facts count.

76

Herakles behaves badly in the Underworld, the world of images. He chokes Cerberus, the three-headed dog who guards the entrance to Hades, wrestles with the Underworld herdsman, wounds Hades, and strikes at ghosts even while Hermes explains that his sword will pass right through them. Other heroes go down to Hades to learn. Herakles goes down to Hades to take, dragging Cerberus back up to fulfill one of his Labors. You act like him when you think of the imagination as a mine to exploit and dreams as only messages to *me.* To the Greeks dreams were individuals who stood at the end of the bed, spilling their contents to the person sleeping. They had a life of their own, often unconnected to the life of the dreamer. The Dream World is a place to interact with the gods, who may appear in the guise of animals or of people you know.

Herakles's attitude gives industry a license to use up the world's resources, because surely everything exists for the sake of humanity. His attitude makes scientists measure a dog's intelligence by its obedience, even though my chow-chow never chased the ball because he didn't want to, not because he was stupid.

Hades punishes this literalism with guilt, sending the very hang-ups that the Hero wants you to leave behind. Herakles can't deal with images because he has no sense of metaphor about himself. He is unable or unwilling to see through his own actions to the fantasies informing them. As a friend of mine on Wall Street used to say about an egotist, 'he believes his own bullshit.'

Herakles rules monotheism, religions which demand belief and forbid graven images, because images transform any god into only one image among many.

Herakles and Aphrodite

Herakles is violent and exaggerated in love as well. He gets this from his mother, Hera, because the Goddess of Morality has mixed feelings about Aphrodite.

He is the prude. You are like him when you aren't

comfortable with nudity, sex, or getting down.

He has none of Aphrodite's subtle allure or the animal mafnetism of her lover, Ares the Fighter, a gorgeous, hot, and outgoing guy. Herakles exaggerates his sexuality as if he has something to prove, like the time he sleeps with 50 women in a single night. You are like him when you think of lovers as conquests instead of as individuals.

Statues show a hulking man with surprisingly small genitalia, like bodybuilders in tiny trunks. When the crew of the Argo docks at an island of sex-starved women, Herakles stays away from the party, preferring to stay at camp and talk big like a frat boy. He is sexually shy because he makes you think of sex as a performance or as something you must master to show your superiority, not as a way of being vulnerable, fantasizing, or improvising. For him, sex requires too much interaction to be tamed like all the freaks he maims.

Aphrodite does not want to be conquered. She'd rather be seduced or grant a lover his fondest wish. Thinking you are heroic brings too much muscle and ego for sex to be spontaneous.

Herakles is a stalker and he's thick headed about love. He can't understand why the beautiful island boy, Hylas, flees when he tries to take him as a lover after he kills his father for refusing him as a guest due to his bad reputation—thereby proving the point. During his flight Hylas stops to rest at a beautiful spring and feels someone grasping at his feet. It is the lovely nymph of the spring who falls in love with him at first sight and makes him her captive partner.

Herakles stubbornly searches for Hylas for days even though the islanders offer him their best sons. He refuses to stop until Zeus sends him a dream in which Hylas tells him that he is happy and to forget about him. When the Hero is around, things have to be spelled out loud and clear. The Hero is immune to hints and subtlety. He makes you mistake stubbornness for perseverance.

There is a vast literature chronicling Herakles' long career, because this hero talks about himself a lot. In one strange episode, he is sold as a love slave to Queen Omphale of the Amazons, who keeps him in her harem dressed in bracelets, a turban, a girdle and purple shawls.

78

Spinning thread at her command with his clumsy fingers, he trembles at her voice as she beats him with a golden slipper, scolding him to tell her stories.

This is the strange femininity of bodybuilders, with their posing in the mirror and their hourglass figures. Herakles is not easy in his masculinity like Ares, who acts friendly instead of aloof, because testosterone makes you friendly for the obvious reasons. Nor does he have the natural build and grace of Hermes, Ares and Apollo, gods with sporting physiques rather than exaggerated muscles. Herakles seeks to impress, not to seduce, because he has to be the best and weights can be easily measured.

The Zeus of Battles

This is Herakles' darkest aspect.

Carl Jung, the psychologist, warned that when an individual cannot recognize his projections, the Unconscious gets a free hand to create delusions. Projections like racial prejudice are then seen as actual facts, isolating the individual from his environment and from reality.

While Hera makes you think of your problems as God singling you out for suffering, Herakles makes you attack them head-on as though they are external enemies. He spends his career killing monsters, washing out stables, draining swamps, and dominating nature while self-righteously calling it progress.

He is xenophobia and the tribal impulse to blame some group for problems instead of looking in the mirror, the way some white people project violence onto black people while supporting capital punishment and calling for more wars, as if wars don't count as violence.

Like Hera trying to keep Zeus to herself, Herakles seeks permanent solutions for things that only need attention and maintenance. He is talking when you say something will never happen again or will be taken care of 'once and for all'. This is dangerous when you're talking about hang-ups and insecurities because they may be the only things keeping you from acting like a madman.

He bullies so-called bullies and is fond of suitable

punishments, like denying prisoners self-improvement or even television instead of teaching them a trade so they can earn an honest living. The Past Master of Monstrous Works lets you claim the high moral ground no matter how badly you treat others.

The Zeus of Battles is selfishness and its civilization. Herakles' world is full of identical sub-divisions and McDonalds' food that tastes the same whether you're in New York or Moscow, because to him, things and people are interchangeable. He wants predictability because it hints at immortality.

He is the guy in the advertisement who would rather take a pill than stop eating the fast food that's giving him heartburn. He wants you to beat symptoms over the head instead of changing your ways or accepting that you are not perfect. He is art that is only self-expression and the conviction that art is just a matter of taste, because 'it's all about me'.

Moving On

You put Herakles in perspective when you stop needing to be the best at everything and focus on acquiring god-like Excellence at one or two things. That focuses Herakles in your life like Athena guiding him instead of letting him run amok. Seeing your ambition and achievements as the work of Herakles frees you from the literalism of selfishness, because everyone shares the desire to be outstanding at something and to befriend a god. Encouraging and mentoring others leads straight out of this quagmire by focusing your energy on improving the world, which is why Athena, who embodies strategy, recognizes the potential of this extraordinary hero. Put him in his place by admiring others and feeling authentically glad for their successes, remembering that you are all humans like Psyche.

You can counter Herakles' hyper-activity by spending some time with Pan the Lazy and living without a goal for a while the way animals do. Pan is the body's wisdom of knowing when you've taken on too much.

Hades is Herakles' true opposite, because dwelling in images takes you out of the realm of action. Accepting the finality of death instead of planning some endless sojourn in an imagined future world helps keep Herakles in perspective, because as the Greeks said, *remember you are only human.* The desire for 'immortality with *me* in it' is a symptom of Herakles taking over, so remind yourself that Apollo's science says we are only animals and nothing more—only exquisite animals. That should bring you back to Earth.

PART THREE: GODS OF POSSESSION

Some gods control you subtly like Athena, Hera, and Apollo, so that you hardly know they're around. Other gods possess you and cause disruptions in your everyday life like Aphrodite, Poseidon, and Dionysus.

Aphrodite is Sex, Love, and Beauty. In the Classical era, being in love was considered a kind of madness, but Aphrodite's gifts were also counted among the greatest joys of life. She personifies your sexuality, your love life, and your perceptions of beauty as a lifelong acquaintance.

Dionysus is intoxication and passion. He is ecstasy and the freedom to *do what you want to do,* as his followers proclaimed. Dionysus leads you to the edge and the extreme in any activity so that you lose yourself. He is passion as if it had a mind of its own—which is the very nature of passion.

Poseidon is the emotional self. This tempestuous god fights with Athena, who is *Mind and Thought (Noos kai Dianoia)*, and with Hera the Goddess of Society, because emotions fight reason and can be deeply antisocial. But Poseidon's great gift is authenticity and emotional excellence—which is the ability to experience any emotion without judging it, identifying with it, or telling yourself that 'I mustn't feel that way'.

Ares is the Fighter. He is fighting anger and the ability to be present in the moment. Ares brings intensity, immediacy, and vigor. He is the second wind, and you are like him when you surprise yourself with an extraordinary effort. Ares is the one to turn to for zest in any activity and when you need to light a fire in whatever you are doing.

82

APHRODITE

Aphrodite is Sex, Love, and Beauty, personified. She is your love life--all of your fantasies and love affairs, and your sense of *Beauty* as a lifelong acquaintance. In the Classical era, being in love was considered a kind of madness, but Aphrodite's gifts were also counted among the great joys of life.

When she is your friend, Aphrodite makes you charming and pleasing to others, which is a huge advantage because beautiful and pleasant people are always in favor. When you cooperate with her, she can help you pursue your desires with sweetness and persuasion.

But when you resist her, she compels you to perversions and degradation, especially if you have a low opinion of sex and beauty, feel ashamed of the naked body, or judge others for their sexuality. Your attitude towards sex, love, and beauty matters more to Aphrodite than how much action you actually get. She doesn't like people pretending to be asexual or innocent, especially when it involves a great deal of forgetting of the past, because that's a snub in her book. You can't be a whore your whole life and then bake cookies in your old age and act shocked by other people's behavior.

Aphrodite can often be satisfied by flirting or by appreciating the beauty of others or of beautiful things like the objects in a museum. The trick is to please her without getting burnt, sick, or broke.

Birth of Aphrodite

Before the age of the gods, when the monstrous Titans ruled the world like formless instincts, Cronus viciously cut off his father Uranus' genitals and threw them into the sea, seizing his throne. A foam, or *aphros*, grew around these monstrous parts. Out of this foam emerged Aphrodite, the Goddess of Loveliness, accompanied by lovely friends, fluttering birds and blooming flowers, as shown in Botticelli's *Birth of Venus*.

She is Beauty, personified, including the desire to feel beautiful. She makes your partner more beautiful as you grow to love her.

83

Aphrodite

Aphrodite's job in the psyche is to make beautiful the brutal, shameful urges of Cronus and blind instinct. To her, humans are sexual creatures like all other animals and we honor her when we make it look good.

Uranus' severed genitals are sexuality cut off from feelings—the secret sex life that is completely separate from the rest of the personality. For Cronus, love has nothing to do with it and the naked body and sex are dirty. His real castration is the inability to be intimate. Cronus makes it difficult to be sexually attracted to someone you care about, because he sees sex as a monstrous act inflicted on others.

You honor Aphrodite when you think of Beauty as a person and a friend. Beauty may only be skin deep, but everything needs a surface and not just a profound interior. Ugliness and an ironic attitude towards beauty belongs to Cronus.

Goddess of Sex

Aphrodite is Sex as a lifelong acquaintance. She is the Goddess of Copulation, the Goddess of Honeyed Kisses, the Lover of Genitals, the Goddess of Beautiful Buttocks, and the Giver of Joy. Her name was shorthand for orgasm and sex. *Venus* means She Comes.

She is *maklozenae*-- the pervading atmosphere of desire, like on New Year's Eve or Valentine's Day. The movie, *A Touch of Venus,* captures this feeling when everyone around the goddess falls in love as she passes by. It isn't personal, it's in the air and it happens to everyone, including other animals.

Aphrodite decides what you find beautiful and whom you find attractive. She cannot be forced. Denying your attraction to someone angers her. She pulls Helen by the hair when she forces her to fall in love with Paris, starting that terrible war in Troy. She treats those under her spell like slaves.

Yet Aphrodite is thoroughly charming. She is Charm itself and the sweet, inviting ways of flirtation and personal allure. Aphrodite prompts you to bring the best to your lover: a low, relaxed voice, elegant posture, an open smile, and lively eyes that invite approach. She is the joyful sense of melding with a lover and being open to erotic entanglement. Aphrodite can grant any lover's wish and bless any union, whether it's a man going to a prostitute or an old couple trying to spice up the relationship.

The Greeks prayed to She Who Postpones Old Age, *Aphrodite Ambologera,* because they correctly believed that sex helps people stay young. She gives lovers' faces that fresh, flushed look as though they've just come from running or dancing.

But Aphrodite cannot be owned, not even through marriage. She never has sex with her husband, Hephaestus the Craftsman, and carries on endless affairs with other gods and men. Aphrodite appears in many combinations with other gods, whose nature colors the sex. Having sex with an obese spouse out of loyalty shows that Hera the Goddess of Marriage is around, for she is *the soul of loyalty.* Thinking of sex as a series of conquests indicates Herakles the Hero, while Hermes is the Friend With Benefits.

Aphrodite is an unpredictable goddess who is dangerous to resist and quick to mete out punishment. She can make you impotent or send you unquenchable neediness, like repeating 'I love you' as a magical incantation. She can cloud your judgment, lead you into bad situations, torment you with jealousy, or ruin your reputation for a passing obsession.

Aphrodite especially punishes anyone who thinks he is above sex or who is afraid to love for fear of getting hurt. She destroys those who judge others for their sexuality and punishes moral fanatics with shameful compulsions, which is why priests and Evangelicals have so many sex scandals. Most of all, she hates anyone in love with himself, or who acts condescending because of personal beauty, which is a gift of the gods and only on loan.

Her love of going out is semi-delinquent. Aphrodite knows all the clubs and party drugs and stays in close touch with her friend, Dionysus the God of Intoxication. Forbidding her to go somewhere makes her want it all the more. A week after New York City banned smoking in the bars, personal ads appeared seeking sex with smokers.

Aphrodite

As lovely as she is, Aphrodite does not care about your wellbeing or happiness. Your sex life has no stake in your peace of mind or health. Aphrodite wants you to serve her without thinking about the consequences. The gods are selfish and see us as expendable. Aphrodite comes and goes in relationships at whim and she bores quickly. When things get stale, she wants you to take a break from your partner and consider ways to seduce her rather than taking her for granted.

When lovers move in together other gods move in alongside them. You might marry Aphrodite for her cute body and find yourself living with bickering Hera the Spouse or Hestia the Homebody, a virgin goddess who sees you eating directly out of the refrigerator, hanging around in a robe, or getting sick.

Some couples try to re-discover Aphrodite by escaping the house and its familiar gods and going somewhere sensuous like the Caribbean. If you hate the loveseat in your living room it's unlikely to become a place of seduction. You can spice things up with Dionysus' fantasies, alcohol, and drugs—anything naughty to satisfy Aphrodite's need to transgress with a partner again.

You act like Aphrodite renewing her virginity in the bath when you think of Sex as an independent person instead of trying to control or force it. If it feels like obligation or if you talk things to death, Hera the Spouse is in charge, not Aphrodite. To the Greeks, sex and love were mysteries that cannot be explained away, just as you can't explain away your friends. If you get aroused in the kitchen at an inconvenient moment, you honor Aphrodite by setting aside whatever you're doing, because Aphrodite doesn't like to be put on a schedule.

Goddess of Love

Aphrodite possesses you and your partner when you are in love. She is the third person in the relationship—she is the Love itself. This love is personal but it isn't human because it comes from a god. When you look back at your romantic history you are looking back at your long friendship with Aphrodite, whoever was involved.

Magic spells are woven into her waistband, like a low-slung Miss America's banner or a sexy negligee. Aphrodite casts love spells with magic trinkets including a spinning top, which is a lot like some love affairs. The Greeks called her *Aphrodite Automata*, Spontaneous Love, *Aphrodite Epistropheia*, Who Turns Hearts Away, and *Aphrodite Apostropheia*, Who Turns You Towards Her, among many other names.

Her entourage includes her son, *Eros*, or Love, and his friends, *Himeros* (Reciprocation), *Pothos* (Longing), and *Peitho* (Persuasion). Aphrodite likes doves that coo like lovers. Her star is Venus, which greets lovers at dawn and crosses paths with the moon and its lunacy.

The ancient Greeks considered love a whammy that can lead those under its spell into blindness, madness, and terrible consequences. When you are in love you are not your normal self, because that is Athena and she is a virgin. Aphrodite sends the delusion that you and your lover are a star-crossed fit that is unique on the planet. She is the madness of thinking that out of all the billions of people on earth, you are destined for each other. She makes you vow to love someone forever when you know you won't live forever. The words *always* and *forever* signal that the person talking is a god and not *you* as a mere human being, or Psyche.

Yet Aphrodite is never cynical or self-absorbed. She chooses her lovers freely and only goes along when the feeling is mutual. She never pines after anyone like Apollo's gay boys at the mirror bar, who want someone until the feeling is reciprocated. And she is never in love with herself, so if you're stuck on your own looks and enjoy being envied, you're probably with Hera, who glories in the admiration of others. Aphrodite likes to be noticed but she wants to be known intimately and not from afar or as a superior. She heightens the senses when you are in love, creating a golden aura that separates you and your lover from the rest of the world. You can see her when you look into someone's eyes as if you are looking at the goddess herself, while remembering that the person is only human at the same time.

Aphrodite

Goddess of Beauty

Aphrodite is Beauty personified. She is the quality of beauty wherever you see it. Aphrodite *Morpho,* the Shapely One, has many ideals of beauty, so there's nothing conventional about her.

She is there whenever you lean closer and realize how beautiful someone or something is. She is the leaning closer itself—not to analyze like Apollo the Intellect, but to appreciate what is in front of you and to cast a memorizing glance upon it. Aphrodite loves compliments and friendliness because those are ways of sharing beauty rather than keeping it to yourself.

The word for Aphrodite the Golden, *Chrysippus,* has linguistic ties to *semen*. She is the golden boy and the golden girl and golden moments of unexpected flirtation or the sight of something enchanting. She is the Golden State where blonds have more fun and movie stars never grow old. Aphrodite loves romantic cities like New York and Paris where people hold hands or kiss in public without shame. Aphrodite the Side Glancer (Parakyptousa) is the make-up model in so many ads who looks at the camera and then glances down, giggling shyly. The Smiling Goddess lights up a face or a room, making just the right amount of eye contact to be inviting but not brazen. Her voice is low and close and never the public microphone voice of Athena the Citizen, Apollo the Know-it-all, or Hera the Social Self—gods who want you to be overheard. By contrast, the Roman Venus can be brash with her furs and sexual confidence like Ivanka Trump.

It's easy to identify with Aphrodite because her friendship is so intimate, but she is a goddess and her gifts are on loan. You can maintain her friendship after you lose your looks looks by cherishing the memories of love, dressing with care, and admiring beauty in others and in art. There are many ways to please a goddess.

The Charms

Aphrodite is more than just good looks.

She is Charm itself (*Charis*) and her friends are the Charms and Graces, lovely goddesses who embody a sweet smile, good grooming, beautiful clothes, easy posture, and all the various charms of your person. The Charms bathe and moisturize Aphrodite with magic oil that restores her youth and wrap her in the ambrosial robe they wove for her, as shown in Botticelli's *Primavera*.

In the Greek view, charm is as much a noun as a verb. You can work at charm by putting effort into your self-presentation. Just kicking back and 'being yourself' shows no desire to please others. Charm is the face you make, not the face you are born with, because a beautiful face can be marred by habitual scowls and grimaces, and a smile makes any face more appealing.

Aphrodite has a jar of cream called Beauty that makes its wearer irresistible. She gave some to Phaon the ferryman in thanks for rescuing her when she was stranded in a bad scene on Lesbos. It made him the most beautiful man in Greece, desired by both sexes. You put on this cream not only by taking care of your skin but also by holding your face beautifully, not pursing your lips in disgust like snobby Apollo or Hera. You display Aphrodite's charms with good, easy posture, an unforced, low voice, and graceful but not ostentatious movement. You can see her relaxed face in models who smile without scrunching their faces like a Kennedy on a yacht.

The Charms are the beauty of personality and the '*it*' quality of movie stars. The ancient Greeks considered sex appeal a kind of divine magic and a gift of the gods.

Charm only happens with other people around. You can't do it alone, because cultivating Charm is not self-improvement or self-involvement. It is improving the landscape for everyone else. Charm makes those around you feel special, for they sense the closeness of a goddess. Charm flourishes in quaint restaurants, flower boxes, and beautiful objects that adorn a room. It dwells in the desire to make things pleasant even when there is disagreement. Charm is the grace and loveliness of human life, from bird feeders to beautiful dresses, and it was considered a public virtue in ancient society and not a personal affair as it is today.

Aphrodite

The Hours

The Hours, *Horae,* are the order of life from birth to death.

These doubles of Aphrodite wear golden necklaces. Each jewel on the string is another pleasant memory. The Greeks never thought of happiness as one giant realization, but as little bits of fun along the way to the grave.

The Hours are lifestyle. They are around when a prestigious job doesn't matter as much as how you spend your day. The Hours want you to forget the time and they are happiest when you love your job because then life is a breeze. The luxury of the home matters to them as well, since you spend so much time there. For the sake of the Hours, a good mattress is in order, for we spend so much of our life in bed.

You honor them when you stop to smell the roses or indulge in luxuries of time like a massage or bubble bath. The Hours are the bigger picture: no one on his deathbed ever wished he'd spent more time worrying or watching television. You honor them when you do things you enjoy until you have had enough, gathering those experiences as so many lovely jewels on the golden necklace.

Aphrodite and the Virgin Goddesses

The three virgin goddesses help you resist and moderate Aphrodite. Athena, Artemis and Hestia are parts of the psyche that must not be polluted by sex or a prejudice towards beauty. Pay attention to them when you need to bring Aphrodite into proportion in your life.

Aphrodite and Athena

Athena doesn't like how sex makes people lose control. She sees sex as a healthy part of life and nothing more. She is the source of second thoughts about an attraction or a liaison--she is the second thought itself, warning you of the risks. Athena the Right Mind steers you away from sex and love because she would rather you throw yourself into work than into a love affair. She wants to keep you at the office and in your

90

professional persona, planning your future and safe from romance and risk.

Aphrodite did try working once—a bit of weaving, Athena's province--but Athena quickly put an end to that and confined her to love making. Athena the Professional is the reason that low cut dresses and muscle t-shirts are frowned on at the office (Athena does the frowning), and why sexual harassment lawsuits re-enact her laying down the law.

The two goddesses work together when Athena helps you strategize your love life, because Athena says, 'there's a time and place for everything'. And Athena *Hygeia*, the Goddess of Hygiene, always reminds you to pack a condom.

Aphrodite and Hestia

Left to her own devices, Hestia the Goddess of the Home would keep you from ever going out or inviting anyone new into your life. She would rather you take care of things and stay in where you are safe. Hestia loves the simple joys of home, where you don't have to be charming or brilliant and no one judges you by your looks.

You can please both goddesses by making your home beautiful. Even a token gesture—perhaps one beautiful object as the focus of a room--can stand for an alliance between the two.

Hestia likes privacy, and all of the gods like some of that. Aphrodite has her own apartments in her husband's palace and her own separate entrance. You honor her when you don't ask your partner what she is thinking about and respect each other's privacy. Hestia would have you sleep on the couch away from your partner once in a while as a welcome break without needing to turn it into one of Hera the Spouse's crises.

Hestia is easy enough to escape by going out of the house where you can be among other people.

Aphrodite and Artemis

Artemis the Bachelor is a self that remains single no matter how married you get. That is the nature of her virginity.

91

Aphrodite

This self can cheat easily because she sees love as just another game. This 'cheating' might involve simply admitting that you feel attracted to someone besides your partner and not feeling bad about it, or it might mean withholding a part of yourself from your partner, which creates an air of mystery that makes you all the more appealing. The Greek ethic was never to confide everything in any one person, not even your spouse.

I have a straight friend who wouldn't take a dance class because he would have been the only straight male in the class and in his mind that would constitute cheating on his wife. Not so in the gay world, where emotional fidelity is most important, and where Artemis' independence is often welcome in a marriage.

Artemis is not willing to die for love. Her anthem is 'I will survive'. To her, sex and love are supposed to be fun, including the thrill of the hunt and keeping score. She has no time for insecurity and is repelled by neediness. She is only attracted to confident people like herself who do things for their own sake and not for the sake of guarantees like Hera, who wants you to talk about the future on a first date.

You can keep Artemis in check by turning her harsh standards against yourself. Your partner may have love handles, but Psyche knows that you are only human, too. And Hermes helps you keep a sense of humor. You reconcile Artemis and Aphrodite by being honest—at least to yourself--about your desires, because the Goddess of Genuine Desires won't pretend for the sake of Hera's commitment.

The Goddess of Purity and Health scorns anyone who is careless about sex, like the time she turned Callisto into a bear and sicked her dogs on her for getting pregnant. Artemis is your good health as a person in your life. She would just as soon you put your energy into sports as into love, for you will get the same flushed face that Aphrodite gives you but without the complications and risks of sex.

Aphrodite and Hera

The gods of sex and morality are often at odds because sex disrupts so many marriages. The very idea of being loved for your body

92

seems superficial and depressing to Hera the Goddess of Marriage, who wants Zeus to love her for herself, not for her 'merely physical' attributes.

These two are at odds when you wish you were attracted to someone you care about but you just aren't. Hera's loyalty makes you want to work at the sex while Aphrodite wants nothing to do with sex that has to be worked on. Hera is in charge when you refuse sex for non-sexual reasons like revenge after an argument.

The truth is that Hera envies Aphrodite's freedom and popularity. When people become too promiscuous and sport like gods, she sends venereal diseases to check Aphrodite's power. From Aphrodite's point-of-view, Hera is moralistic and controlling, but she would never say so to her face because she doesn't like confrontation like Hera, who takes everything personally. Aphrodite likes sex for its own sake--not for the sake of the relationship--and she bores easily. She would never settle for a sexless relationship or one in which she has to remind someone to sleep with her. She might have you manipulate someone into loving you--she casts love spells with trinkets--but only for the sake of the love and the sex, not for some other reason like a mink, prestige, or loyalty.

Statues in ancient Greece show a combination goddess, 'Aphrodite Hera', the goddess of newlyweds and romance, who loves wine and candlelit dinners, followed by lovemaking with that one special person. Gay men like me usually do this in reverse—sex first, dinner later--because who wants to have sex on a full stomach? We generally try out Aphrodite first, starting with the sex to see if there's any reason to invite Hera with her romance over dinner. Aphrodite Hera had a temple for virgins and a sacred spring that made women fertile. This was a bridal cult, which lives on in 'the pledge', a chastity movement among Christian young people, except that with Aphrodite chastity has nothing to do with sinfulness or prudishness, only with saving yourself for someone special.

You can please Aphrodite Hera by continuing to date your partner even when you are already married and being your best for each other. You can put on a sexy self the way Hera puts on Aphrodite's negligee, perhaps by wearing sexy underwear, leather, or something naughty but nice.

Aphrodite Hera is also the Goddess of Mistresses and Widows—people who have been around the block and just want some intimate company and friendship. She is a goddess of unmarried couples who live together with or without sexual fidelity. You can honor her by flirting so long as you respect the rule which satisfies both goddesses at the same time: once it's understood that nothing can happen, the more outrageous the flirtation the better.

Dione

Some myths call Aphrodite the child of Zeus and Dione, a sea nymph and double of the goddess.

Dione is the Hollywood romance and its ritual re-telling. Two friends slowly fall in love within familiar surroundings as one sees the other in a different light, and the relationship changes forever.

You honor Dione by admiring longstanding couples and being grateful for their happiness—or by being part of one. You can hang out with her by reading romance novels or watching romantic movies. And you can be on the lookout for her just by keeping an open mind about love and its strings.

Venus

The Roman Aphrodite is--like everything Roman--harder and coarser than her Greek counterpart. Aphrodite looks girlish in comparison to this war goddess who takes no prisoners in love. Botticelli's alluring Venus is more like Aphrodite than Venus.

Venus is the Sexual Provocateur, with a taste for role-play. Her doubles include a long list of brassy blonds like Mae West, Ivana Trump, and Zsa Zsa Gabor as well as brunettes like Madonna the Material Girl--individuals with high style and uptown manners, furs, diamonds and sexual power.

Venus can be like a drag queen with her over-the-top defiance. She wants you to slip on that slutty outfit and plaster on the makeup so that everyone knows you mean business.

Aphrodite and Poseidon

Greek sailors kept an image of Aphrodite the Protector of Sailors on board to keep horny old Poseidon happy, like the poster girls on GI's lockers. In her honor, the prows of ships bore statues of the goddess and ships are still dubbed *she*. Aphrodite's natural connection with the ocean is why the Miss America Contest was held for years in Atlantic City and has always included a swimsuit contest.

Aphrodite and Poseidon are sexual freedom. Their excellence is possible when your emotions and your sexuality are free of your own meddling—that is, when you see them as belonging to someone else, a friend whom you do not tell what to do.

Aphrodite's festival was the *Aphrodisia*, wild days of abandon after the festival of Poseidon when ships returned to port, which was like a combination of Fleet Week and Spring Break. You can spend a weekend in Las Vegas to get a feel for this sensuous and slightly tacky couple. The Goddess of the Haven is the special atmosphere of harbor towns and beach resorts, where beautiful people congregate and romance abounds. You can honor them by spending a day relaxing at the beach and watching everyone go by half naked, or by 'cruising', contemporary slang that reflects her connection to the sea. Aphrodite of Fair Sailing, *Euploia*, is success after a setback and the calm after the storm. She is around when you feel lucky and optimistic in life.

She is one of many Greek gods of salvation—which in Greece had nothing to do with being a good person and everything to do with how much a particular god liked you. Aphrodite saves Boutes from drowning when he jumps overboard because he is handsome, not because he is a 'good person', a concept foreign to Greek sensibilities. Indeed, the Greeks would say of a wise man that 'he knows wisdom' and of a strategic woman that 'she knows strategy' rather than attribute personal qualities to a single Self.

Beautiful people have it easier than the rest of us, and being

Aphrodite

loved by some god—any god: a talent, a friendship, or an abiding passion—makes life fair sailing and worthwhile.

Aphrodite Watcher from the Sea Cliffs is the special mood of promontories, widow's walks and lonely hearts. Missing or remembering love after a separation or death—including the love of a pet—can find refuge by the ocean, with its constant waves and sense of immortality, or at any place that feels like the end of the world.

Aphrodite and Hephaestus

Poseidon and Apollo vied to marry Aphrodite but Zeus preempted the quarrel by marrying her off to Hephaestus, the smithy with deformed feet. Their marriage was never consummated because that was not the nature of their relationship. They represent the marriage of Beauty and Art.

Domestically, they are the arrangement, the understanding that distinguishes between sexual and emotional fidelity that keeps so many marriages going beyond the honeymoon years. As long as you stay together, you are free to roam or to fantasize about someone else.

Aphrodite comes and goes as she pleases but she is discreet about it, because consideration for her partner is part of her loveliness. Hephaestus spends most of his time at work anyway.

She likes having it both ways: being married but not acting like a couple. Aphrodite doesn't want you to be half of anything, especially anything predictable or conventional. Nevertheless, she wouldn't want an open relationship because she likes the illusion of fidelity too much. Aphrodite needs the romantic white lie of 'the one and only' in order to feel secure in her position. Besides, the guilt of cheating is part of the thrill to her.

Hephaestus fascinates her because the God of Craft is so different from other men—so completely strange and full of original ideas. He makes her exquisite jewelry and creates art in her likeness. Hephaestus' skilled work provides amply for them both. Their recent doubles are Aristotle Onassis and Jackie Kennedy.

96

Hephaestus' interiority and complexity are the opposite of Aphrodite's surface charms and the reason we attach more gravity to an artist than to a runway model. She easily gets handsome men to chase her, but she is thrilled to inspire in Hephaestus the creation of beautiful art, which is so much more than mere prettiness. She loves being his Muse because it makes her feel uniquely beautiful.

This couple is not like Hera and Zeus, who argue all the time and try to work things out. Their marriage has surprisingly few blow ups, because Hephaestus knows his own good luck and would never leave her. Mostly they live a peaceful co-existence, with Hephaestus providing an emotional home base and not asking a lot of questions.

You are like them when you give your partner space, whether it's taking separate vacations, having different friends, or just being able to be alone together. When these two are around, you can resist asking your partner who was on the telephone or where she is going, because silence is the secret of this marriage. Theirs is a pleasant fiction that keeps the peace and lets each go his way freely.

Aphrodite and Hermes

These two are the Cosmopolitan who desires to experience everything that life has to offer, culturally and erotically. You are like them when you enjoy luxury and know how to splurge once in a while.

These gods think of dating and sex as great varieties of pleasure—pleasures that have nothing to do with obligation or childbearing. They make you feel at ease with new people, and to find Aphrodite the Stranger particularly alluring.

Hermes the God of Travel has one in every port. He may love truly and be a good friend, but he has no interest in settling down with one person because his priorities are good times and friendship, not guarantees. Hermes never tries to control Aphrodite, because this freedom-loving god has no desire to dominate others and would never limit someone to playing the same role all the time. He likes change and he encourages you to like change too.

Aphrodite

They share the nickname Persuasion, *Peitho.* Hermes Persuasion is smooth talk and humor, while the Lady of Persuasion, *Potnia Peitho,* convinces you to fall in love and manipulates you with vows of love and games of jealousy. *Aphrodite Psithyros,* the Whispering One, speaks to you and you alone, perhaps through pillow talk.

Their child, Hermaphrodite, was born with male genitals and the breasts, thighs and hair of a female. Some say he was a handsome young man who attracted the eye of the nymph, Salmakis, who conjoined her body with his while he bathed in her spring, whose waters were thereafter said to make men effeminate.

You honor Hermaphrodite by not judging women who are masculine or men who are feminine. Or you can imagine being of the opposite sex or of the opposite sexual orientation for a little while as you go about your business. No one has to know, because Salmakis did not ask for Hermaphrodite's consent.

Aphrodite Courtesan

Aphrodite Courtesan, *Hetaira,* is another mix of Aphrodite and Hermes.

Aphrodite Hetaira is the friend who is easy going and fun to be around. She is a geisha—a sophisticated party girl who can speak in depth on any subject, often in more than one language, and usually has some musical or other talent to liven up the party. She may be a high-class prostitute, a trophy wife, or a cosmopolitan friend who is lively but of somewhat dubious character—but who doesn't judge your character either.

You honor her when you enjoy a variety of pleasures and think of yourself as an artiste, with or without a medium. Aphrodite Hetaira is the goddess of Metrosexuals and jetsetters. The Greeks prayed to her to *make us amiable in words and deeds,* the way you put yourself in the right mood before going out to dinner or to a party.

She's the kind of friend you can confide in about personal things like your love life and your health, but in a light way like the girls at the beauty parlor or the friends at the barber's or the coffee shop—

wherever groups of friends meet casually. These friendships cannot withstand arguments or unpleasantness, but they love gossip. They are shallow but pleasant friendships in which you can treat plans loosely in case a better offer comes up.

Aphrodite the Laughter Loving is the pleasant MTV commentator discussing the personal lives of the stars with a smile and the obligatory cockney accent. She is the charming date, the laughter and squeals of children playing, the loveliness of flowers and butterflies, and the frolicking of animals. She is the impulse to make a fuss over small treats, to coo at babies and puppies, and to scream and jump in delight like co-eds reuniting after summer vacation.

Aphrodite Pandemos

Aphrodite of the People, *Pandemos*, is the Worldly Venus of Botticelli's *Primavera*--the one with the clothes on because she knows shame, as opposed to Heavenly Aphrodite, *Urania,* who stands in nude innocence.

Plato called Pandemos the *common physical love*--heterosexual love, that is--as opposed to Heavenly Aphrodite, who is homosexual and platonic--but then again, Plato was a follower of Apollo the Gay Perfectionist, who prefers longing for someone out of reach to actually getting to know someone real. He has old Socrates share a bed with Alcibiades the athlete without making a single move all night just to prove that he's above physical sex.

Pandemos is the Political Activist, especially concerning sexuality. This goddess shows up with Persuasion, *Peitho* to plead causes for the common man alongside Hermes of the People. She is the animating force behind ACT UP, NOW, Planned Parenthood, and GMHC—a goddess of tolerance and good health, notably sexual and women's health.

Pandemos is a friend of Athena Health, *Hygieia,* who sees the treatment of epidemics as a civic duty and not a moral issue. These days, she leads efforts to make condoms available and to get young women vaccinated. She is a friend of health plans that cover contraception and a

Aphrodite

proponent of safe and legal abortions.

You befriend her when you talk freely about sexual issues and take a political stand that defends women, gays, and other common citizens. You insult her when you judge others for their sexuality or have a negative view of sex, which denies our common animality.

Heavenly Aphrodite

Urania, the Queen in the Heavens, is an ancient goddess of the Eastern Mediterranean. The Daughter of the Sky is the oldest of the *Moira,* or Fates.

This is Aphrodite's spiritual side, which is similar to New Age spirituality with its emphasis on relaxing meditation, sensuous baths, soothing massage and magical oils, candles, and scents—all in the name of inner peace. This spirituality is materialistic and superficial, staying with the body while claiming to rise above it, because that is Aphrodite's nature. She doesn't ask you to fast for a cause or build housing for the poor but she will lead you towards peace, especially freedom from stress, guilt, and tension.

Venus of the Lighthouse, *Phosphoros*, is the guiding light in your life, a beacon shining in the dark, the light at the end of the tunnel, and the inspiration from afar, like a dream of retiring or an artistic project that keeps you going.

Heavenly Aphrodite is the Muse and the Eternal Feminine of great artists, whose beauty is uncanny, rich in meaning, and inspiring. Like many ancient goddesses, Urania is a virgin mother who was worshipped with incense and dove sacrifices. She is the intellectual love of the soul and the soul's longing for beauty. Answering her call creates art that is less personal and narcissistic and more noble and heavenly in its aspirations. She is Aphrodite from Apollo's point of view, so there is always plenty of longing when she's around, especially the artistic longing for perfection. Urania's temples were off limits to common people, sometimes even to the keeper of the temple.

And yet there is a certain vulgarity about her. The

100

conservative Greeks considered eastern gods effeminate and barbaric because they made people lose control of themselves in orgies and dances or give in to laziness. In Corinth, the Las Vegas of its time, the temple of Urania housed the *Daughters of Persuasion*, sacred prostitutes who offered their services for a donation to the temple.

Yet, considering a prostitute a priestess of Aphrodite changes the act from debasement to sex therapy. As with all behaviors, the Greeks never tried to eliminate prostitution. They just tried to find a place for it and to make it look good. To them, sex is a holy act because it belongs to a god. It is only dirty if that is part of its fantasy, as with sadistic Chronos, a raping Centaur or selfish Poseidon.

Urania is a decadent beauty like Rembrandt's *Flora*, a faded grand hotel, or the atmosphere of *Death in Venice*. When you completely immerse yourself in art, the actual world seems tawdry in comparison.

I have friends who attend art openings and theater with a kind of desperation, surrounding themselves with fabulous individuals as if trying to prove that their lives are above the common folk and that things aren't as squalid as they seem to secretly fear. The ivory tower looks down upon green fields and quadrangles, but it also looks down upon teeming slums and human garbage. Aphrodite is a world but she is not the World, for that is Zeus and he includes all things.

Warrior Aphrodite

When Aphrodite was born on the tiny island of Kythera, she gave it the once over and skipped on to the larger island of Cyprus, taking its name as her own because Aphrodite *Kypris* is too beautiful and likes going out too much to stay cooped up in the middle of nowhere. The natives welcomed her like a celebrity and crowned her Aphrodite the Queen, *Basilis*.

She arrived on the Greek mainland as Warrior Aphrodite with an invading navy bringing scandalous rituals from the decadent East, because sex invades the rational mind of Athena and feels foreign like Dionysus, another invading god.

101

Aphrodite

Warrior Aphrodite combines Aphrodite with Ares the Warrior. She is the aggressive side of sex—its fight—and the appeal of men in uniform, from soldiers to the UPS guy, and the erotic nationalism of Nazism and send-in-the-boys mentality. She is the women who travel alongside the army, including the female soldiers, the prostitutes, the poster girls, and the letters from back home.

Aphrodite Victory, *Nike,* is the love that conquers and the surge of testosterone that comes with victory, like GI's at the liberation of Paris or the well-documented testosterone peaks following a winning sports competition and affecting entire cities. Her longtime boyfriend, Ares, is hotness itself. He brings his rock hard lance to battle, not as a sweet and loving thing but as an angry and demanding thing.

Aphrodite satisfies his aggressions or abets them to intensify the lovemaking. In many Renaissance paintings, Mars, the Roman Ares, sleeps next to the waking Venus, not because Venus answers strife with love, like flower children or Christians, but because she wears it out until it runs its course.

Peace follows satisfaction, not a withdrawal from fighting, so the way to be like these two is to pursue release before the soul turns upon itself in neurosis. You honor them when you think of sex as hot and not just as romantic, as Hera the Spouse would have you do. You also honor them when you fight for something or someone you love instead of withdrawing like a frightened nymph or rising above the fray like Apollo, releasing stress.

The children of Aphrodite and Ares are Fear, *Phobos,* Terror, *Deimos,* and Harmonia—these emotions are familiar to those in love. Phobos can be any phobia or fear and Deimos can be the sound of fire alarms, racing ambulances and the panic of the poor soul riding inside. Recently they were 'Shock and Awe', but usually you know them through the fear of losing your lover and being alone.

Aphrodite tends to like men who aren't good for her-- masculine and moody guys like Ares, who make better lovers than husbands. Studies show that just before their period, women are attracted to bad boy types and that the rest of the time they want a reliable man,

102

because the bad boy may offer genes related to more aggressive behavior but the reliable man is a good provider.

Anthea

Anthea is the Garden, as a place and as a state of mind. She is the paradise of gardens with inviting niches, statues and rooms. She is also the enchanting bouquet, centerpiece and idyllic, leafy suburb. You honor this Goddess of Fruits and Herbs when you create lovely floral arrangements, sachets, and fruit baskets, or when you lovingly tend a garden.

Flowers are sex organs and gardening is a kind of public sensuality made to look as natural and inviting as possible. In England, Aphrodite is largely confined to Antheia, which is why a traditional English woman will grow flowers and talk about them in great detail, but would never dream of putting one in her hair.

Antheia makes you care what the world actually looks like. She is *the woman's touch* that brings loveliness to the ordinary. She is the magic of flowerboxes and mini-parks that bring charm to an otherwise shabby neighborhood like Greenwich Village.

Aphroditos

The famous Bearded Venus is Aphroditos the Transvestite, shown in statues as a man in a dress. At his festival on Cyprus, men and women exchanged clothing. You can wear a bit of underwear of the opposite sex to get into his mindset. Or you can pretend to be of the opposite sex or sexual orientation for a while. No one needs to know because *the gods love to hide.*

Aphroditos liberates because it is completely arbitrary that women wear dresses and men do not, since everyone used to wear togas.

You can honor him by letting your inner voice—the one that narrates—belong to the opposite sex for a while. Of course, going to a drag show is a real treat for this persona.

Aphrodite

Aphrodite and Anchises

Zeus got so annoyed at Aphrodite for making him horny all the time—and even tempting him herself--that he arranged for her to fall in love with a mortal, his son and double Anchises.

Aphrodite Mistress of Beasts was out walking through the forest and putting all the animals into heat when she came upon Anchises, a shepherd with the body of a god. She told him she was a princess from far away and looked down coyly like *Aphrodite Parakouptousa*, She Who Looks Away. Anchises hesitated at first until her inviting looks led him to take her by the hand to his tent.

These two are the Enchanting Love Affair, as a person you will always remember and seek to find again. Aphrodite is the lover you feel lucky to have and who seems out of your league, like a Hollywood star on the cover of a glossy magazine.

After sex and a doze, Aphrodite reveals herself to Anchises, growing taller until her head reaches the top of the tent and her face bathes in light. Terrified that he has defiled a goddess, Anchises relaxes when Aphrodite tells him not to worry, only to keep the affair a secret. Sadly, one night at the bar Anchises boasts about sleeping with Aphrodite, and Zeus strikes him lame with a thunderbolt. Not one to stick around during the tough times, Aphrodite soon tires of nursing him and moves on to someone else.

When someone looks like a god or a movie star, try to remember that he or she is also a mortal and subject to the same gods as you. Anchises wants you to ask that person out. Anchises' mistake is to tell everyone about his sexual fulfillment, and Zeus strikes him down because telling people about things like your fabulous sex life or your incredible wealth only makes people jealous and by extension, the gods. Zeus stands for the order of the world and he puts great effort into keeping his own affairs secret.

Nerites

Nerites is the name of a small and marvelous cockleshell. He

104

was once Aphrodite's lover and the handsomest of men and gods.

They lived together in the sea until Aphrodite moved on to the flashy crowd on Olympus. She invited Nerites to join her and even offered him wings but he chose to stay in his old home. Eros got the wings. Poseidon then took up Nerites as his own lover and drove around with him in his chariot on the waves like an old letch in a convertible showing off his trophy lover.

Nerites is puppy love and crushes. He is the first person you loved and the person you were when you did. Remembering him is a way of being loyal to that self and that time of innocence. When he's with Poseidon, he is the desire to recapture youth and innocence by dating someone half your age.

He is the high school steady, the houseboy and the kept surfer. He is the group of young friends in the old photograph, the teen memories of trolling up and down Main Street, and the way the old schoolyard looks so small when you go back to visit, like the marvelous little shell. Nerites is the old skill or interest from long ago, like playing guitar or a forgotten coin collection. You honor him by looking up old friends on Facebook, visiting your old stomping grounds, or showing your loyalty to the past in some way. Nostalgia is a gift to Nerites, even if it's just listening to your old favorites on the stereo on a rainy day.

Adonis

Smyrna's mother foolishly boasted that her daughter was more beautiful than Aphrodite, so to punish her the goddess made her sneak into her father's bed at night.

When he realized who was carrying his child, Smyrna's father chased her in rage with his sword as she cried out to the gods for help. Feeling sheepish, Aphrodite turned her into a myrrh tree, which the striking sword split right down the middle. Out tumbled the baby Adonis.

Aphrodite put him in a basket and entrusted it to Persephone. When the boy grew into a beautiful young man, Persephone made him her lover. Aphrodite acted morally offended when she heard this and

Aphrodite

demanded custody, but she just wanted Adonis for herself. Zeus took no part in this unsavory dispute and referred the matter to a lower court presided over by Calliope, who worked out a deal in which each goddess kept Adonis for a third of the year, with the young man free for the other third to rest from these insatiable lovers. Naturally, Aphrodite didn't play fair and used her magic girdle to make Adonis yield his free season and begrudge Persephone her share as well.

In revenge, Persephone told Aphrodite's boyfriend, Ares that she was sleeping with a mere mortal—*and an effeminate one at that.* Ares appeared as a boar while Adonis was out hunting and gored him to death right in front of the weeping goddess.

. He is lost youth. He is your long lost younger self, following you around, the teenage self you encounter in dreams and the innocent pretty boy or pretty girl within.

Adonis is the name of a fast growing lettuce with shallow roots. During the *Adonia,* his yearly festival, the Greeks grew sprouts in a flat bowl called *Adonis gardens* and observed alternating days of happiness and sorrow, like Easter week.

Adonis is a lightweight--an adolescent self who wants excitement but isn't ready for the hard world of men like Ares. His attraction to danger causes his death, like teens killed in car accidents while drinking or speeding. His doubles include Keats, Shelly, and James Dean—people who are 'too beautiful for this world' and are remembered as much for their early deaths as for their achievements. Adonis is the melancholy mood of lost promise and summer love doomed by practicality. He is your adolescent voice--higher than your grown up voice--and the tendency to dance on your feet instead of standing firmly on the ground.

For all the tears, Adonis is more poignant than tragic. This unformed self must be gored to death, because there's no time for mortals to cling to the past or to dwell in innocent sensuality. Aphrodite demands that where once there was a passive young man, there must now be the virility of Ares-- and a dead boy.

Underworld Aphrodite

The Queen of the Underworld and the Dark Goddess, *Malainis,* is a double of Persephone, the self who is married to death, or Hades. She is sexual darkness, including cruelty, disease or loss. The French call orgasm *le petit mort,* the little death, remembering the connection between death and sex. AIDS brought back this association, tainting every liaison with the possibility of death. Aphrodite Death in Life is the love that dies before the lovers do. She is also the dying lover, like my partner who died of AIDS. Aphrodite on the Graves is the lover who is now dead. You honor this goddess by keeping the memory of past lovers alive, perhaps with a photograph or keepsake or by staying in touch with lovers from whom you have separated.

It gets more sinister than this. Aphrodite the Dark One, *Skotia,* and Aphrodite the Unholy, *Anosia* are dark sexual compulsions and perversions, like 'gift-giving' and 'bug-chasing'—passing along a venereal disease intentionally. These dark goddesses want you to relish shame and humiliation in sex and to leave far behind any sense of Hera the Person and Athena the Mind. Aphrodite the Watcher, *Parakuptousa,* is coldness towards a lover and voyeurism. She looks upon her dead lover in artwork, possibly counting her inheritance. You can invite her into the relationship by discussing how you would spend your lives after the other one dies.

Aphrodite *Gorgo* is Sleeping Beauty frozen in slumber—or in death. She is the face of the lover sleeping next to you in a distant mental state. And Aphrodite the Man Slayer, *Androphonos,* is one of the Furies, monsters of outrage and revenge. She is the love that becomes hate, as in *Fatal Attraction* and so many Lifetime movies.

The Sirens

The sirens are bird-women who lure sailors to rocky shoals with enchanting voices and pick over the bodies of the living and the dead with their gigantic beaks. Only Odysseus has heard them and lived to tell about it, because he had his crew tie him to the mast as the ship sailed by, stopping their ears with wax and ordering them not to release him no matter how much he begs. Twelve step therapies and interventions are a modern equivalent.

A Siren is a dangerous pleasure or addiction that takes on its own life in your experience. It might be cigarettes or drugs or any destructive pleasure. By seeing this compulsion as a Siren and a person in its own right, you create some space to maneuver. You can relate to that person, the one who does the drugs or smokes the cigarettes. You can get angry at that person without picking on yourself, or beg them to leave you alone. You can remember that person in a 12-step program or through personal rituals, like having a cup of tea instead of smoking a cigarette without denying what you'd rather be doing or trying to get rid of that self, which will only make it dig its heels in.

You surrender to the Sirens when you follow an addiction to your doom or become co-dependent with someone else, so that you become Sirens to each other.

Moving On

You identify with Aphrodite too much when you think that looks and love are all that matter and age is only a reason to despair. However much she may love you today, Aphrodite is fickle and we all grow old. You know you're in trouble when Love and Sex are making you broke or wrecking your health or reputation.

The virgin goddesses are best at resisting her insatiable demands. Athena wants you to work and to adopt a practical approach to life. Hestia wants you to stay in at night and be at peace. Artemis doesn't want you falling in love because she likes her freedom too much.

Other pleasures appeal. Turn to Hermes for the hedonistic fun of going out, traveling, and being in a crowd, or to Artemis, who enjoys being physical in other ways than sex, like team activities and sports. Or try entertaining Aphrodite with the beauty of objects in a museum. There's more than one way to please a goddess.

Psyche deepens Aphrodite by reminding you of your mortality. Maintaining a double consciousness by seeing the other person as both

Harriet/Tom and Aphrodite the Lover helps to put Aphrodite's superficial ways in perspective. Or you can do something artistic for Hephaestus, who sees beauty in the created thing more than in actual people.

Clinging to Aphrodite only annoys her because she won't be held still. She prefers you to act charming and to give her some space the way she does with Hephaestus. That means setting aside your friendship with sex, love, and beauty sometimes and paying attention to other gods.

DIONYSUS

Dionysus is the God of Wine and Madness.

He is ecstasy. He is intoxication. He is who you are when you are drunk or high, and he is the drugs and the alcohol itself. Dionysus is the freedom to *do what you want to do,* as his followers declared. He is passion as if it had a mind of its own, which is the very nature of passion.

Dionysus is a god of the arts, especially the performing arts in which the artist seems possessed by his role. Nietzsche pairs him alchemically with Apollo in *The Birth of Tragedy.* In Hellenistic times, artists and thinkers banded together in guilds called *Dionysus flatterers* to recognize the greatest among them in the name of Delphi—the equivalent of our Oscars and Kennedy Center Awards.

Turn to Dionysus when life feels dry and predictable or you feel restrained by social identity or rationality. You can follow the Lord of Freedom to excess in anything from yoga to sex to art—Dionysus is the impulse towards the extreme in any activity.

But passion isn't all fun and games. Remember the Saints. No human can pursue Dionysus alone, unfettered by any other god. That leads to burnout or worse.

Dionysus possesses his followers and leads them into madness, tearing them apart through humiliation, disease, and addiction—or a hangover, withdrawal, and low blood sugar. Dionysus comes and goes, because you can't always live like it's 1999. The Greeks welcomed his return in the spring with great festivals, because Dionysus makes everything old seem new again.

The Liberator

Dionysus the Liberator is a god of freedom, often through drugs or alcohol. He frees you from your usual selves and the life of routine.

He is the God of Intoxication. The Greeks called anyone drunk or high *Another Dionysus*, because when you are drunk, you are a double of the god himself. Dionysus is the only god who breaks down the barrier between gods and men. To the Greeks, wine was a miraculous gift from the Giver of Joy to mortals, rivaled only by Demeter's food and immortality cult. The new bunches of purple grapes are Dionysus in a Basket and the crushing of the grapes is the martyrdom of Dionysus the Vine Cluster.

The God Wine turns the world upside down and brings the arrogant down to earth, because everyone has to let go sometimes. His very presence makes rocks split open and water gush forth. *Time for Dionysus* is time to throw back a few and let Dionysus the Deliverer and Healer free your tongue and clear the air. As the Greek poet said, *Wine is a look-see into a man.*

He is the normal, healthy desire to be liberated from the normal healthy self (usually Athena or Hera) once in a while, bursting through habits and limits that have become bondage and routines that have become a rut. Dionysus tumbles down walls and turns chains into vines, freeing you from the constant goal setting of Herakles the Hero, whose great strength and focus on action can be monotonous. He wants you to live without a goal the way animals do.

The wise old seer, Teiresias, sets an example for society by following Dionysus willingly, shamelessly wearing the outfit of his female followers, the Maenads, despite his age and dignity--because it is better to get down once in a while than to be torn apart all at once.

With Dionysus, the aim is always ecstasy, never curing anything or getting things done. *Ekstasis* means *to stand outside oneself*, like when you've been dancing so long it becomes automatic or you do any activity with such passion that things seem to happen by themselves. He is the urge to be someone else and to see your self as someone else. Dionysus rules the theater because his consciousness sees a world populated by masks: there are many eyes shining in the darkness. Dionysus sees your identity as a cluster of masks and roles with even the true self of Apollo as just another mask.

Stranger yet, there is no one wearing the masks. The masks speak for themselves, a point brought home by the famous stone masks of

Dionysus

Dionysus carved as big as a man. This is completely with Evolutionary Psychology's observation that when we look at the brain we see behaviors but there's 'no one home'—no 'ghost in the machine' or area of the brain that describes a center or self.

Prince of the Blessed

Dionysus is passion as a person who comes and goes in your life.

The original party boy *loves banquets and bouquets* and all kinds of fun. He likes sex for pleasure, not for procreation, although he is also a loving father. You are like him when you pursue something you enjoy to its utmost, insane extreme, whether it's a love affair, a hobby, a talent, or a job.

When Dionysus takes over, the normal safe world is gone and you find yourself on the edge—which is exciting but also frightening and insane. He may lead you to the wrong side of town and to the wild places and caves of the city—or to the wrong person's apartment. At his best, Dionysus brings you the quiet good that comes from satisfaction and the wisdom to accept the new. He is the cure for Hera the Moralist who is full of resentment because she isn't getting any and feels righteous about it.

When Dionysus goes away, life is dull, the libido drops, and routine takes over. He *dies* when you stop dreaming or touching or when you try to act like an adult Athena and not a sissy. Dionysus goes missing when you watch the clock during an activity instead of pursuing it to satisfaction.

Artwork shows a young man of great beauty and refinement, wearing a royal purple robe or other feminine attire. Sometimes he is a bearded man with horns, looking grave and tranquil with flowing hair and holding the *thyrsus*—the burning pine torch--a wine cup and a spray of ivy. In later years, he is shown with his head drooping with long hair, his gaze downward, and his limbs softened in a languorous buzz. Nevertheless, his images always radiate inner life and dignity. Dionysus has the powerful presence of Another Zeus.

The Greek Gods Among Us

The symbols of his festivals are a wine jar, a vine, a goat, a basket of figs and a phallus. His two major festivals at Athens began with the Festival of Flowers, *Anthesteria,* which opened with the crowning of three year olds with flowers—for the Greeks considered infants to be hedonistic creatures of Dionysus. Later in the day, men pushing carts hurled insults at bystanders in a reversal of the social civility of Hera and Athena, reveling in Dionysus' power like the carnival clown who insults people while they throw balls to dunk him in a pool below. At the end of the day, Dionysus arrived in an elaborate ship on wheels like a parade float with a masked actor onboard playing the god, who would sleep with the Queen that night. Then there were prayers over the new wine.

The second day, everyone brought his own bottle and drank in silence. According to legend, a famous misanthrope when asked by his silent drinking companion at the end of the day how he enjoyed the afternoon responded, *It was fine except for you being here.* That was spoken like a real Silenus, the cynical satyr who is any drunk crying in his beer or singing *Is That All There Is?*

On the third day the underworld spirits, the *keres,* were invited to dine with the living and then ritually swept out of the house with brooms at the end of the festival.

The second fest, the Greater Dionysia, started off with a procession led by a large wooden phallus through the city. Phalli were hawked everywhere and paraded past all the important landmarks of the city amid boisterous dances and jokes. Later that day, large numbers of bulls—Dionysus' animal--were slaughtered for a citywide steak dinner. The classes intermingled freely amid the optimism of the city.

The Athenians went to these lengths because tradition had it that when Dionysus first showed up, the Athenian men did not eagerly accept him and he cursed them with impotence.

Dionysus cannot be controlled or put on a schedule. With him, arousal follows desire and not instruction or duty. If your sex life with your partner is sagging, you can't schedule Dionysus' passion; you have to act when the interest shows up, even if you're in the kitchen. Dionysus

113

Dionysus

likes role play and theatrical elements like masks, war paint, and costumes to get you out of Athena the Normal Self or Hera the Dutiful Spouse.

The theatrical performances at Dionysus' festivals grew to include three tragedies, a satyr play and a comedy, which made for a long day. The audience drank and ate throughout the plays, grabbing at the nuts and raisins the actors threw at them during the comedies. There was lots of hissing and booing and kicking of heels in approval, yet it was all very religious at the same time.

The Greater Dionysia was a huge success in ancient times among citizens and foreigners alike. But by the time it moved to Rome the party became a true sex orgy and was eventually banned.

The Foreign God

Dionysus means *the God from Nysa*, the name of a mythical paradise. It can also translate as *Zeus' Limp*, because lightning killed Dionysus' mother and he was sewn into Zeus' thigh until he was born.

The God Wine and his crew conquered India by making their enemies insane and causing them to panic rather than engaging in direct combat. Then they invaded Greece, although in time aristocrats would claim pride of lineage and ownership of the original vines from Asia. In actuality, images of Dionysus date back to Mycenaean times, so his *newness* is psychological, not historical. Dionysus the Foreigner indicates something new in the personality or in the body that makes normal life difficult to continue, like an addiction, a disease, or a desire that takes on a life of its own. He is a sense of sudden urgency in an otherwise orderly existence that, if ignored, grows only worse or violent. He provokes xenophobia in those who would resist change.

Dionysus adopted the rites of the Earth Mother, who cleansed him and initiated him into her mysteries. He is the mystical aspect of religion, like identifying with the Passion of Jesus or with ever-suffering Mary.

Unfortunately there were no extra seats at the Olympian table, so modest Hestia yielded hers to Dionysus—something none of the other

114

gods with their Hollywood egos would ever do. Hestia was willing to sacrifice because she is the Center and that must be set aside in order to know Dionysus.

He has two story lines: he is kind to those who accept him willingly and merciless to those who refuse him. Yielding to Dionysus wins his blessings of happiness and even a light buzz and some action. His presence makes life seem to spin out of control—or at least the room -- because the Warden of the Gate brings you outside the city walls of your life and into an underworld of dreams and fantasies.

This clears the air. Amid the swirling dance, the flinging torches and the primal drums, the God of Madness fixes his calm eyes on you, and you can't turn away from the terrible truth of whatever you are denying or dreading. Dionysus is there when you wake up at three in the morning, filled with dread.

The Greeks admired the wisdom of the modest and gentle temper that knows how to give in occasionally rather than to cling to socially upright selves all the time. Nobody looks back on his deathbed and wishes he spent more time at the office instead of having fun.

The Womanly Stranger

Dionysus is The Womanly One.

He is the pretty boy in purple who is just too beautiful, too talented, or too fascinating to be 'one of the guys'. He is your inner femme-boy or girly girl and he is fabulous.

Prince Paris in *The Iliad* is like Dionysus. He poses in his dashing armor to impress the women, not because he's eager to fight at Troy. Dionysus can be overwhelmed on the battlefield and in the corporate office by the tough masculinity of Ares the Fighter and Zeus the Businessman. He is the only Greek god whose followers belonged mostly to the opposite sex. He leads these *Maenads* away from the daily drudge of home life and off to the mountains with their arms flung over their heads in wild abandon.

Dionysus was raised as a girl or an effeminate boy with Eros

115

Dionysus

and Aphrodite for companions. His priests were transvestites. He is your sensuous and receptive nature. Fifty years ago he invaded America with the Beatles and their long hair and a generational revolution of sex, drugs, and non-conformity.

One day Dionysus was walking along the beach as a beautiful young man with strong shoulders and long hair, wearing the purple cloak of royalty, when some passing Cretan pirates seized him and bound him for sale. But the ropes didn't hold. The helmsman realized he was holding captive a god and warned the crew, but they ignored him.

Courage, divine Hecator, said the god, *I like you. I am Dionysus, the Ear Splitter,* and he promised the helmsman wealth and luck as a reward for recognizing him without force. You act like Hecator when you allow someone else to lead or allow events to change your course rather than fighting stubbornly.

Suddenly, wine bubbled miraculously out of the woodwork, vines laden with luscious grapes climbed up the masts, and the oarlocks turned into garlands. Dionysus appeared on the upper deck as a roaring lion while a bear attacked the crew below. The captain was slain and the crew jumped overboard, turning into dolphins.

You honor Dionysus by accepting and respecting traditionally feminine qualities in yourself—whatever your sex --and in others. You respect him when you do not mistake beauty for weakness and when you honor true desires and fantasies. Dionysus has no patience for anyone who pretends that he's so heterosexual he can't tell if another man is attractive. Dionysus is bisexual. To honor him, you don't have to literally sleep with someone outside of your sexual preference, but you have to be able to be affected by beauty, wherever it shows up. Even straight men gather eagerly around a handsome leader. Most of our presidents have been good looking and most fascists like David Duke are typically handsome.

The effeminate self wants you to be open to new pleasures and longings, especially those denied by Hera's morality and Athena's pragmatism. This doesn't mean you have to degrade yourself—unless that's your secret desire—but it does require following Dionysus by indulging your fantasies once in a while and living truly.

The God Who Arises From the Earth

The Earth Father in the early Mediterranean area was depicted as *the Worthy Bull,* and identified with both Poseidon and Dionysus. Artwork shows Dionysus riding a bull, a tiger, or a leopard, sometimes alongside Poseidon. While Poseidon is Force, personified, Dionysus is Flow. Both are overwhelming like their animals.

Dionysus is fluids like wine, blood, semen, sap, and honey. He is the god who gets the juices flowing. He is the Tree God and He Who Lives In A Tree—and the reason ancient trees matter. The Giver of All Good Gifts is the fruit of the tree, the fruit of a pursuit, or the fruitfulness of a lifetime.

Dionysus keeps things happening.

He is spontaneity and flow. He parallels Poseidon's emotional freedom, which allows the sea creatures of monstrous emotions to frolic without judgment or control. When Dionysus is around, things flow in the here and now like leaves sprouting in springtime. You're like him when you don't hold back in an activity.

Dionysus the Roarer, *Bromios* is the power and immediacy of loud noise, like a heavy metal rock concert, because the loudness is the power of the music. The Loud Shouter shares the Earth Mother's love of noise, liveliness, and whirling lights, because loud music alters consciousness and takes you outside of yourself.

He is your inner rebel, the one who hates schedules and decorum and wants you to break the rules and live more truly and naturally. The God Who Wanders at Night is the reason people wait until dark to reveal their wilder sides, far from the watchful daylight selves of Athena and other judgmental gods. Dionysus' doubles include androgynous bad boys like David Bowie, Kiss, Prince, and Queen.

There is a built in conservatism to this idea of wildness. The workers drinking and celebrating their freedom on Friday nights will be back in the factory on Monday morning. That is Dionysus' tie to the Earth

117

Dionysus

Mother, who keeps us bound to the order of life and limits rebellion to altered mental states.

Dionysus and Hera

Hera the Goddess of the Yoke fears Dionysus because he frees you from obligations and morality. The Goddess of Marriage wants you to be the same person all the time—married to your life—and not turn into someone else like this unpredictable god. Dionysus threatens other order-loving gods like Herakles the Hero, Apollo the Law, and Athena the Normal Self because he is just too crazy, too dangerous, or too effeminate to take seriously.

Dionysus is experienced through possession. He is the possession itself. He can show up in sex, acting, exercising, cleaning house, or creating art—anything you do as one possessed. Dionysus is intimate but impersonal: you cannot take personally the words and actions of someone drunk, because anyone carried away with what he's doing is outside of Athena the Normal Self or Hera the Personal Self.

His appearance can be startling. Dionysus makes establishment types cringe. What mayor really wants a Grateful Dead concert in his city with all the hippies and club kids around? These days, we fight Dionysus in the wars on drugs and terror, seeing 'foreign' devils out to destroy the system. Dionysus makes controllers paranoid.

To resist him is dangerous. The daughters of Minyas stay home weaving while the rest of the city goes off to worship Dionysus when the room suddenly fills with wild beasts, the weaving turns to vines, and wild music and loud shouting engulf them. Insane, the women draw lots for their little boys and the winner tears her son to pieces. The women of Hera's city of Argos who refuse him fare no better, eating their children in madness. You offend Dionysus when you can't even imagine certain desires, never mind act upon them.

However, Dionysus never forces anyone to be promiscuous. Surprisingly, the artwork never shows the god drunk or engaged in sex. Instead, the god remains calm and removed amid the writhing and dancing

around him. It is his followers who act crazy, not Dionysus—when you are
drunk, he is the knowledge that you are drunk

Dionysus' sole demand is that you *do what you want to do.*
He dares his followers to be free just as he dares you to pursue your heart's
desire, even if it hurts someone's personal feelings, including your own.

Dionysus and Apollo

Apollo and Dionysus are the famous opposites in Nietzsche's
Birth of Tragedy, which describes how they work together to create high art.
The two gods are intellect and intuition imagined as friends or lovers.
Apollo is the delicate line of awareness that separates you from experience
like a pane of glass over experience, while Dionysus is the lyric cry of the
self caught in suffering.

Apollo's clarity of mind opposes Dionysus' possession by a
god. The god who commands *know thyself* and *nothing in excess* opposes
freedom, losing yourself, and finding truth in excess. Dionysus *Paideios,*
the Educator, is the liberal arts that free the mind while Apollo is systematic
learning, like law, math, and science.

The two are friends and rumored to be lovers. On some
vases, they hold hands across a bay tree.

When Dionysus arrives at Apollo's city of Delphi, he is not
resisted. Instead he is recognized and moderated and turned into an
institution and even buried there.

This is because it is rational for the rational self to let go once in a while.
Apollo symbolically goes north to the land of the Hyperboreans every
summer, leaving Delphi to Dionysus, because it's important to step out of
the long-term plan once in a while, like taking vacations.

Both gods inspire prophecy and the arts. Apollo is the
prophecy of insight while Dionysus inspires artists with enthusiasm and
spontaneity. Both *lead the Muses* and are essential to art, because
Apollo's clarity refines Dionysus' gut instincts. For Apollo, art is an end in
itself. For Dionysus, it's only Art if it moves the soul and shakes you to the

Dionysus

core. Studies show that genius is as much a question of god given talent as of a manic obsession with detail and practice. The genius of a literary work requires obsessive re-writing.

This is a very democratic idea of genius. In the Classical World, every individual had an abiding genius or *daimon*, like a familiar spirit. Socrates used to talk to his soul, whom he called Diotima, just as Michelangelo had Vittoria and Dante his Beatrice. Personifying your talent or genius lets it take on its own life, for the mind has many independent selves that function better without your conscious interference.

Pentheus

Pentheus, the king of Thebes, is the poster child for those who refuse Dionysus. His name means *full of suffering*.

He tries to stop the women of his city from running off with Dionysus when he comes to town and refuses to even mention his name in public rites. He is the reactionary, the self who resists change. He is anyone who resents whatever is new simply because it is new.

After Pentheus arrests Dionysus the chains fall off like loose vines and Dionysus possesses him with madness. He has Pentheus dress up as a woman and leads him to spy on the Maenads, Dionysus' female followers.   He climbs a tree to watch them and is quickly discovered. The Maenads shake the tree and bring him down, tearing him limb from limb as they do small animals. Pentheus' own mother, Agave, rips his head off and carries it around with her until the spell wears off and she comes to her senses and sees their tragic fate.

You are like Pentheus when you try to thwart new or strange moods or desires to protect the status quo. If you don't deal with a self who is trying to get your attention—for instance, through a symptom or a recurring thought--it gets angry and expresses itself in an ugly form. By resisting Dionysus and playing a rule-obsessed Apollo, Pentheus becomes the pervert peering through the keyhole and is ultimately humiliated and destroyed.

Maenads

The *Maenads,* the Mad Women, and the *Thyiades,* the Rushing Distraught Women are the housewives whom Dionysus calls away from the humdrum life to go running through the hills and partying all night.

They are the women Freud diagnosed with hysteria and who today have chronic fatigue syndrome or fibromyalgia: middle aged women who suffer from boredom and psychosomatic—but not imaginary—complaints. They are anyone whose deadened soul cries out for a good dose of Dionysus and a jolt of excitement.

To be a Maenad is to *do what you want to do,* as Dionysus urged them.

You don't have to run to the hills or be sexually wild—unless you really want to. To be a maenad means to reject Hera's morality as the basis of your actions and to live truly. It means imagining the unimaginable and thinking the unthinkable, whether it's an erotic fantasy or a nightmare. The Maenads bring you to the edge and make you say, *I do not want what everyone else wants.*

The ritual started with a fast. Then the maenads worked themselves into a frenzy by chewing psychotropic ivy, drinking wine, dancing wildly to a primal drumbeat, and twirling their torches to psychedelic effect. They performed strange miracles like carrying fire in their hair, resisting all weapons, and making water, milk, wine, or honey flow from the ground where they struck it with their burning pine torches. These are useless miracles because Dionysus is a god of art, not pragmatism.

The maenads suckled kids and fawns lovingly one moment and tore them apart the next to commune with the god. When they get exhausted, they sank to their knees with face in hands, experiencing the strange *silence of the Bacchi*, with heads tossed back and throats turned up in a collective 'what have I done?'

All the while, Dionysus stands calmly among them, his eyes closed or half closed until suddenly he is gone, like a buzz wearing off. The women ritually search for him and report that he is hiding in the marshes

Dionysus

with the Muses. This may mean that the wild life he wants you to live is best experienced vicariously through Art, because marshes are inaccessible. They are not literal places you can stand on.

Dionysus is a difficult god to satisfy because he likes such extremes. Physical exertion and sex are primary to his followers and can require as much energy as some people give to their jobs. The One Born of Fire and the Fiery One can make you a burn out. Dionysus is fun while he's around and that joy feels eternal, but it is always framed in suffering. When Dionysus disappears, your sexuality may disappear or you may find yourself bored and feeling empty. This only makes Dionysus' eventual return feel like discovering the fun all over again.

He is a god of recovery and of the sick and dying. He is any physical suffering that teaches you limits and possesses you directly, like a disability or a cancerous tumor. He is the stranger dwelling within. You remember the god when you personify your suffering and dedicate it to him, instead of bearing it yourself.

Palaimon

Jealous of Zeus' affair with Semele, Hera drove Lykurgus the King mad. Grabbing an axe, he chased Semele's sister, Ino off a cliff into the sea while she held the baby Dionysus. The two were transformed into Leukothea and Palaimon, gods of the sea who protect sailors in distress.

Palaimon is enthusiasm, a word that derives from *en theos,* 'a god within you'. The Greeks believed that enthusiasm shows that a god has taken an interest in you—and not the other way around. You are like Palaimon when you leap into something with the passion of Dionysus—with everything you've got--whether it's a marriage, a job, or a sport.

He is the watery element of the psyche that can be harmed by the hard masculinity of the man with the ax in the form of harsh criticism, cruelty, and rejection.

By seeing those tender feelings and *girly* enthusiasm as Palaimon's and not your own, you give yourself some room to maneuver. Dionysus permits all feelings and fantasies, even the shameful ones that are unacceptable to

122

more sociable selves. You are only responsible for how you relate to them.

Dionysus is the God of the Double Door and the Twice Born, taken from his mother when she was struck by lightning and sewn into Zeus' thigh. He is ambiguity itself, for he was born of a woman and also of a man. Palaimon helps you deal with uncertainty, whether it's living on commission, in an undefined relationship, or with intense internal conflicts and contradictions.

Ariadne

For years, Athens sent a tribute to Crete of seven young men and women to King Minos of Crete. The wicked king locked them in a labyrinth to feed the Minotaur, a monster half-man and half-bull, born of his wife's perverse intercourse with a bull.

Theseus vowed to put an end to this and boarded the ship as one of the intended victims. On Crete, he seduced Minos' daughter, Ariadne, who helped him escape by giving him a ball of thread to unravel his way out of the labyrinth. As they fled by boat, she taught the young people the *crane dance,* because she was a follower of Dionysus, God of Dance.

When they anchored at Naxos, however, Theseus conveniently forgot his promise of marriage and deserted Ariadne on the island. Some say she hanged herself in desperation or that she died in childbirth at the hands of Artemis, the Killer of Women, acting on orders from Dionysus, whom she rejected earlier.

Ariadne is emotional drama--the feeling of being betrayed, knocked around, or abandoned by the world. She is distinct from Hera's Drama Queen because she does not exaggerate her emotions in order to get attention. She's more of a victim. Ariadne combines Dionysus' passion with Poseidon's emotions, which makes for a bumpy ride as you swing from bliss to sorrow. She is your inner Miss Mess.

Dionysus and his crowd showed up just in time to save her, cutting the rope from her neck and taking her as his bride. He gave her the Corona Borealis as a wedding gift, which is wildly romantic. Despite his

123

Dionysus

reputation, Dionysus remains forever faithful to Ariadne—because that is what he truly wants.

Some say he led her to the top of the mountain on Naxos, where they both disappeared into immortality. Ariadne is *Arihagne*, or *Aridela*, Utterly Pure and Utterly Clear, a name shared only by Persephone, the self married to death—the real you without all the hype and pretense. Ariadne is a vulnerable and authentic self who feels everything intensely, even too intensely.

In ritual, young men would dress and act like women, pretending to give birth and wailing in mock pain. The festival of Ariadne and Dionysus on Naxos pairs a gloomy day with a joyful one like Good Friday/Easter Sunday to reflect her mood swings.

Ariadne is a dark view of love and life. She is your inner drama queen, but not in a self-absorbed way like Hera the Person, who is really looking for attention. Ariadne feels things deeply and needs true love. She can make you want to run away with someone or something, even if it seems foolish, like deserting the royal life she had in Crete. She agrees with the maenads when they say, *what the world calls wise I do not want.*

Seeing your emotional turbulence and personal drama as Ariadne separates you from it and gives you some perspective and options. Let Ariadne have the problems and emotional turbulence instead of owning them on top of enduring them. You can just stand by while they swirl around you like her partner Dionysus, calm and supportive amid the turmoil—until he disappears.

Eater of Raw Flesh

When Dionysus is born, Zeus pronounces that he will be cut into pieces amid great honors. This is the crushing of the grapes and the reason Dionysus is associated with cannibalism. His sacrifice is raw meat.

Dionysus Omadios, the Eater of Raw Flesh, is whatever is eating you. The Man-Renderer is the feeling of being torn apart, whether by a disease, worry, or addiction.

With Dionysus, the gods are not just concepts or 'parts of

124

myself'. Consistent with evolutionary psychology, each self is independent. The gods are real intrusions in 'your' life, like a bull bursting in from the dark—or a diagnosis or accident. Dionysus is the intense suffering of the victim and he resides in any strong, pervading physical presence like paralysis or deformity.

He is dismembered when your life falls apart and you can't get your act together—when you can't be Herakles the Hero anymore. Dionysus is the nervous breakdown and the end of the rope.

At the Feast of New Flesh, the crowd tears apart a live animal—a goat, fawn or bull—and eats it raw to share in the life of the god, just as Catholics claim to eat their god and not just a symbol of him. But you don't have to eat your pets or bite a cow to know Dionysus. You just have to remember that life is tragic and to imagine the unimaginable, because sometimes that's what happens. People in nursing homes staring blankly with tubes sticking out of their bellies were once proud athletes, professionals, and lovers. By simply imagining that you are paralyzed— even for a minute—you can better appreciate how remarkably lucky you are today. Dionysus can compel people to do drugs, drive recklessly, or have unsafe sex just to feel the reality of danger. Life ends badly for all of us, and remembering that makes today more vivid and worthwhile.

Dionysus can be vicious and impersonal like some drunks. The Raging One, the Frenzied One, and the Crazed God can turn on friends in a moment and tear them to pieces with violence or cruel comments that would never be spoken in sobriety.

A good cry is a blessing from Dionysus, like a good belly laugh. It clears the air. He is the elation that can accompany terrible news, because then life is real. He is the wounding that saves you from the flat boredom of thinking 'this will go on forever' or feeling stuck in one or two personas. He makes life exciting by making it feel temporary, which is the truth.

Semele

Zeus lusted after the mortal woman, Semele, and

125

Dionysus

impregnated her as a yellow rain. When Zeus granted Semele a wish, she foolishly wished that he reveal himself in his true form. Bound by his oath, Zeus appeared as lightning that consumed Semele in a fiery burst. He saved her child, Dionysus, by sewing him into his thigh until he was ready to be born.

You are like Semele when the truth about someone or something destroys you. She is the experience of being overwhelmed. You are like Zeus with Semele when you completely dominate someone else.

The Lord of Souls

The Greeks called Dionysus *Another Hades* and *A Second Zeus*—meaning Zeus as an Underworld god. Artwork shows Underworld Dionysus holding a vine and a pomegranate, the fruit that looks like a graveyard inside. Him Entwined Around the Pillar is the ivy on the grave and the feeling of death closing in and binding you. The Greeks used pine and cinnamon to mask the odor of decomposing bodies, and they hung masks painted with blood from tree limbs to send power in all directions.

The Lord of Souls resides in dark fantasies, sexual or otherwise. He pushes you to experience humiliation—to go as low as you can go to get beneath Herakles' idea of life as heroic progress and glory. 'Humiliation' comes from the Latin *humus* or *earth* and it represents a darkening of outlook that acts as a counterweight to identification with one's daytime identity. Dionysus is a god of life as fantasy and role-play. Down in the Underworld among extreme images the soul can breathe, free of social pretense, superiority, and self-importance—things that will not matter at the sad moment of death that is surely on its way.

Cerberus the three-headed dog guarding the entrance to the Underworld licks Dionysus' feet when he visits, because Dionysus makes you feel comfortable in Hades world of images, which turns out to be quite an interesting place. Most of us need a friendlier attitude towards sleep and dreaming and the third of our life that waking gods like Athena and Herakles ignore or judge as useless.

126

The Greek Gods Among Us

The Lord of Souls dwells in forbidden sexual fantasies like sadomasochism, which breaks the identification with the daytime, respectable persona. He is the reason the guy tied to the wheel at the fetish bar may very well be a banker during office hours, the masochistic fantasies freeing him of all pretenses and leading him below the persona he wears in the world of society. If you don't actively seek humiliation it will find you on its own through aging and the inevitable betrayal of the body.

Dionysus hides in terrible secrets and shameful longings. He wants you to resist smoothing things over or pretending not to know something about someone or something just to keep the peace. This self knows there is a place for pain, contradiction, and sorrow in life.

The Lord of the Night frees the soul from the self-esteem that binds it to Herakles the Heroic Ego and his denial of death, epitomized by Christian Heaven. From this point of view, Herakles is the true sadist --not the guy with the kinky fantasies or the neurotic obsessions. The Hero looks out on a world of freaks to bully and problems to solve, manhandling moods and desires while ignoring the voices hiding within them. He wants you to get rid of your hang-ups, straighten your life out, and live in literalistic fantasies of health and success in some bulldozed suburb of a psyche.

Dionysus is a god of immortality, for he went down to Hades to fetch his mother, Semele, and his wife, Ariadne--myths that informed several ancient cults. But this immortality has nothing to do with a future life in some imagined future world. It is the Greek immortality of knowing the gods in the here and now. Dionysus appears in moments that you know you will never forget, moments when you say, 'this is what it's all about' or 'I want this to go on *forever*'--a word that signals the presence of a god.

Dionysus the Black Goatskin, *Malanaigis,* is the self who will ultimately accept your death, imagined as a black goatskin cape. He is the antidote to a life seen through rose -colored glasses. You can sense him in self-pity and self-hatred and every form of self-flagellation. You honor him when you stop taking those legitimate feelings personally and give them back to him.

Underworld Dionysus is *Ploutos*, the Giver of Riches and the

127

Dionysus

boundlessness of the imagination. He rules the Underworld of the theater and cinema. He is the strange feeling of emerging from the movie house and discovering it's still broad daylight and you are yourself again. Dionysus makes your life and the person you think you are seem like a stranger or a dream about someone else.

As the Greek poet said, *I am but I am not* and *he does but he does not.* Odysseus says at the end of the story, *Odysseus. There was a man, or was he all a dream?* Helen says, *There was a world...or was it all a dream?*

Dionysus *Another Hades* is this uncanny experience. As James Hillman said, *"I am not real"*, for the self we think we are is only one of many selves and no more real than the rest. As the Greeks prayed to Dionysus, *be good to us.*

Moving On

Dionysus can take over your life through addiction and cost you your health and reputation. He always disappears just before the party crashes, leaving his followers to deal with the mess and the consequences. Dionysus is dangerous.

He proposed marriage once to Hestia Goddess of the Home, so she's a good person to turn to when you need to feel centered again. Stay home, tidy up, stock up, review your mutual funds, and feel safe with your pets like Hestia if you have been too free.

You can also spend time with Dionysus that has nothing to do with partying by taking a dance class, dwelling in the painful positions of yoga, or doing anything to the extreme and with passion, which brings the god into the experience. You can even honor Dionysus and Hestia the Homebody together by cleaning house *like a maniac.*

Apollo can direct Dionysian impulses in a productive way through creative work. This can be in the arts or it can be in an artistic approach to your job, no matter how mundane it is.

Hermes is a great refuge because he's also at home in the Underworld and comfortable with images and fantasy. Just tune into his

128

sense of humor and remind yourself that 'this too shall pass'. Or look to Artemis and Hekate, who give you the courage to change, for they are gods of doors and gates that lead from one part of life to another. Going to 12-step meetings and honoring the god by recounting your adventures with him is another way to escape the literal acting out of his impulses without trying to reject him, which only makes him angry.

POSEIDON

Poseidon is the God of the Ocean and Streams. The turbulent brother of Zeus is the emotional self---your emotions as a person who tries to boss you around. Spending time with Poseidon can be as refreshing as a trip to the beach if you feel overly restrained by Athena's reason or burdened by Hera's personal touch and Demeter's relatedness.

Many emotions precede our humanity and not all of them are personal. They are subject to illness, hormones, medications, and the weather. Emotions can make you act monstrously and lead to terrible regrets, just as Poseidon brings endless humiliation upon himself through his rash, vengeful behavior.

But the original Earth Father is a source of vigor and earthiness with dark roots in our instincts and appetites. The bearded man with *blue-black hair* embodies a primeval masculinity available to both men and women. More animalistic than other gods, he lives through our sensations, especially touch, taste and smell. He is in the physical nature of emotions, like a blush that flushes the cheeks.

The great gift of Poseidon King is emotional excellence-- feeling like a surfer hanging loose in life. In the artwork he surveys his watery realm from his golden chariot while strange sea creatures frolic around him on calm seas. This is your emotional core expressed freely and without personal interference, judgment, or identification.

You are not responsible for how you feel, only for how you act. That's where gods of reason like Athena and personal consideration like Hera come in. Saying, 'I mustn't feel that way' only teases the monsters and makes them angry, setting up for the inevitable storm.

God of the Ocean

Poseidon is more concrete than other gods. He is not a god of deep thought like Zeus, Athena the Mind, or Apollo the Intellect. He's more physical than that.

Poseidon means Ocean. He is the Ocean as a person in your life. He is who you are at the ocean, because everyone is different there.

The ocean's power over human beings is both physical and emotional. He is the invigorating salt air, the negative ions that make you hungry, the sound of the waves breaking, the sunburn, and the sand in the sheets. He is the power and mood of weather and other physical forces that intrude into your life, altering your mood.

Humans have loved the beach for timeless eons. At the beach you are at the edge of the world and at the edge of social restraint-- and scantily dressed. In the waves, you find your core nature and animal vigor. The ocean washes away feelings of mediocrity, passiveness, and over-refinement, because when you are wet and in the waves you connect to vast reserves of sensations and unvisited moods. As a human Poseidon is animal magnetism. He is the physical touch or scent of someone who enters your personal space with the immediacy of an intruder. He is raw sexuality and sex appeal.

Ancient artwork shows a rugged, mature man, either clean cut or with facial hair, often standing with one hand on his thigh and one on his trident. Poseidon is typically shown nude or with a towel draped casually over his leg as though he is in a steam room. He is the natural, hedonistic love of sensation and freedom from reserve. He is your inner nudist.

Earth Shaker

Poseidon is Zeus' inferior brother. You are like him when you let your emotions take the reins. While Zeus brings civilization and prosperity, Poseidon brings storms, volcanoes, and earthquakes.

Poseidon is rage. He makes people erupt all the time. He can make the ground shake beneath your feet with emotional upset and inner turmoil. When he has you in his thrall, he can make you abandon reason and get you into the kind of trouble that is always plaguing him in the myths. The Greeks lived by the sea and were used to the ocean's impetuous change from peaceful seas to raging swells. Water takes the form of its container, like emotions that change shape depending on how they are perceived. Poseidon's stories highlight the mayhem caused by his lack of self-control—in sharp contrast to Zeus' superior restraint and

Poseidon

success. He is your emotional life personified as a lifetime friend.

To the Greeks, *you* do not have emotions—emotions have *you*. Poseidon can shake and possess you beyond your control, shipwrecking your life with rages, jealousy, and spite. Rage doesn't need a reason to exist. It has its own life and feeds on itself. The shallow waters are your personal emotions while in the depths lurk the bizarre creatures of memories, feelings and dreams—including feelings you'd rather not own up to but which are better recognized than left to fend for themselves.

In the artwork, Poseidon's forehead looks swollen and troubled, with deep eye sockets and thick locks of hair littered with seaweed. He is a moody, defiant god who loves revenge and is as unpredictable as a storm at sea. He has his brother, Zeus' noble brow but his cheekbones are stronger, as though he is clenching his teeth. When Poseidon looks off in the distance, he is not lost in some great thought like Zeus or Apollo. He is probably on the lookout for someone trespassing on his property.

Poseidon is a god of old-fashioned ways and under educated people, a god of the Red States with their resentment and self-righteousness. He is around when you feel threatened instead of inspired by other people's confidence and success. He makes you see conspiracies everywhere, carry on grudges, and act aggressively while claiming to uphold to be the victim. He is irrational, destructive, and difficult to deal with. Poseidon the Flooder, *Proklystios,* is the feeling of being overwhelmed by tidal waves of anger, hatred, or sorrow. He can make you eat because you're bored or yell at your spouse because you got annoyed at the bank teller. As my mother used to say when I cried as a baby, "he's just tired."

Poseidon can infect entire groups of people through terrorism, Tea Party nihilism, and crippling strikes--impulses that destroy everything in their path and shake society to the core. He resents Zeus' superiority and his rules, government, and civilization, just as he resents being confined by Zeus to the ocean the way emotions are confined by reality. Poseidon makes you think you got a raw deal in life. He is the god of Donald Trump and his followers, nihilists who resent social order and politeness.

His appetites are huge because they are linked to his emotions. He can give you excessive desire at any age, making you a letch, a wastrel, or a compulsive eater. This god expresses through a surge of hormones, his chemical manifestations. Poseidon wants you to inflict your emotions on others, dominating friendships and conversations with moods and crises and reasons to take offense.

Potidan

Poseidon's original name means *Husband of Da*, an ancient name for Demeter, the Goddess of Grain. He is the Earth Father to her Earth Mother.

Potidan is physical force--a terrible fall, a blow to the jaw, a rush of emotions—as a person intruding in your experience. The jolt of a car accident is Poseidon. He is intense storms, cold, and heat as both physical and emotional forces, affecting your moods. He is a friend of Helius the Sun, which is not the Sun of Apollo's divine brilliance, but the sun as a brutal, whirling power--the sun as it actually is.

The Lord of the Waters is the god of springs and rivers. His animals are rams, bulls and horses—charging creatures whose striking hooves were believed to break the earth and cause it to spring with water. Grappling with emotions does not lead to clarity and illumination, because Potidan is the struggle itself, living through you. Emotions exist for their own sake and you are better off just trying to step away and let them be themselves. These animals are unstoppable.

Poseidon presents a brute masculinity associated with lumberjacks, truck-drivers, and farmers. He wants you to get *dirty* physically with blood, mud, and sweat or unsafe sex and pornography. He is blue-collar men with hairy chests and tattoos who are prone to liquor and excesses like whoring, gambling, and fighting. Poseidon is a sweaty impatient Yosemite Sam who sees other men as rivals, and you are like him when you feel defeated by other people's success.

133

Poseidon

Acheloos

The Prince of River Gods is Poseidon's double, shown in artwork as an old man with water flowing from his hair like an aging Fabio. He was pictured hanging out with the other river gods like a gang of Ernest Borgnines.

Acheloos is wetness, a feeling that focuses your attention on sensation, especially base sensations. The River God is sensation, including the pleasurable sensations of sex, elimination, and washing in water. He is the discomfort of cramps, urgency, and dull aches. He is sensation as a person and a presence in your life.

Taking a shower or going to the bathroom always changes your mood. The bathroom is a veritable temple of Poseidon where you can experience the primitive pleasures of being wet and playing in the water anytime you want—an unimaginable luxury from the perspective of human history. Just close your eyes while you shower and you might as well be a sea monster, frolicking around Poseidon's chariot.

Streams wash away impurities just like flushing the toilet. Acheloos *Aspropotamus* or Clean White River is the god of flowing water. He is hydration that gives you a sense of wellbeing and makes your urine run clear.

The Greeks used to clip a bit of hair and toss it in the local stream on occasions like graduations and weddings to thank Acheloos for leading them from one part of life to another. You can toss a bit of hair or nail clippings into the toilet as a symbolic gift to this self and flush away some other self or mood in your own version of a lustral (cleansing) ritual, or take a nice long shower or bath to mark a change in mood or self.

Poseidon and Zeus

Poseidon is Zeus in Water. Although he claims to be his brother's equal, he lacks his spiritual and ethical dimensions.

He is inferiority. He is your inferior self. You are like him when you sulk and brood and feel tossed around by 'life'—meaning Zeus, who is the very pattern of events. He is self-pity and the belief that life

The Greek Gods Among Us

(Zeus) is unfair. He is like an old uncle, because there's something old fashioned about being grievance and resentment, like the 'heartland' Red States. Poseidon can make you quarrelsome and greedy, or bring you over to base addictions and indulgence.

He is cynicism. You are most like him when you are ungrateful. Poseidon wants you to think you got cheated and that your happiness depends on the failure of others. He is the god of *schadenfreude,* and he secretly wishes for Zeus to be confined to the sky as he is to the ocean.

Both gods commit many rapes, but these are metaphorical. The Christian Church made much of these *rapes* but only literal minded people actually believe the Greeks were a bunch of rapists. After all, don't Catholics insist they are *literally* eating Jesus' body at communion?

Zeus' rapes happen when reality intrudes into your life, like when you realize, achieve, or fail at something. Poseidon's rapes happen when your emotions harm your judgment—when Poseidon violates Athena the Normal Self—or when they hurt your personal loyalty, violating Hera the Personal self through arguments and grudges with the spouse or with loyal friends. While Zeus' lovers go with him freely and proudly, Poseidon is more of a molester. This rogue self will say anything to get someone into bed—or to get you to let emotions and base pleasures run your life.

The Soul needs civilizing up from this level. Who wants to be like Poseidon when he's raging bottomless anger or sabotaging his own interests? The Greek ethic was largely aimed at making people act more like Zeus than Poseidon, his unpredictable and inferior brother.

Poseidon and Aphrodite

Ancient art shows Poseidon riding over the waves with the White Goddess in a chariot drawn by *Hippocampi--* half horse and half fish-- and attended by Mermaids, or *Nereids.* His queen is Amphitrite, the Queen of the Waves and Mistress of the Sea, whom he made as jealous as Zeus did Hera with his many affairs with both women and men. Their nuptials were like a wedding attended by the Opera Society and the Hell's Angels.

Poseidon

He seduces Tyro by appearing as the river god she is in love with and then violating her while she sleeps. A dark wave of the river curls over the couple to hide his action, because Poseidon thinks of sex as something to get away with. When Tyro wakes up and realizes what has happened, she is furious, but instead of apologizing Poseidon scolds her and tells her she is pregnant with better children than her boyfriend could ever give her.

Poseidon is the sexual knave. He is sexual robustness and the desire to take advantage of innocence. He lives in primitive sex roles--macho men and busty women, butch/femme, sadomasochism, and sex-is-dirty mentality. To him, every woman is the Eternal Feminine and every man a stud—which makes his partners interchangeable. It's impossible for this self to be only friends with someone he finds sexually attractive.

For him, love has nothing to do with it--no candlelit dinners with Aphrodite the Date or Hera the Spouse for him. Poseidon is the deep-sea voice in chocolate advertisements repeating the orgasmic, *oh yeah*. He is there when you care more about the sex act than about whom you do it with, because he's more interested in sensation than in the person. He makes you feel at home in the whorehouse.

When a lover acts like Poseidon, psychologists say he has *gone archetypal* and acting out of pure instinct. This is because psychologists serve the interests of Hera the Person, and it hurts her feelings to be treated impersonally. But if you're in a sexually bored relationship, treating your beloved as a sex object or a piece of meat may be just what is needed, like Rhett Butler carrying Scarlett O'Hara up the stairway.

He is the swagger in sex. He is Falstaff's excess and appetite. He makes people obsess over freakish muscles and genitals, breast implants and other bulging exaggerations, because they put the focus on sex and away from the personality. Poseidon can bring a welcome change when there is too much emphasis on personal feelings and relating when what is needed is physical relief.

136

Poseidon and Athena

Athena the Mind restrains Poseidon the Emotions whenever you use your judgment before you take action. She invents the bridle to his horse and the ship to his sea. One of her greatest successes was the British Empire, where Athenian assertion over the sea symbolized a nation's steady grip on its emotions. Poseidon strikes back when your emotions invade your faculties and disrupt your intentions. You see this struggle in people who try to compose themselves during terrible grief or resist being baited into an argument while the camera is sadistically rolling.

In the first round of squabbles, Poseidon thrust his trident into the Acropolis and claimed all of Attica, Athena's home territory. A saltwater spring bubbled up where the trident broke the ground—an impressive but not very useful gift to the city. Athena answered his challenge by planting the first olive tree—an economic boon to Attica and to all of Greece. As the two readied for combat Zeus intervened and ordered them to arbitration. All the goddesses voted for Athena and the gods for Poseidon with Zeus abstaining, giving the victory to Athena. Poseidon felt that the vote was rigged against him so he flooded the plains, which happens whenever your emotions flood your reason.

Poseidon and Hera

These two are at odds when Poseidon's emotions conflict with Hera's personal feelings. Emotions have a life of their own and cannot always be taken personally, like when someone gets nasty when he's drunk. Poseidon calls the Goddess of Society *that bitch who married my brother* because social manners work to suppress emotions, like when Hera tries to give Poseidon's rightful seat at the Olympian table to Aeolus the God of the Winds. To Hera, Poseidon is too low class for society, because emotions cause conflict and upset. To her, emotions have no loyalty or values. To Poseidon, they don't need them, just as rage needs to reason to exist and can spring up out of nowhere. You can see these two fighting full force when an old argument boils up to the height of emotional drama, as in *Who's Afraid of Virginia Woolf*. The Destroyer of the Rampart on the Shore

Poseidon

gives you boundary issues just as the ocean fights with the land.

The two argue over Argolis, a beautiful and fertile peninsula. Feeling burnt by his dispute with Athena in which all the goddesses teamed up against him, Poseidon refuses to let his fellow gods pass judgment, so Zeus appoints a tribunal of the four local river gods, who rule in Hera's favor anyway. Once again, he is furious, and since he is forbidden to flood the land again he dries up all the rivers instead, causing widespread famine. When Hera's personal feelings fight Poseidon's emotions, you may find yourself acting impersonally or coldly towards someone who expects otherwise. Poseidon is the silent treatment.

Hera the Personal Self wants you to feel special and to be loved for your own sake. She judges emotions and even questions their right to exist, as in 'how could you even think that?' This infuriates Poseidon, who wants emotions to be free to be themselves. After all, you don't choose your emotions. You only choose how to relate to them. Letting yourself have feelings without identifying with them gives Poseidon the dignity he longs for, because emotions may have nothing to do with your personal life and they don't always have to be acted upon.

Hera the Personal Self can be turned to advantage here. All you need is some manners, which are especially meant for people you don't like. You can help keep the peace between Poseidon and Hera by saying whatever you need to say, but pleasantly and politely and without the intention to dislodge the other person. One good practice is to take people at their word instead of digging for motives or looking for offense— and letting them know that you are, indeed, taking them at their word.

Poseidon and Apollo

The emotions and intellect also come into frequent conflict.

Apollo sees the big picture while Poseidon gets you caught up in the moment. Apollo wants you to stay calm in an argument while Poseidon turns up the heat. Apollo tells you to leave the room when things get uncomfortable and to rise above your emotions. He is the reason that when two people are arguing, the one who stays calm looks right, even if he's on the wrong side of the argument.

When they cooperate, these gods can be dangerous and seductive, like well-educated terrorists or Nazis who blend intellectual mythology with emotional fervor.

But both gods can be healers. While Apollo is medicine and his focus is on disease, Poseidon Healer, *Iatros,* is the god of health spas, chiropractors, Jacuzzis and aqua-size, focusing on sensation and physical wellbeing—on how you actually feel.

Poseidon Savior

The Master of Fishermen, the Helper of Fishermen, and the Savior of Ships is not just a great guy handing out favors to sailors. For a seagoing people like the Greeks, Poseidon was more often a problem than a blessing. They called him Savior just to convince him to leave the ship alone, like saying 'nice kitty' to a wild cat.

Poseidon Savior is catastrophe, personified. He is the thing that can go wrong and the disaster that awaits you, as if it had a mind of its own. He is especially any catastrophe that could have been avoided by planning and consulting with Athena's strategic Mind.

The Greeks called many gods Savior, *Soter,* because there are many kinds of salvation—'save my life', 'save my stock price', or 'save my marriage'. Deciding which god to pray to depends on the nature of the rescue you need. Christians would never pray to Jesus for a good marriage or business deal, because Jesus specializes in spiritual and medical healing like Apollo. In the Greek view, if you survive an accident with a tractor-trailer at an icy intersection, you owe thanks to Zeus, who is 'what happens'; to Athena, who is clear thinking in the moment; to Hephaestus, who is the brakes and the air bag; and to Hermes the God of Good Luck.

. Just to be safe, you also owe thanks to Poseidon, who is the ice and the blow of the truck—for not finishing the job. There's a lot to think about after surviving an ordeal. You can get some distance on the experience by thinking of the ordeal itself as Poseidon and his violence, so that it can be its own thing instead of keeping it to yourself.

Poseidon

Triton

Triton, or He of Wide Force is a frightening half-fish-half-man who lives in Poseidon's palace and leads his advance escort, like the wind before a storm. Triton is an extreme version of his emotional father. He is the self who runs amok. You know Triton when you completely lose control. You are in his hands when you are rowdy and self-destructive and dangerous to yourself and everyone else like a storm at sea.

Triton hangs out with a gang of tritonesses and *nereids,* or mermaids, like a bunch of motorcycle rowdies spreading terror through a small town. He leads people astray with his conch horn, which he sounds in various directions to confuse his victims like conflicting emotions or an addiction pulling you this way and that. He leads you to debauchery and cynicism and makes you act like a cold fish. Triton's gang is an ugly crew of walking fish that rapes women and boys and wreaks havoc on the world in the cold way that fish eat other fish without hesitation or remorse or even seeming to know what they are doing.

The Greeks honored him just to keep him away. Men would dance around wearing fish tails to get this god's anti-social party impulses out of their system—not by fighting them but by experiencing them to satisfaction, in typical Greek fashion.

The Cyclops

These one-eyed giants are the children of Poseidon who inhabit an island paradise where the fruit grows untended on the trees and no one needs to work. The race of the Cyclops has no society, customs and laws. Worst of all to the Greeks, they have no market to exchange goods and conversation.

The Cyclops are self-absorption, which is distinct from Hera's loneliness, Artemis' serenity, Demeter's reflection, or Hestia's centered time alone at home. The Cyclops want you to cocoon and live only for yourself. They live a selfish, utterly suburban existence with few streets to walk and nowhere to meet other people. The single eye in the forehead is

140

identification with one point of view--in this case, oneself. It is the Third Eye of New Age spirituality, which values simplicity and inner peace over social involvement and a complex world.

You can counter the Cyclops' mentality by getting out among others, especially where you can meet people who are different, foreign, or who don't share your values and sensibility. You can escape the narrow mindedness of the Cyclops by participating in any communal activity that gets you outside of your usual concerns.

Dolphin

Poseidon's messenger is the Dolphin, *Delphinus,* a combination of Hermes the Messenger and Poseidon the Emotions. The Dolphin saves many lives from drowning and is a beloved figure in Greek mythology. In his human form, he is the good king of a blessed island.

Just as Hermes is the ability to change moods, the Dolphin is the ability to manage your emotions while maintaining their authenticity. He lets you provide the right tone at the right moment—on command and when needed, as though you are an ambassador from your emotions. Dolphin helps you turn it on and off without being false, like the best salespeople who represent their products with genuine enthusiasm.

The Dolphin is the emotional ally. He is the friend who stands up for you or looks out for your interest, and the emotional bonds that come with loyalty and common goals. He is the best man at a wedding and the person who knows and honors your good intentions, despite yourself.

After Poseidon built his magnificent underwater palace, he needed a wife who wouldn't mind living at the bottom of the sea. After a few false starts, he noticed Amphitrite dancing with the mermaids, the *nereids*. At first, he scares her by either ravishing her or at least coming on so strongly that she runs off to the Atlas Mountains.

Poseidon sends Dolphin after her. Dolphin courts Amphitrite with all his charm and wit on Poseidon's behalf, and when she finally consents to marry the God of the Sea, Poseidon sets Dolphin's image in the stars as the constellation of the same name.

141

Poseidon

Poseidon the King

Poseidon the King, *Basileus,* surveys his kingdom from a grand chariot drawn by white horses with golden manes and hooves while the waves calm and sea creatures frolic around him.

Poseidon King is emotional excellence. He is the Aloha spirit of beach towns. Poseidon King gives heart and diversity to emotions, which can become flat and monotonous when you try to censor them like Athena, rise above them like Apollo, or own them personally like Hera.

He is emotional freedom. You befriend him when you allow yourself to have any emotion, so long as you don't identify with it. You might want to kill your spouse sometimes, and to admit that feeling is healthy so long as you don't identify with it or act upon it. Rely on Athena's judgment, Hera's caring, and Zeus' reality to suppress the action, but there is no need to suppress the feeling.

Emotions are the strange sea creatures of Poseidon, so marvelous and inhuman and so dependent on physical chemistry and the weather. They don't need you to justify them, take their side, or even understand them. They exist on their own already and everyone has all of them, even the socially unacceptable ones. If you imagine them as wild sea creatures, you allow yourself some room to maneuver around them, because then you have a self that is different and separate from the one experiencing the feelings. You can be Poseidon the King, surveying his realm.

Like emotions, Poseidon has an impressive gravity that borders on comic grandiosity. He likes physical paradises with brutish simplicity like luxury spas and resorts that promise a return to voluptuousness, gated condos on the golf course with no need to go anywhere else, and advertisements that say 'it's time', 'you owe it to yourself', or 'only the best', because emotions take themselves quite seriously, even comically.

To Poseidon, happiness boils down to money, sex, a tan, and white teeth, because emotions are materialistic. He wants you to kick back by the pool like Hugh Hefner in his bathrobe and feel like you've got it made, meaning that you are free from the need to work, which comes from Zeus the God of Necessity, whose rule he has always resented.

Pelops

Pelops is the original surfer dude. He is so comfortable in his skin and so naturally athletic that he can maneuver his way around anything. You can see his intriguing charisma in Billy Budd, Lord Jim, and Keanu Reeves.

Pelops is the easygoing self. His likeability is a gift of the gods and a great advantage in life.

Poseidon fell in love with Pelops over dinner and took him up to Olympus. He did well by the boy, taking a genuine interest in him and setting him up with a beautiful wife and a kingdom, like a kindly sugar daddy. Pelops did not resist. This opportunistic self can finely tune emotions to take advantage of any situation, like loving someone who just happens to be rich. Pelops is the secret of many marriages and unions.

You are like him when you can fall into manure and come up smelling like a rose. When Pelops is found guilty of murder, the Delphic Oracle cleanses him and he goes on to have many children, found the Olympic games, and rule southern Greece, named the Peloponnesus after him.

Pelops always paid honors to the gods before he did anything important, and he always honored the dead. In other words, he kept the other selves in mind in every experience and it served him well, because that is a friendly attitude. Young men used to cut themselves at his altar and offer their blood for his favor. His rites were the nighttime counterparts to Zeus' rites during the Olympic games, so he has dark aspects like selfishness and secrecy.

Pelops lets you manage your emotions to your advantage— and to do so without being malevolent or unloving. He is a self who can befriend the boss in a genuine way while knowing that his advancement is also at stake.

Poseidon

He is materialistic like Poseidon. Pelops wants you to have the house, the family, and the car as material proof of your success. He eagerly marries a prominent woman who kills her own suitors and who offers to sleep with his rival as part of the deal—a rival he murders by shoving him off his chariot with a spear. Pelops is the two-timing survivor within—and a part of you that can get away with anything.

Theseus

Theseus, or *Disposes/Orders,* is the founding hero of Athens. Like many heroes, he has two fathers, one mortal and the other immortal. It was said that his mother slept with both Aegeus and Poseidon on the same night, but Aegeus is likely a mortal double of Poseidon.

When he came of age, Theseus went to Athens to serve his father, the King, fighting the invading Amazons and performing many services for the city. But his greatest feat was challenging King Minos of Crete, who demanded seven young men and seven virgins as a yearly tribute to feed to the Minotaur, the monstrous creature his wife bore after having sex with a bull Minos kept trapped in a labyrinth.

Theseus sailed off in a ship with black sails that he was supposed to change to white on his return to let his father watching on shore know that he survived.

On board, Minos started harassing one of the virgins and Theseus stopped him. Angrily, Minos boasted that he was the son of Zeus, which a flash of lightning promptly confirmed.

So if you are really a son of Poseidon, fetch this, he said, throwing a golden ring overboard. Theseus dove under water for a long time, visiting Poseidon's palace where Amphitrite wrapped him in a purple robe and placed a wreath of roses around his neck. Then he floated up out of the water perfectly dry and holding the ring.

On Crete, Minos' daughter, Ariadne, fell in love with Theseus and helped him escape the labyrinth by giving him some yarn to unravel as he walked in. He killed the Minotaur and fled on ship with Ariadne, whom he promised to marry.

144

However, when they stopped on the island of Naxos, Theseus stranded Ariadne--either on purpose or because Dionysus put a spell on him, meaning that he probably got drunk. As the ship approached Athens, he forgot to change the sails, so his broken hearted father leapt to his death from the Acropolis.

Theseus is the ability to forget and let go. This self never looks back and drops things without regrets. Studies show that centenarians typically do not dwell on the past. Theseus gives you the ability to move on without having to resolve things, whether it's forgetting people you once loved or forgetting your own bad behavior. Theseus doesn't even get wet when he jumps in the water.

His best friend is *Perithoos*, or Run Around, with whom he shares a series of adventures like a couple of frat boys. They start off as enemies. When Perithous drives away Theseus' cattle, he takes up arms against him. But when they see each other, they size each other up in admiration and offer their hands in friendship, putting aside their quarrel.

These two get away with a lot of shenanigans and derring-do until they try to kidnap Persephone the Queen of the Underworld. When they come calling, Hades receives them patiently in the Underworld and bids them sit on thrones carved in a rock by the palace while he goes to fetch them gifts. But these are seats of *Lethe,* or Forgetfulness, which hold them fast and make them forgot why they had come to Hades and even who they are.

Herakles the Hero later drags Theseus out of Hades, but he leaves a bit of his rear end sticking to the chair, which is why Athenian men are said to have small behinds--a literal detail about how Theseus doesn't look behind. You are like Theseus when you overcome emotional pain by changing the subject, dropping excess baggage, moving to another town, and forgetting the past.

Moving On

If you spend all your time with Poseidon, your life is going to be a mess. Grappling with emotions doesn't get you anywhere and living in

Poseidon

emotions is infantile. Poseidon is difficult to deal with and difficult to set aside, but seeing your emotions as a separate person from you is a good start, because emotions are like the ocean, and it's your choice whether to plunge in or to stay dry.

Athena the Normal Self and Hera the Personal Self emphasize your right mind and your social connections. Apollo counters Poseidon by letting your intellect bring you above your emotions. Zeus is reality and the ultimate check on emotions, because acting out will likely land you in court, just like Poseidon.

Hestia can bring some relief. Poseidon wanted to marry her once, but she refused him, because the Homebody is the sense of a center and she doesn't like being dislodged by emotions. Honoring Hestia by putting your home life in order can help even out Poseidon's unpredictable behavior.

And then there's Hermes, who is your sense of humor. Laughing at life and at yourself gets you out of identification with your emotions, because Hermes is the self who knows that 'this too shall pass'. Poseidon doesn't laugh at himself; instead he feels humiliated. Rather than resenting other people's success like Poseidon does, Hermes wants you to get a piece of the action. You can approach Hermes from Poseidon's perspective through affiliations, like the Lion's Club or the local choir, because there you can find emotions that are shared by the group and moderated by structured friendship.

ARES

Ares, the God of War, is the son of Zeus and Hera, who are in eternal conflict. He has Zeus' courage and Hera's individualism. You're like him when you fight others, fight a disease, or fight to stay awake.

Ares is arguments, fighting anger, violence, and terrorism. He is the fight itself and the war itself. He is the bombs, the violence, and the casualties. He is gang wars and bar room brawls, 'roid rage and road rage. Ares is there whenever anyone threatens, challenges, or calls a bluff. When he's around, the fists and weapons take on a life of their own.

This self doesn't need a reason to fight. Ares likes fighting for its own sake. He wants you to feel intensely alive and to roil in the thick of things, gripped by moods, surprised by your own anger, and unable to let go. He possesses with rage and intensity. He is Rage itself as a person in the psyche.

The Chariot Driver changes the personality of anybody who gets behind the wheel of a car. He makes even mild people who don't use profanity swear at other drivers just by getting behind the wheel. His children with Aphrodite, *Phobos,* Fear, and *Deimos*, Terror, help drive his war chariot and can craze you on the highway.

All of the gods fight to some degree. Their turf battles help define and contrast our various selves. The gods keep a fragile peace but they do not avoid each another. They never hesitate to take sides in a quarrel—except Apollo, who wants you to rise above uncomfortable circumstances.

Our lives are full of Ares's violence. Career ambitions may fight the love of a hometown. Laziness may battle the need to exercise. Dieting pits one persona against another, as do addictions. Ares of Superior Force often decides the outcome.

But he is not evil. The Greeks considered fighting and war a natural part of life, not something to bemoan, renounce, or get rid of. They would never pray for universal peace, because that sounds to Greek ears like nothing is going to happen anymore. In the *Iliad*, a book about war, Zeus is happiest when all the gods are fighting each other, each one

147

Ares

asserting his utmost against the others. In the Greek worldview, balance is not achieved by standing still, as in spirituality, but by going in all directions at once like a dancer doing an arabesque.

Leave inner peace to Apollo. He can rise above life in a way that humans cannot. Ares sees life as a big fight and he wants you smack in the middle of it so that you know you're alive.

Ares the Soldier

Ares the Soldier is the military identity.

He hails from Thrace, a wild land to the north of Greece. For such a major god, Ares has relatively few temples or mysteries, because the battlefield is his holy ground and the men killed in war are his blood sacrifices. He has always been well provided for.

His only real friend is Hades, the God of the Underworld, because he sends him so many fine young men from battle. Ares the Dispenser of Youth's Sweet Courage does not spare the brave man, but the coward. The Greeks prayed to him to keep them away from the action and to leave them in peace.

You can see Ares in the hyper-masculinity of skinheads, tattoos and boot camp workouts. He is the opposite of softness. The military buzz cut thrusts forward the features of the face, emphasizing masculine traits, although sometimes Ares is bearded to underline his manliness. His shield is a set of ripped, six pack abs, the ultimate sign of hotness because he is psychologically mean and lean, like ancient hunters bringing home a large catch after chasing prey and living on only meat for days. He is the mean, sculpted look of intense bodybuilders of both sexes and the hardness of their faces.

Ares makes you never want to apologize for yourself, even when you're wrong or pig-headed. He wants you to take a firm stance--chin down, eyebrows low, and the voice at the deepest, relaxed and most commanding end of its range. To imagine his voice, say *No* the way you would to a misbehaving dog. Ares abhors up-speak as a coward's way of talking.

148

The Greek Gods Among Us

You can see his mean good looks in Billy Idol, Clint Eastwood, and Grace Jones. Ares is the edgy hip-hop and gangsta rockstars. You can watch him in military movies or visit his crowd at West Point. A gift to him can be anything from learning how to fire a gun to doing your abs with military fervor.

Ares Helper of Mankind

Ares' intensity is a boon to any activity. The Helper of Mankind is zest, passion, and energy. He is the intensity of the battlefield, the boardroom, and the bedroom. He is the burn in the muscle, the raging erection, and the latest hot craze. He is hotness itself.

His gift is *menos*—a word used to describe runaway fire and bounding animals. Menos is the second wind that lets you surpass yourself. It is the adrenaline rush that floods your arms and legs with superhuman strength when you're past exhaustion. Menos is a light step and an eagerness to get down to business, whether it's closing a deal, taking action, or getting into bed with someone.

Ares goes best in combination with other gods, giving them the fight they need to achieve Excellence through you. Ares with Apollo makes Beethoven rage (*Mars Furibundus);* with Aphrodite he makes sex wild (*Mars Ferus);* and with Hermes he makes your hunger for travel rabid (*Mars Lussa*). These qualities can apply to any combination of gods. You can even pair him up with Hestia the Homebody and clean the house *like a maniac*, or with Demeter the Goddess of Food to make a recipe insane (Mars Insanus). Ares gives that extra oomph that kicks things up a notch like red pepper.

With Zeus by his side, Ares is the Helper of Justice and the Leader of Most Just Men like the heroes who fought the Nazis in World War Two or for our civil rights in the Sixties. He is rarely shown alone in the artwork, because there is usually something else at stake in any fight besides the fighting.

Turn to Ares when you need vim and vigor in the present moment. He is the present itself as an onslaught of the senses—the *din of*

Ares

battle that is mentioned with his name. Ares is presence in the moment, undistracted by future plans, distracting fantasies, or errant thoughts. His intense presence is a virtue for any fighter, lover, or dancer, all of which are his specialties.

Get to know Ares when you need a hard edge. He is the cure for feelings of mediocrity and listlessness. Seek him for intensity and endurance in anything: at the office, in romance, and in sports. Ares is the zest of life.

Ares Courage

The Greeks prayed for Ares to shake off *cruel Cowardice*, which keeps you from living life.

Ares is Courage personified.

The Greeks never considered courage a personal virtue. Instead of saying, *I was brave,* the Greek would say, *Courage drove me on, Zeus filled me with courage, the gods sapped their courage,* and so on. People who act courageously in extraordinary circumstances often say, 'I don't know what got into me' or 'I just had to do it.' They never say, 'I was courageous."

That's because courage comes from the gods. It can inhabit individuals or groups, which is why it's so contagious. The troops of Leonidas and Napoleon won because of their high spirits not because of their numbers. Courage keeps people fighting when they're wounded. Losing courage also comes from the gods, and it can panic investors, derail an actor's or athlete's performance, and infect whole armies and populations.

Courage applies to many things besides fighting. The courage to seize an opportunity comes from Mars Who Jumps On It, *Mars Deprensus.* Ares can make you lion-hearted and able to face anything, even your own death.

Confidence is a kind of everyday courage, and it also comes from Ares. His presence makes confident people so appealing.

The Greek Gods Among Us

Confidence means *with faith*. Like all virtues, the Greeks saw confidence as something external and not a personal virtue. Virtues were *known* not owned. For instance, what we would call a wise man, the Greek would say that *he knows wisdom*. What we would call a brilliant woman, the Greek would say *she knows brilliance*. So if *you* don't have confidence you can let Ares have it for you, just be knowing Ares. Confidence and courage don't have to be personal for you to experience them and turn them to your advantage.

These days, people have a low opinion of aggression because it offends Hera the Personal Self, who's always worried about personal feelings. Hera has mixed feelings about her violent son, even though she has a violent temper herself. To Ares, aggression is the essence of courage and confidence because it is aggressive to be friendly, to introduce yourself to someone, to break conventions, or to start a business.

Boasting and mutual admiration also come from Ares. A certain amount of boasting can be virtuous and effective, as I experienced when I used to box. You can be like Ares by giving a firm and friendly handshake with a direct but quick look in the eye that shows mutual respect. Ares makes it natural and easy to put your arm over a buddy's shoulder in friendship.

Wanton Ares

Wanton Ares is a thrill seeker. He makes you come alive when the adrenaline is spiking. He makes you want to be where the action is, whether it's in a battlefield, in bed, or in a big city, and to sneer at the pampered life of safety. He is the injured athlete in the Nike ads who says, 'just do it'.

Ares draws people to risky occupations like oil and construction and encourages them to depend more on luck than on long term planning. His friendship requires a life lived vigorously and without guarantees. That is his zest.

151

Ares

The parts of the brain responsible for inhibition which develop after adolescence begin to erode in men in their Forties and Fifties, when a new rebellious spirit requires greater risk taking: Ares is back. He might be an untamable urge in a previously dull life, like Ed Norton in *Fight Club* befriending his Brad Pitt Ares persona. You can thank Ares the Killer of Men, *Ares Androphones,* when the parachute doesn't open or the Ares the Murderer, *Ares Maiaphonos,* for deadly accidents and crimes.

Sometimes he is just what is needed, especially when social gods like Hera, Demeter, and Athena make you feel hemmed in by life. Ares gives the soul the air it needs to keep from suffocating in hyper-domesticity.

Ares Hard with Spear

Ares Hard with Spear carries *the staff of manhood,* as the hymn calls it.

He is the erection personified.

His tutor is Priapus, the little gnome with the giant backwards-facing penis, who teaches him how to fight and how to dance—which must have been quite a sight. Priapus is the confident stud, whether you're a man or a woman. The manliness that he teaches Ares is one of his gifts. Indeed, one of the prizes in the Athenian athletic contests was for *manly deportment*—the masculinity of men as they move, speak and gesture.

Ares loves Beauty in the person of Aphrodite-- but not in the intellectual way of Apollo, in whom Beauty inspires longing. Ares wants the real thing. To him, sexual attraction comes first and the 'relationship' (Hera) comes later. He's the strong and silent type who's probably thinking about football and hooters. He has no interest in sex that is 'safe' or 'sane'.

While his mother, Hera, sends you Haagen Dazs to keep you from cheating on your spouse, Ares takes no substitutions in love or in anything else. He gives you the ability to treat your lover like a sex object to be honored and enjoyed. Ares treats himself like an object as well. That is his world. What he lacks in imagination he makes up for in actuality.

152

Ares and Aphrodite have a longstanding affair on Olympus. Ares never asks Aphrodite to marry him and he doesn't begrudge her marriage to Hephaestus, the artist. For them, sex is the heart of the relationship. The God of War comes to Aphrodite as an ardent lover not a rapist—unless that's the fantasy possessing the lovers. He brings intensity to sex with an aggression that is hotness itself and can only be quelled by satisfaction. Aphrodite abets or slows down the aggression to prolong the lovemaking. Her job is to feel beautiful.

Hera the Personal Self and Athena the Normal Self may find Ares frustrating because they are the impulse to tame and 'improve' him. But when the wild Ares of the lover was what attracted you in the first place, turning him into 'marriage material' will only alienate Wild Ares and cause him to rebel through drinking, abuse, or other forms of revenge.

Ares the Straight Limbed

The Greeks considered athleticism a part of courage because it takes courage to get out there and compete.

Ares is the athlete.

He's a natural. Ares is the kid in high school who was on every team and made everyone swoon. The *straight-limbed* god is limber and lanky, muscular but not muscle-bound like Herakles. In their body building contests, the Athenians would judge which man had the best of each body part—biceps, quads, or pectorals—and then say that if you put them all together, you'd have Ares.

He is athletic virtue, like a challenging workout and clean movement with no flourishes. Ares would never have you make fun of your own instincts like Woody Allen or think that there is any such thing as a mind/body split. That's Apollo's game, because he makes you think you are somehow disconnected from or above your body. Naturally, Apollo has a generally low opinion of his half-brother.

Ares the Din of Battle

153

Ares

Ares is the *din of battle.* He is the present moment with its overwhelming onslaught of information.

He is the present, personified.

You are like Ares when you fight to pay attention or to stay awake. You enact him when you stay in the moment and avoid slipping into fantasies, perseverations, or thinking about the past or the future. Ares would never have you stare at your phone when other people are surrounding you. He's the one to turn to when you spend too much time being anywhere but here and now. This explains why yoga, which brings you into the present moment, was originally a martial art.

Ares is your gut reaction and your first impression—and the reason those matter so much. He is your ability to size up an opponent or a challenge by observing it directly. He lets you actually see the ball land in your hand as you catch it, rather than generalizing a trajectory and hoping for the best. Ares makes you less self-conscious simply by plunging you into the present moment, using up all your attention so there's no nothing left to be self-conscious about. He frees you from thinking about who's watching because that's Hera's concern, not his.

When I took up boxing, my coach emphasized the special vision that boxers develop which requires avoiding visual generalizations and remaining focused in the moment. Feints and fakes take advantage of the tendency to standardize what you are looking at and to rely on patterns instead of paying attention to what is actually going on in front of you. You can't role-play Ares in the ring because being in the thick of the fight is Ares himself.

He rushes into your life when you are thrust directly and sometimes painfully into the present through an accident, bad news, or physical pain. Ares is the heightening of the senses that arises in acute situations, making you notice concrete details, like when a truck is heading towards you at an intersection. He is the reason most people remember what they were doing on 9/11 and how pleasant the weather was that day when Ares struck with sudden violence.

154

Mars

Mars was bigger in Rome than Ares ever was in Greece because the Romans were a warlike, conquering people. He had two festivals, a magnificent temple, and two months named after him—including our March. Mars is the Red Planet, the planet of fire and blood.

Mars and Ares are hotness--the hot new dance, the hot fashion trend, the hot movie star, or the hot idea, because hotness is intensity in the moment. Each hot new thing does a kind of violence to what preceded it by taking its place or turning it upside down. In the arts, Ares is a rebel and a troublemaker. The avant-garde is the front line of his invading army, because innovation breaks with the past like Ares breaking things, clearing the air, and making room for something new.

There is a contradictory side to the Roman Mars, if you think of war as only destructive. Mars is also the Builder of Cities and the father of Romulus and Remus, the founders of Rome. He is a god of old ways and attachment to the soil. Mars the Archaic, *Priscus*, is an agricultural god—an old fashioned and conservative type, now one of the major gods of the Red States along with Hera.

His names include:

The Rough, *Asper*
The Unarticulated, *Confusus*
The Savage, *Saeuus*
The Horrible, *Atrox*
The Foul and Obscene, *Turpis,* and
The Blind, *Caecus*.

Ares and Zeus

Ares is Zeus' lesser self.

Ares the Destroyer, *Aidelos,* kills all sense of order, defying Zeus, who is Order itself. A sharp word can kill a love affair and a violent act can nullify a reputation--all thanks to Ares. He is the reason that groups of people who once lived together peacefully can lose all fellow feeling once

Ares

certain taboos are breached, like the sectarian violence that followed the collapse of Yugoslavia or the bombing of the Golden Mosque in Fallujah.

You are most hateful to me, of all the gods; forever strife is dear to you and wars and slaughter, Zeus proclaims when Ares comes whining from a lost battle. All the gods shun him and look uncomfortably away in this scene. Zeus recognizes Hera's temper in Ares, as well as her vengeance, and he doesn't like what he sees.

No Greek general would ask Ares for victory, only for courage, enthusiasm/*menos*, and a fair fight. He would never claim that God was on his side or take credit for victory. The Greeks were never sure whose side the gods were on or if a god was out to mislead them into false confidence. Ares may be a fighter but Zeus decides victory because Zeus is the God of What Happens.

After a battle or victory in life, the Greeks would typically thank Zeus, Herakles the Hero, and Ares' son, Fear (*Phobos*)for routing the enemy and motivating the victory.

When the Greeks did win a battle, they offered the gods a symbolic share of the spoils, like building a memorial on the Mall or giving away your ashtrays when you quit smoking. Sometimes they thanked the local deity for improving his own territory, which you do when you improve the neighborhood in some way. A victorious soldier might hang miniature gold shields around the house like commemorative plates or pile up the losing army's gear, but he would never give away the winning arms, because they are lucky and should be kept.

Ares and Hera

Both Ares and Hera are quarrelsome and give birth to dragons. The distinction is that Ares is never righteous or self-dramatizing like Hera the Personal Self. He just likes to fight while she always needs to be right, even if it requires playing the martyr.

He is the god of the individual, especially rebellious individuals. He is the god who stands apart from others, which is the definition of being an individual. While Hera is the god of heroes, Ares is

156

the ability to not care about other people's approval, for he stands in defiance of the gods while Zeus berates him in front of them. He is unapologetic loyalty to your own nature. Ares carries a shield in the artwork because this self doesn't need to explain himself.

He's a rebel who embarrasses his mother and stands for everything she hates about Zeus. He's just too sexual, too unreliable, and too given to violence for her taste. And he's a little too hot and sexy to bring to a family reunion, because he doesn't know how to act innocent. Ares scorns Hera's society and morality as phony pretense by people who probably just aren't getting any.

I remember being shocked and pleased when I first moved to New York City and saw lovers quarreling on the bus in front of strangers. It was so refreshing after living under the rule of Hera the Suburbanite who makes everyone watch each other closely but seldom clash openly or even know each other.

Ares is no stranger to self-pity. "I coulda been a contender," he moans with regret. But he never weeps for physical pain or apologizes for his aggression. His courage has less to do with maturity than with sheer defiance. He is an anti-social self in Hera's eyes and, therefore, a force for the independence of each self, fighting to be itself.

To the Greeks, everyone is a *son of Ares stained in blood.* You can't play innocent even if you take yoga every day, eat hydroponic celery, and leave no carbon footprint. Being an individual is a hostile act because it requires separation from others--at least enough to create your own space.

Americans are far more comfortable with Ares than are Europeans, with our gun culture, cowboys, and entrepreneurial spirit. Ares gives us an edge that appeals to the world and makes us so innovative in the arts.

Eos

Eos is Dawn, the Goddess of Sunrise, a time for lovers and for armies to attack. She is the morning moon, greeted after a night of

Ares

revelry. This moon is wilder and more turbulent than her sister, Selene, the romantic moon of moon/spoon/June and *Moon River*, but it is not as wild as the crescent moon of Artemis the Wilderness and Hekate the Witch, gods of the uncanny and of possession.

Eos is compulsion--the uncontrollable urge, the late night seduction enabled by drugs or alcohol, or the shopping spree. She is the violent need to have something or someone simply because you don't have it yet.

Aphrodite cursed her with compulsion after she caught her in bed with Ares, her boyfriend. She made Eos desire and abduct one man after the other, including *Kleitos*, the Renowned, and countless other unnamed handsome young men. She is *Looking for Mr. Goodbar* and one reason that many gay men seek Ares in promiscuity.

Eos loved one young man, Tithonus, so much that she begged Zeus to give him immortality. Zeus granted her wish but Eos forgot to ask for eternal youth as well, so Tithonus shrank and shriveled into a cicada, which she keeps in a jar. Tithonus is the idealized lover from a past love affair, the one that some people spend their lives trying to find again in someone else. Looking for him keeps them going with Eos even as the sex becomes fetishized and the personal connection is lost, because the spontaneity of Ares has been forgotten.

Eris

Ares' sister, *Eris*, is Strife. There is always trouble when she is around.

Like many gods, she is both a person and a thing. She is the self who causes strife and she is Strife itself as a person in your midst.

Eris spreads rumors and cultivates jealousy in order to bring about ruin, which is her delight. Zeus upheld Eris' right to exist because he wanted humans to always have Strife and *Neikos*, Quarreling, her sister, among them.

The Greeks believed that in the olden days, men and gods mingled freely in a world without strife. But Zeus chose to separate the

them *so that the gods could take their accustomed places apart from men.*
In other words, he made them metaphorical, because the gods are
imaginary people just like Ego and Id. That is why it violates Zeus to
believe in the gods literally or to speak as if you know what they are
thinking.

Eris thrives in conflicting accounts, ambiguity and alternate
meanings. She is competition, which was as prized among the Greeks as it
is among Americans today, who make contests out of yoga or baking a
cake.

She is a friend of many great artists and individuals who are
admired for their ability to embrace contradictions, as Maslow observed.
Her friends include families who argue a lot, especially when it's considered
the normal state of things and nothing personal.

The way to honor her is to personify all strife as belonging to
her. That way you can live with the strife without identifying with it or
seeking to eliminate, cure, or resolve it. The gods are always striving
against each other, both in yourself and in other people, so seeing Eris as
normal and necessary means you don't have to do anything about it, only to
learn to live with it as one god among many.

Otis and Ephialtes

Poseidon impregnated the wife of Aloeus when she scooped
water up into her bosom and she gave birth to twin boys. Otis and
Ephialtes grew into giants on Mother Earth's corn. Only Orion was ever as
big and strong and macho.

They are bullies. You are like them when you push other
people around.

When the oracle tells them that *no man or god can kill them*,
they declare war on Olympus and swear by the River Styx to rape Hera and
Artemis. But first they go after Ares to break the fighting spirit of the gods.

Ares is only a child at the time. The twins grab him, pull out
his sinews and shut him up in a bronze jar, where he lies helpless for 13
months. Finally, Hermes finds him, restrings his sinews, and sets him free.

Ares

You are like young Ares when you are a Helpless Victim but you want to fight, like when you have a broken leg or your position in a company prevents you from speaking up.

Apollo comes up with a plan to defeat them. He tells the giants that his sister, Artemis, will gladly offer herself to Otis on the beach at Naxos, but he doesn't offer Hera to Ephialtes, which makes him jealous. When Artemis appears as a white doe on the strand, the brothers throw their javelins at her, but she slips their aim and they strike each other instead. As the Oracle predicted, *no man or god could kill them,* for they killed each other.

Now they sit tied back to back by living snakes in Tartarus, the worst part of the Underworld, while the grim owl, Styx, perches overhead reminding them of their unfulfilled oaths.

You are like Otis and Ephialtes when you abuse your power or physical strength. They are Ares in the extreme as unchecked force and aggression.

You are like Ares locked in a container when you are too weak to defend yourself physically or psychologically, especially when you think of aggression as a dirty word. Ares is hamstrung when wars are completely overlooked as Americans do today, when everyone around you talks in up-speak, and when life becomes a trance of food and television. Ares is paralyzed when you are always looking at a screen rather than living in the real world, and when you avoid all conflict and assertiveness as taboo.

Amazons

These children of Ares and Harmonia love war so much that they cut off their right breasts to shoot more accurately with bow and arrows.

They are the gang, depicted in art as horsewomen who keep men as domestics or keep away from men altogether. This self fights for the tribe and feels persecuted because of tribal identity.

160

The Greek Gods Among Us

One tribe met with the men from the other side of the mountain every year for orgies at the summit. They would send the baby girls to the Amazons and the boys to the men--or the boys' limbs were broken and all of the children sent to the Amazons.

The Amazons are a female version of the male Ego, and they tend to clash with that all-time Male Ego, Herakles, who has to be the best at everything. As one of his Twelve Labors, he goes to fetch the Amazon Queen's girdle, but when the two meet they jump into bed together and the Queen gives him the girdle freely out of love. Others say that Herakles killed the Queen in battle and took the girdle. They are the battle of the sexes.

You are Herakles with the Amazons when you are both attracted and repulsed by something at the same time, like when you change your mind from one decision to its complete opposite, or when you love and hate an addiction at the same time. One self might go on a diet and another self eats chocolate anyway, or one self might want a career in business and the other in poetry. It's not enough to want something. This crowd wants you to choose sides and you are stuck in the middle with no room for negotiation.

Seeing an impossible conflict as Herakles with the Amazons gives it a life of its own and separates you from it. You can try to satisfy each desire in turn by giving each your absolute attention when you are with it, but knowing there is another self who wants the opposite. You're doing the same thing as before, but at least each self knows the other one exists. You can even say out loud what you're doing to both selves: "I am smoking cigarettes even though you don't want me to" so the two selves can get to know each other.

Some remote tribes of Amazons lived in a distant paradise in the West where there was no need to work, like neighborhoods with a Bohemian flavor, full of coffee shops, artists, and alternative life styles. You are among the Amazons in any milieu where traditional sex roles and expectations are set aside and you wonder, *does anybody work in this town?*

161

Ares

Moving On

Ares goes best with some other god in company rather than as violence for its own sake. Instead of fighting his aggressive impulse—which locks you into fighting anyway—you can pair him with some other god or activity. Bring Ares into sports or into any discipline as fight or zest, and do it until you are satisfied and worn out, like he would do.

You can contain Ares by personifying your anger as him and imagine him standing beside you as you go about your business like the gods who stand by as Zeus rebukes him. You can honor him by not giving a damn what other people think of you. And you can assuage Ares with a little Aphrodite by keeping your sex life alive--but only by giving him the real thing and what your true heart desires.

PART FOUR: GODS OF SOCIETY

Hera, Athena, Demeter, and Hestia form a traditional grouping in Greek art, shown together in many friezes and vases. Athena has already been discussed under 'Gods of Action'. According to Evolutionary Psychology, multiple selves are 'orthogonal' or at right angles with each other, meaning that they do not simply slice up the pie evenly; they embody competing behaviors in entirely different modes of being. For instance, you don't 'act' like Ares the way you act like Athena, for you are never possessed by Athena, only obedient to her.

Hera is the Goddess of Marriage, Society, and Morality. She embodies both the burdens and the glories of civilized life, inspiring greatness among individuals and groups. The Queen of the Gods is the self who is *married to God* and who sees your life as, indeed, *your life* and not just an arbitrary situation in a random universe. In the age of Facebook and hyper-individualism, she has become an infection and is crowding out other gods that offer a respite from self-centeredness.

Demeter means *Grain Mother.* She is the God of Motherhood and the God of Food. Demeter is your family and who you are with your family. She is food and your relationship to it.

Hestia is the Goddess of the Home. She is the house itself and who you are at home, especially when you are alone. She is the sense of a psychological center and self-sufficiency. Hestia is a peaceful goddess who likes to support others and to work in the background rather than be the center of attention. She is privacy.

While Hera was more feared because of her rages, Hestia and Demeter were beloved throughout Greece, rivaled only by Hermes the God of Friends.

163

HERA

Hera is the wife of Zeus and by extension the self who is married to God. She gives you the sense that your life is a matter between you and God and that it is *your* life to begin with and not just an accident in an arbitrary universe.

'Hera' is the feminine for 'hero'. She is the strong and willful champion of great individuals. Hera fosters ambition and dreams and often works with Athena to strategize the hero's way to success.

She is the Chosen One, for she was chosen by God out of all others to be his wife. Hera makes you believe that your life matters more than others and that you are special to God. She is American exceptionalism and all the many forms of feeling chosen or more important to God than others, because feeling chosen requires that others be *not* chosen.

She lives and breathes self-esteem. Self-esteem values you for yourself, not for any charms, talents, or capacities you may offer the world. Hera values you 'just for being you' and makes you believe that you are far more than your body and attributes and that no one can replace you, just as she tells herself that no bimbo will ever replace her in Zeus' true affections.

Hera looks for comfort in the personal exception, like the stories of the handful of survivors of the tsunami that killed a hundred thousand people, because secretly she convinces you that you would have been one of them. She is the voice that urges you to take the medication whose benefits take seconds to list in the advertisement and whose side effects take two minutes, because surely you'll be fine. She makes people prone to magical thinking and sentimentality. One of the few miracles in Homer occurs when Hera gives the horse, Roan Beauty, the ability to speak, which he does for a short time until Zeus stops him. You can see Hera's wishful thinking in the need to believe in miracles like Heaven rather than to find meaning in reality.

Zeus causes Hera terrible suffering through his endless affairs with women, men, and youths. To Hera, God is disloyal when events don't

164

go your way and everyone else seems to get the looks, love, talent, or money. Hera makes you feel that you're missing out when someone else gets all of God's attention.

Her suffering was painted in the most terrible colors, but the Greeks never really condemned Zeus' infidelity until later times when he became more conceptual. Asking the sky god to be monogamous would be like asking it to rain in only one place. God cannot only love one person, no matter how special. For his part, Zeus never apologizes for his affairs and lets Hera know that he would ignore her anger even if she ran away forever.

At one point, she convinces the gods to revolt against him. She drugs and binds Zeus with many knots to a couch but soon enough, the gods start arguing over who will take his place. At Zeus' bidding, his ally, Briareus, one of the Hundred Handed Ones, unties all the knots at once, freeing Zeus to grab his thunderbolt while the other gods beg for mercy.

He hangs Hera from the sky with weighted gold chains on her ankles, which happens when reality forces you to stretch out of your personal narrative. After Hera cries all night Zeus frees her so he can get some sleep, but only after she swears never to rebel against him again. She is the sense that God is picking on you and that Life (Zeus) makes you suffer more than others.

Zeus faults her for trying to read his thoughts, but he knows she will never change and can't help herself. Hera ultimately submits to Zeus, who is Reality. You do this when you let things follow their own course, whether it's a conversation or a new friendship. You stretch when you stop spending all your time worrying about how you are going to react to some feared future event—a worry cumulatively worse than the event itself. You stretch when you face reality instead of wishing for magical events to save you from it.

The Great Lady

Hera is the Great Lady and the Queen of the Gods.

In artwork, she stands tall and stately in beautiful, flowing

Hera

robes, wearing a crown or sporting a diadem in her blond hair and carrying a wreath or scepter like the Queen of England. Her cult included some of the greatest temples ever built and is native to Argos, one of the wealthiest and most fertile regions of Greece.

Hera is the Goddess of Nobility. She is classiness and your better nature. She is noblesse oblige.

Hera is the Leader of the Original Settlement, which carries as much prestige today as it did back when the settlement was Sicily. The Goddess Worshipped on the Heights loves prestige of address and wants you to live in a glorious house on the top of the hill or in a penthouse with a view. Hera wants you to have all the status symbols and to glory in the eyes of others. In her cherished role as Zeus' wife, she is the feeling of being a *somebody* and not part of the great unwashed. She is the shining face of celebrity. Follow her exclusively and you will find yourself sitting on a high horse looking down on others and acting like a queen at court.

Hera of the White Arms, *Leukolenos* has white arms because she doesn't have to work in the fields like the commoners, just as today tanning is déclassé. Statues show a mild and benign face with lips slightly parted in gentle nobility. This self loves leisure and shopping and especially top shelf items. 'You get what you pay for' is her nobility projected onto merchandise.

Hera is the founding spirit of volunteerism and the desire to improve the world, which is pleasing to Zeus. The Benefactress of the Land stands up for human dignity and her loyalty reminds others that they have not been forgotten. Her followers are the ladies who lunch, who support the arts, and who run voter registration drives for the benefit of society and civilization. Her doubles include Eleanor Roosevelt and Jackie Onassis and women of power and position who promote culture and causes.

Volunteering shows the world your nobility and it suits Hera to a tee. Volunteering is a sign of class because it signals a superior social position (requiring leisure time), which is why you can always get a whiff of condescension among volunteers.

The Romans, whose religion was a matter of state,

worshipped Hera's double, Juno, a matronly goddess who combines Hera's society with Athena's practical wisdom and industry. You honor these goddesses when you cherish traditions, holidays, and anniversaries—not least because they give you a chance to dress up and show off a little.

Goddess of Marriage

Hera the Uniter, *Hera Zygia,* is the Goddess of Marriage. She is who you are as a spouse.

Zeus shames the aristocratic Hera into marrying him by appearing as a little cuckoo bird shivering in the rain. When she scoops up the pitiful creature in delight he takes on his human form and ravishes her. Their wedding night lasts four hundred years on a fresh bed of flowers and grass, but after the honeymoon Zeus goes back to his philandering ways and the relationship devolves into one long, exhausting discussion about the relationship.

No one would blame Hera if she cheated on Zeus the way he cheats on her, but the Goddess of Marriage could never do that because it would contradict her nature. Hera can help you withstand a sexless marriage but never one in which there is no emotional loyalty. She needs you to feel as though you are someone's *One and Only.* If you find yourself in a bad marriage Hera would have you end the marriage rather than betray it. Her usual tactic is to have you substitute one thing for another like staying together for the sake of the children or eating Haagen Dazs when the sex stops happening.

She rules untrammeled in the suburbs, where spouses generally can't have friends with the opposite sex --unlike in the city where one's comings and goings are not so easily observed. When a spouse dies in the suburbs, the survivor often loses the couple's old friends because to Hera, 'three's a crowd'.

She and Zeus bicker constantly, so when you find yourself bickering with your partner, remember it is only Hera and Zeus at it again, enacting the ancient quarrel. You may need to indulge it a bit out of

167

Hera

politeness to the gods, but it can turn into a divine whirlpool that preoccupies you and chases out all other gods. The flip side of marital bliss is the feeling that the other person is limiting you. See it as Hera and Zeus, at it again, and let it be their quarrel, not yours.

Her jealousy is terrible. When Zeus carries off Aegina, the nymph of an island, she sends a dragon after her that kills all of the inhabitants. When he seduces the lovely nymph Callisto by appearing as her girlfriend, Hera turns her into a bear that her own son kills while out hunting.

Her festivals are more like social crises than celebrations. One time, Hera flees in a terrible rage to her mountain home, vowing never to return. This time she seems to really mean it—until Zeus announces he is going to marry the local princess, *Daedele,* or Cunning Work—which is a block of wood dressed up in a gown. Indignant Hera leads all the wives of the town into the streets in protest. When the puppet is uncovered and the joke revealed, Hera has a good laugh and forgives Zeus immediately--but she burns the puppet anyway.

This myth was re-enacted at the Daedela festival. A puppet dressed like the goddess is hidden in the bushes while everyone goes out looking for it and society breaks down in ritual panic. A goat eventually finds the puppet, which is then wrapped in willow branches—an anti-aphrodisiac--and forcibly returned to the people amid a procession of maidens. The goat is then sacrificed for treason because Hera always has to blame someone, as anyone knows who has ever intervened in a couple's quarrels or tried to help someone with his problems who values them too highly.

Hera and Aphrodite

The Goddess of Marriage resents Aphrodite the Goddess of Sex for breaking up marriages and wreaking havoc on families. But once in a while, Hera borrows Aphrodite's magic sex girdle and seduces Zeus— which you do when you change persona by putting aside playing the spouse and become a lover to your partner again.

Aphrodite doesn't sleep with anyone out of obligation like Hera does. Aphrodite likes to be seduced, not nagged into sex with Hera's, "You don't want me anymore." She wants you to have sex for its own sake, while Hera usually has some other thing in mind besides the sex—perhaps a vacation or a mink, or just securing the relationship. You follow Hera rather than Aphrodite when you have sex with your partner because you love him rather than want him.

In revenge for harassing her, Aphrodite sends her child, *Penia*, or Want, upon Hera's followers, turning them into consumers and over-eaters who want one thing after another out of pure sexual frustration. Hermes the Persuader, Aphrodite's hedonistic paramour, colludes with her through advertisements that sell cars, chocolate, and materialism as pleasurable substitutes for sexual freedom. Aphrodite's revenge on Hera is to get you to spend on credit and stand in the mirror hating your waistline.

A combination goddess, Hera Aphrodite, is the spouse as lover and the mood of honeymoons. Zeus and Hera had sex after their wedding for four hundred years. Most couples find it's hotter in the beginning when everything's new and *when Love and the Graces set up house.*

Hera and Artemis

These two are the opposition between duty and freedom. Artemis is the Goddess of the Gate and the freedom to change, which naturally threatens Hera's loyalty. Hera would rather you remain a predictable 'good old so-and-so' while Artemis lives for fun, authentic desires, and adventure.

To Artemis, what you do is more important than whom you do it with, because she likes you to relate to others as teammates, buddies, competitors, or members of a club. Artemis knows that you won't really keep in touch with your friends at the office when you take another job. This self is never really surprised when people disappoint and she's not interested in forgiveness and reconciliation, which Hera can do all day.

To Hera, Artemis seems irresponsible and cut off from others.

169

Hera

Doing things purely out of choice rather than obligation or duty looks like pure selfishness to her, because the Goddess of the Yoke wants you all tied up. She is the one who keeps you sleeping with your spouse even when Aphrodite has lost all interest.

During the battle of the gods, Hera smacks Artemis on the nose with a slipper and sends her crying back to Olympus, saying *take that, you Missy.*as though upbraiding a puppy. Hera envies pleasure seekers like Artemis and Aphrodite, who are always out having fun while she's stuck with a smile plastered on her face at church, family outings, and other social obligations.

The Cow Eyed Goddess

Cows were a measure of wealth and establishment in ancient societies. But the eyes of a cow are not the first image that comes to mind when you think of a beautiful woman. They are large and shallow and kind of stupid like a deer in the headlights.

You see cow eyes in people who regard themselves with too much familiarity, especially when they talk about themselves. You see them in young people who fall in love and show not an ounce of irony or separation from it, and in parents who talk about their children as if they are a wonder upon the earth.

Cow-Eyed Hera lives in statements like 'why me?' 'I'm crazy that way', and 'that's our Jason'. She dwells in condos and developments named 'The' like The Hampton because Hera cherishes the personal exception and could never stand to live somewhere called Rich Neighborhood or Exclusive Housing.

The Cow-Eyed Goddess is the personal self. She is the feeling that the world revolves around *me* and that human history has culminated in your existence. The personal self takes everything personally, by definition. Hera wants you to cocoon in your personal world with your personal feelings. Her sense of life as a personal journey can trap you in maudlin sentimentalism, like the advertisements for banks and airlines that bring tears to your eyes with their bald vows of loyalty and

170

swelling hymns. Giant corporations manipulate Hera's personalism through complex matrices of data including your shopping habits and on-line viewing—proof of how impersonal the *personal touch* can be.

That's because *personal* does not only mean only *human*. It comes from a god—a god who is personal *and* inhuman, like an illness. To get a good idea of Hera the Personal Self, practice your Oscar acceptance speech, thanking everyone for the roles they've played in your amazing success as you tearfully accept the world's grateful—if belated--recognition. Or make a list of your greatest humiliations, because Hera dwells in the spectrum of fulfillment and despair. Either way, 'it's all about me.'

Her sensibility feeds on confession, closure, and cathartic joy, like spouses making up after a fight. Hera wants to put Zeus' infidelities and life's pain behind her for once and for all. Her followers spill their hearts on talk shows, misty interviews, and weight loss programs because Hera lives in personal relatedness and wants people to hash things out until we know absolutely everything about them and wish they would go away as soon as possible.

Hera controls people by keeping them stuck in personal feelings. She is the spouse who answers when you complain she's spending too much money that, "you don't love me." Her courtly laugh is the embarrassed laughter of a celebrity roast, with its highly contagious and self-conscious smiles like the grimaces of submissive monkeys, fearful that the spotlight will turn on them next.

But the personal self cannot contain the soul. The soul contains the personal and much that is not personal, like dreams, sensations, compulsions, and emotions that precede your humanity. You don't need Hera the Personal Self when you're driving a car. In fact, if she's there you will take every lane change personally and risk going into road rage.

One way to put Hera on a diet is to not to take anything personally for one day, even if it is meant that way. Seeing your personal feelings as belonging to Hera frees you to break out of the personal pattern, for the Soul needs air and freedom and cannot be confined to a single

Hera

narrative about *me*.

Goddess of Morality

The most striking aspect of statues of Hera is the enormous amount of clothing draped on her body. She appears stately and wealthy in rich materials, but never sexy or alluring.

She is morality. The conflict between Hera's monogamy and Aphrodite's sexual freedom is the basis of morality and the sina qua non of monotheism. While sexual attraction depends on fleeting things like chemistry and youth, Hera wants you to follow the rules and to make sure that others do the same.

She is the desire to judge others and to consider yourself an example for all to follow, even if you're unhappy. She is Nancy Grace with her hands on her hips and anyone who wags a finger, because *good* people need *bad* people for contrast. Hera will do anything to convince you that you are not a mortal animal and that 'those others' are the animals who die. She is the impulse to project characteristics that we all share upon others and the source of racism, because Hera makes you define yourself against others as their superior.

Hera is the one who says, 'I hate to tell you but' and then says the hurtful words anyway. Her family values concern sexual restraint and have nothing to do with caring for children, for the same conservatives who obsess over abortion oppose school lunches. Hera the Nurturer of Boys, *Kourotrophos* gives moral instruction, but she was never called *Mother* and never appeared in the artwork holding a child.

Goddess of the Yoke

Hera is the Goddess of the Yoke and the Holder of the Reins.

She is responsibility and obligation—to your family, your reputation, your bills, or your job. The Yoke and the Reins are Hera's marital vows extrapolated to everything that you have to do in order to keep your life going, including maintaining your family and social position. She is the obligation itself, telling you what to do.

The Soul of Loyalty holds us responsible for the events of our lives just as she holds Zeus responsible for the many affairs he has with mortals and goddesses. Hera's loyalty weaves the episodes of life into a personal history like a movie or novel, marrying your individuality to your particular trajectory. Hera is one of the great unifiers of experience.

Indeed, without Hera life would be a series of unconnected scenes and people would be interchangeable. Because of Hera, we have *long friendships to soothe old age*—the old friends who have known you in many guises and are loyal to your shared personal histories.

Ideas about Heaven and an afterlife are Hera's loyalty to God and to your life extended into eternity. Promoters of immortality like Christian and New Age religions don't like to dwell on how you'll actually spend the endless time up there because it sounds so ridiculous and repetitive. Heaven is a place where Hera controls events and Zeus forever and nothing ever changes. In stark contrast, the Greeks sought to know the gods in the here and now, not in some imagined future world.

Hera of Fullfillment

Hera *Teleia* is the Bringer of Fulfillment, imagined as a radiant bride. She is Fulfillment itself, like Oprah on the magazine cover, beaming in a hat and ribbons, hawking slimness and self-improvement in the hope of stepping into the cover alongside her.

Hera picks Zeus as a winner early on even though she is well aware of his amorous adventures. In the end she decides to marry the rich, handsome, and powerful guy after all.

Her double and daughter is Eileithyia, whose specialty is childbirth. But this is not the physical process of birth. That's Artemis, an animal self who is with women during the pain of birthing. Eileithyia is the fantasy of being reborn again and again through different stages of life. To Hera Eileithyia, every decade is a new beginning and the past is always 'just a phase'. Eileithyia is the fresh start, for Hera renews her virginity every year with a bath in her sacred spring.

Hera

You are like her when you drop the argument or drop the past and yield to Zeus, who is reality. Americans, with their strong identification with Hera, are remarkable for their ability to drop baggage and start all over in a new business, a new city, or a new relationship. We adore repentant sinners like Martha Stewart and eagerly allow them to put the past behind them.

Hera Chera

The single self is lonely by definition. Thinking of experience as *my life* automatically separates you from others. Hera is the first god swallowed by her cannibal father, Cronus, and the last one out so she spends the most time alone in his dark belly—although Hestia also claims this distinction.

Hera Chera, the Abandoned One, is loneliness and sulking. She is the widow, the divorced self, and the separated self—a goddess of barren autumn and winter remembered in the *Feast of Lamentation* in Corinth. She is around when you feel frustrated or ignored by life—meaning Zeus--and are convinced that no one really cares about you. Lonely Hera wanders the earth wrapped in darkness or runs off to the mountain of her childhood home, like staying with your parents during a marital blow up.

Everyone feels lonely sometimes but seeing that feeling as coming from Hera breaks the identification with it, for you are not alone in your loneliness. It's just Hera Chera, visiting you now and then. It can be therapeutic to get away from people you are obligated to see, especially if you keep a busy social schedule, because then you can come back to the world fresh and new the way Hera does after her bath.

Typhaon

Hera is so consumed with jealousy after Zeus bears glorious Athena without her help that she strikes the Earth, *Ge,* demanding a child mightier than Zeus'. Ge brings forth Typhaon, a mighty and ugly creature *unlike the gods and mortal men,* like a Titan. In horror, Hera hands him over to the dragoness at Delphi, hoping that like cures like.

Typhaon is jealousy, born of Hera the Chosen, who is naturally jealous of anyone who seems to contradict her specialness. Typhaon immediately goes to war against the gods because envy destroys everything in its path.

He throws mountains at Zeus and Zeus throws them back along with lightning, but it is a stalemate until Zeus tricks Typhaon into eating fruits provided by the Fates which they claim will strengthen him but which actually weaken him. When Zeus prevails he throws Typhaon into Tartarus in Hades, where he feeds Mt. Etna's fires.

Typhaon is a monster because spite and envy can consume your life and turn all the gods against you. Friendship with the gods requires letting them pick their own friends, just like with people. You can't expect the gods to love only you or even to love you the most. Nor can you think of the gods as existing for your sake—not if you want to be their friend.

Resenting someone else's good luck, talent, or success alienates both the friend and the god whose friendship he enjoys. Being close to a friend of a god makes you a friend of a friend and makes you more likely to succeed and to be liked by that god. That's why everyone crowds around a winner and why the ballet corps dances best when a prima ballerina guest stars in the production.

You can keep Typhaon's jealousy in check by visiting Apollo, who is the harsh truth. Rooting for others and sharing in their victories makes you like Zeus throwing the mountains back at Typhaon and quelling his cynicism. Healthy competition has nothing to do with tearing others down and everything to do with admiring the gods in your competitors and honoring your shared field of endeavor.

Typhaon is also the monster in horror movies that carries out Hera's revenge on any characters who dawdle with Aphrodite in sex. He is Hera's sexual envy and rage turned into a Bogey Man.

Goddess of the Peacock

Hera

One of the games at Hera's festivals was the *brazen contest*, in which men run throwing a spear at a hanging brass shield.

Hera's shield is your official public self-- the person you hold up to hide your more vulnerable or embarrassing sides from scrutiny. This shield is the selective memory that allows us to live with our flawed natures and weave a flattering story about our lives. It is the person you think you are, as in 'who do you think you are?' and who you are in the eyes of the world. She is the reason that even people who live in the privacy of the suburbs care very much about which car their neighbors own, even if they don't know their first names.

Her mascot is the peacock, a royal bird with a gorgeous fan of colorful eyes—the eyes of all the people she makes you think are watching you with fascination. Hera the Peacock lives in the eyes of others. She is the Show Off.

I've had the particularly American experience of finding Europeans maddening polite when they speak so low in cafes and restaurants that it's impossible to ever strike up a conversation. This situation pits Hera the Personal Self in America against Apollo the True Self in Europe, which is why I was once advised when going into a gay bar in Paris not to walk into the middle of the room and look around but to slink off to a dark corner and wait, because 'they see you', I was assured.

One of the most famous scenes in Homer is Hera's toilette, in which she sits at a vanity applying cosmetics. Hera gives you the valuable ability to put on a public face—your best face--and to put your best foot forward, which doesn't have to feel authentic for it to be a social virtue.

Hebe the Hostess

Hera's delightful daughter is her double as a young woman. Zeus' cupbearer and personal attendant is eventually replaced by Ganymede, the handsome prince he kidnaps and makes his lover. Zeus marries Hebe off to Herakles.

Hebe the Hostess is politeness and classiness: ever thoughtful, tactful, helpful and friendly. You are like her when you are

176

concerned with the everyday grace and peace of human life.

Think of Hebe when you have to be polite to someone you don't like, because that is the point of politeness. She's talking when you say 'you're no bother' or 'you're not intruding' when it isn't true. The Hostess wants her guests to feel welcome, for kindness to strangers was a social norm in ancient Greece as in many societies, and Greek tradition dictated that the host feed the guest before even asking his name.

A forced smile is better than no smile at all because it shows that you are in charge of your emotions and not the other way around. Courtesy helps keep Poseidon the anti-social God of Emotions in check. A variation, Hera *Anthea,* or Blossom, is the goddess of bouquets, cards, and the personal touch, like remembering someone's birthday or anniversary.

Hebe means *Youth* or *Prime of Life.* She is your ideal self and your inner celebrity, the one you would be if only you could lose those extra pounds, get over that hang-up, or turn back the clock and start over. She is the fabled innocence that Americans lose over and over again. In Greek art, Hebe wears a sleeveless dress--the picture of simple elegance and poise like Jackie Onassis or Audrey Hepburn.

Politeness is a great way to relate to the other selves. It's rude to interrupt, judge, or ignore a self when each of the gods has a legitimate place in the psyche. It's also rude to speak for the other selves, as in 'Aphrodite wants me to wear this dress', just as it's impolite to speak for your friends. It is polite, however, to say 'I'm wearing this dress for Aphrodite', 'I'm going to dress like a goddess tonight', or even 'I'm going to be a goddess tonight', because those statements are metaphorical and do not violate reality, which is Zeus.

The Greeks were far more pessimistic in general than we are. The characters in Homer always presume the worst, because pessimism is a kind of politeness like not thanking a neighbor for a loan he hasn't agreed to give you yet. Acting too sure about something is like walking up to a wild animal and petting it, because then you tempt some neglected god to sabotage everything just to prove its independence. You might make a ruinous gaffe when you are up for a promotion or get an injury at the gym

Hera

when you get cocky and careless—snatching defeat from the very jaws of victory so that some other self can make the point that you are not in charge.

Nephele

Ixion was a lucky but foolish mortal and a regular guest on Olympus until he started making moves on Hera. To test him, Zeus creates a Hera look-alike, *Nephele*, or Made of Clouds. When Ixion tries to seduce her, Zeus banishes him with a thunderbolt to Hades where he spins forever on a wheel in Tartarus.

Nephele is a variation of the Stepford wife. The Cloud Lady is the phony self, like the 'plastic' cheerleaders in high school movies. This cloud version of Hera is an exaggeration of the public persona, all phoniness and pretense but lacking the sincere personal feelings of Hera.

Moving On

The best way to get out of Hera's personal self is to pay attention to someone else. You can highlight Hera's virtues by helping others, making them feel special, and letting them know they haven't been forgotten. Hera wants to please Zeus by making the world a better place and she submits to Zeus' rule when you realize your effect upon others.

You switch from Hera to Zeus whenever you focus on the situation—on reality, which is Zeus—instead of on yourself, because then you are too busy with the matter at hand to be preoccupied with how you look playing the role. You also switch from Hera to Zeus whenever you focus on the result you want instead of on what others think about you, especially if you're waiting around for their admiration or repentance.

You move from Hera to Artemis when you do things for their own sake instead of doing them out of duty, morality, or for show. Artemis gives you authentic desires that free you from showing off all the time or acting only out of social obligation.

Laughing at your self like Hermes puts Hera in perspective as well, which is why so much stand-up comedy is about her self-absorption.

Hermes sees right through Hera's high-mindedness and loves shocking the pretense with a good dirty joke.

DEMETER

Demeter is *Da Meter,* the Grain Mother. As her name suggests, she is Food and Family as a person in your life. Demeter is who you are with your family. She is unconditional mother love and food as love, especially meals shared together with loved ones.

In the body, she is the stomach and rumination. Demeter helps you digest experience through withdrawal. You are like her when you ruminate on experiences. This saves you from having to do the same thing over and over for it to sink in, like rushing through a meal and never feeling satisfied or needing a thousand partners like Don Juan in order to feel sexually free.

This goddess of gratitude and sharing with others was one of the most beloved gods in Greece. She is the impulse to nurse someone or something—like a talent—until it grows big and strong.

Demeter the Mother

Demeter is the family self. She is the entire experience of family.

When you go home to your folks, old habits come back as if they never left, because that self still exists. Your voice rises to its adolescent range, your accent reappears, and you may find yourself eating out of the fridge or drinking straight out of the milk carton like a teenager.

The Mother Bee lives in a personal world, safe from strangers. The Lover of Peace doesn't care who is right, only that everyone gets along, like any mother. Demeter is one of the few gods who ever helped mankind. Gentle and mostly mild, her love is broad and inclusive and truly generous to mankind.

Her festival, the Thesmophoria, marked the autumn sowing. It began with a procession from Athens to Eleusis, the site of her major temple. At one point in the procession, the participants passed under a bridge crowded with people shouting insults and vulgarities at them, which must have been hilarious when everyone was acting so pious about family at the same time. This is the carnival clown who hurls insults while sitting

180

on a perch above a bucket of water, waiting to be dunked by someone with good aim.

Demeter and Kore

Demeter's daughter, *Kore*, the Maiden, was out picking flowers with her young girlfriends when she came across a one hundred petal narcissus that Mother Earth, *Gaia*, created for Hades God of the Underworld, at his request. When she leaned over to pluck it, the earth opened up beneath her feet and Hades appeared on a horse drawn chariot, dragging her down to the Underworld to be his bride.

Demeter heard her scream, as did Zeus, who gave Hades permission to do this. Zeus' complicity in the rape is noted repeatedly in the Homeric hymn that tells the story, because all humans must submit to mortality.

Demeter rushed around like a wild woman for nine days, torch in hand, neither eating nor drinking, looking desperately for her daughter. She is Despairing Demeter, for whom death is nothing short of a catastrophe, because Mother loves her children. Meanwhile, other selves, darker in nature, know that death isn't always the worst thing that can happen to someone. Knowing you are mortal helps you make more informed decisions about how to spend your limited days.

Eventually Demeter came to rest at the Well of the Virgin in Eleusis, taking the shape of an old baby sitter. The four beautiful daughters of King Celeus met her there and found her intriguing despite her age and rags. She called herself Dois and claimed to have been kidnapped by pirates, and the women invited her into their home to babysit their newborn brother.

Upon walking into the house, the doorway filled with a strange and beautiful light and 'Dois' grew taller, more beautiful, and younger in appearance until her head almost touched the ceiling. Revealed, she glanced upon Metaneira, her mortal double, holding the infant. This iconic image was the Greek version of the Madonna and Child. Like Mary, Demeter told the women to *be gracious and pity men,* and then she fell into

181

Demeter

brooding.

Terrified, Metaneira offered her seat but Demeter didn't respond to anyone until Iambe, a servant double of the goddess, placed a stool in front of her with a silvery sheepskin on top. Demeter sat there and pulled a veil over her face in silence for a long time, lost in sorrow.

Finally, Iambe and Baubo, another nurse double of the goddess, cheered her up with some vulgar humor and antics. This was the first time in months that Demeter smiled, laughed, and drank with others. In gratitude, she decided to make the baby, Demophoon, immortal, thrusting him into the fire every night to burn off his mortality. The child grew miraculously without food or water.

One night, Metaneira woke and saw Demeter putting her baby in the fire and screamed, interrupting the spell. Angrily, Demeter called the whole thing off.

Stupid people, she cried, *brainless, you don't even know when fate is bringing you something good or something bad.*

Metaneira fainted and dropped the baby on the floor. Her daughters helped her, but the baby didn't like these new inferior nurses.

In consolation, Demeter offered another gift. She taught Metaneira's other son, Triptolemus, the art of agriculture and sent him around the world spreading the practice. She demanded that the citizens of Eleusis build her a temple to house her other great gift to mankind, the Eleusinian mysteries, a cult of immortality.

When the temple was done, everyone went searching for Kore while Demeter grieved in the temple, causing endless winter and killing all the vegetation.

Now all the gods got involved —not because the people were starving but because their offerings were getting scanty, for the gods are selfish. Zeus sent each of the gods to Demeter but none could change her mind until Hekate the Witch Goddess, brought her to Helios the Sun, who sees everything. Helius told her what Hades had done and advised her to accept him as a worthy and unbelievably rich son-in-law.

Zeus sent Hermes to fetch Kore in the Underworld, where he

182

found her sulking on the bed while Hades leaned in trying to soften her up. She was relieved to see him, but as Hades set her in the chariot and she was preparing to leave he slipped five pomegranate seeds in her mouth.

This changed everything, because having tasted the food of the dead Kore was eternally bound to Hades and forced to return there for five months every year—making Demeter mourn again and bringing winter back to the world.

Kore was now no longer a maiden. She was transformed and became known as Persephone.

The rape by Hades—who is Death--changed her forever, making her stranger and sadder. This happens to everybody whom Death touches, and it is what Zeus wills for mankind and why he allowed the rape in the first place. To be human is to know you are mortal. Eventually, Persephone comes to love Hades and reigns as the dreaded Queen of the Underworld.

Kore

Kore is your innocent self. She is your inner Dorothy.

You are like her when you identify completely with life, health, and personal identity, thinking things will go on the same forever. Kore plays out in the meadow of happy flowers with young Athena and Artemis, and the *big breasted daughters of Oceanis,* as the hymn recounts.

The *big breasts* are a clue that something else is going on here. These young people are seductively innocent, like a perky aerobics instructor. They lack awareness, like someone who flirts unconsciously. They have no mystery, dreams, or longings—but they do have a willful ignorance of their effect on others, like a tourist wearing a mini-skirt on an Arab street. They are consciousness that doesn't know what it is.

Identifying completely with your conscious life and thinking you know who you are makes you forget the other gods who bind mortals, not just the ones you may like. Dreams, Night, Death, Chaos and most of all, Psyche the Night Moth are gods who complete the soul, which is bigger than your conscious self. The daytime selves cannot speak for the people

Demeter

who are around when you're asleep.

You are like Kore when you think you are a sweet thing that can do no harm. She makes you hopeful and loving, but in a sweet, sentimental way like a child, without eroticism, ambivalence, or familiarity with death. She puts tiny circles and hearts over her *I*'s when she writes longhand.

Demeter kept Kore safely in a cave, where she wove a picture of *a world she had never seen.* This is the mindset that claims that the answers lie within and not in the world. It is the cocooned world of the Internet, a virtual world of personal imagery unconnected to others. Kore is willful ignorance.

The myth repeatedly says that *Zeus allowed* the rape, but at the end it says that *Zeus planned* it. Kore is a self that needs to be disturbed. She must be raped by Death, as we are all metaphorically *violated by Death*, because a life that denies death is too closed, too unreal, and not human. It takes Zeus--Reality personified--to break the spell that would have us believe that we are only the face in the mirror --as if the soul and one's life were the same thing.

If she'd had the chance, Hera would have opposed Zeus' decision because the wife of God wants things to stay the same forever. Hera dominates the American psyche, which would keep Kore innocent and optimistic in her cave forever. This is why we can 'lose our innocence' over and over again, despite our violent history: the innocent self remains intact because it is a god.

Kore plucks the giant narcissus because its bizarre beauty speaks to unknown yearnings and unknown reaches of the psyche. She does not know it yet but her soul seeks to be free of the relatedness that chokes her, like when you think you know who you are because everyone around you seems to know who you are.

When she arrives in Hades, Kore is numb and full of hate as she sulks on the couch, for the innocent self sees death as robbing life of all meaning. But once she swallows the seed of the pomegranate, the fruit of the dead, the human knowledge of our own mortality seeds within her.

184

Kore then deepens into another identity--the mysterious and dread Persephone Queen of the Underworld who grows to love Death, her husband.

Persephone is who you are as you face your death, like Hamlet, poisoned and nobly dying in the last act. She embodies a state of mind that does not need to wait until you are actually dying to be known. You can spend some time imagining that you are on your deathbed and assess what you've done with your life so far and you'll see your life as Persephone does. Or you can extrapolate how much of your time your 20 hours of television per week is going to mean in terms of years over a lifetime. This can be very clarifying. Persephone pulls your identity below your life towards the mysterious beauty of that strange flower and the soul's unfathomable and inhuman depths, for *Psyche* was not only an innocent girl but also a strange giant night moth—the soul as something inhuman. Persephone's new depth makes her both beautiful and a hideous gorgon that sees through all self-deception, procrastination, and denial.

When she returns from Hades, Kore is hailed as *a wonder to gods and mortal men*—because closeness with death is transforming. You can recognize Persephone in cancer survivors and refugees who have seen death up close and possess a strange depth and beauty that does not brook lies and avoidance.

Demeter Eleusinia

Demeter's famous religious cult engages the mystic self.

Once her temple was built, she gave mankind the Eleusinian mysteries, which were secret rites of immortality. Despite their popularity, these mysteries commanded so much respect through antiquity that their secrets were never revealed. All we know is that they involved a series of images, bright lights interrupting darkness, banging gongs, and recitations, and that the whole production was lubricated with a Greek version of LSD.

People came out of this experience transformed and hoping for a better life in the Underworld than the average Joe, who is only a fluttering bat in Hades with a squeaky voice. The psychedelic effects of the ceremony helped them to break the identification with everyday reality, and to glimpse a self that is deeper than normal identity--a taste of immortality. Seeing yourself as someone else is liberating.

She Who Dwells in Solitude

Demeter is depression.

Depression is a mystery with many shades, like sorrow, solitude, negativity, withdrawal, and withheld anger. These come from many gods, but the gods most known for depression are Hera and Demeter.

Hera wanders off to her mountain home to escape Zeus and his infidelity, which happens when life is unfair and the gods seem to favor everybody else. Her depression is a kind of sulking loneliness.

For Demeter, depression is a sense of loss and rumination on the past, a psychological digestion that dwells upon things and feels them deeply. Demeter's sorrow helps your soul build stamina by sending it through low points and hopelessness accompanied by love, the way you feel about someone once they are dead and gone and you can't ever hug them or tell them you love them again.

The Greek way is not to fight depression but to treat it as a visitor and spend some time with it. Ignoring depression is like snubbing a friend who then gets annoyed at you and more difficult to deal with. If you think of it as belonging to Demeter the Depressed, you don't have to take it so personally. Then you can relate to it from some distance, as if you were talking about someone else.

There are other selves to pay attention to once you spend some time with Demeter the Depressed. You can take a break for a couple of hours at a time, promising to return to it once you are done visiting other gods. The Greeks were always working out deals with the gods. And to answer Artemis the Pure One's hesitation to use anti-depressants because 'it won't be me', you can consider them ritual pill offerings to the god who sent the depression. Medication does not have to feel like denial or a loss of authenticity. As my psychiatrist once told me when I was covered with

186

cancerous lesions and hesitated to take psychiatric medications, "you have enough reality."

Demeter's depression helps you see through superficiality, like Persephone in the Underworld. The Greeks prayed to her and to Persephone to *give me the kind of life my heart wants.*

The White Goddess of Bread

Da Meter or Mother Grain is blond like barley. The Roman *Ceres* gave us *cereal*. The Barley Mother and Goddess of Agriculture is She Who Fills the Barn, the White Goddess of Bread, She Who Gives a Good Yield and She of the Big Cake.

The Giver of Wealth dwells in the landscape of tilled fields, fertile valleys and gently rolling farmland, which is more like the Hobbit's Shire than the raw wilderness of Artemis. Demeter abides in rich, dark soil and the earthy smell of manure or cut grass.

She is food as a person in your life, someone with whom you have a long relationship.

When the Greeks sat down to eat, they would say *it's time for Demeter.* Any meal can be a ritual in honor of her so long as you are grateful for it, especially shared meals, because being thankful and loving around food honors Demeter.

Diets offend her. Hating your stomach or feeling guilty about food insults her generosity with ingratitude. Demeter wants you to enjoy good food as an instinct, and to eat slowly and to enjoy it with others.

Aphrodite Goddess of Sex makes people overeat in revenge against Hera the Moralist for avoiding sex. Hera is perfectly happy to see you standing in front of a mirror hating your body, because then you are locked in her realm of personal identity and disdain for the flesh.

Eating is one way we experience Demeter. Eating while pretending you are Demeter can be an uncanny pleasure. You can start the pleasure early by anticipating a meal instead of eating the moment you think of food. Anticipating pleasure is a pleasure itself, like looking forward to a trip.

Demeter

Erysichthon

Erysichthon was so greedy for lumber to build a new house that he chopped down a grove of trees belonging to Demeter. The priestess, who was the goddess in disguise, politely asked him to stop but he threatened her with an ax.

Then she revealed herself in terrifying splendor. The man pleaded for mercy but she told him he'd *better make it a banquet hall* and disappeared.

Suddenly he felt starving. He ate and ate but nothing could ease his hunger. Finally his family had to put him out on the street because they couldn't afford to feed him anymore. Erysichthon gorged on filth, all the while getting thinner and thinner.

Erysichthon is the consumer.

He is agri-business, with animals kept in feedlots and never allowed to see the sun. He is the way you see the meat at the grocery store as a product instead of as a dead animal.

This attitude insults Demeter. The poor chicken deserves to live in the sunlight before you eat it. To deny the source of our food is to deny our animal nature. Vapid foods in pretty shapes like yellow twists turn eating into just another mental pleasure for Apollo the Observer.

You are like Erysichthon when you consume experiences and buy things as if they are so many empty calories. He is there when you never give Demeter a chance to fully digest an idea, an event, a problem, or a relationship. He is rampant materialism that seeks happiness in a constant flow of new things. Erysichthon wants you to flee Demeter and her depressing psychological rumination. He would have you take on more debt rather than change your life or appreciate what you already have.

Some people can take a trip and talk about it for a lifetime or have a love affair and savor the memory and guilt for years. Erysichthon makes others need a constant repetition of events to feel anything at all.

Psychological digestion takes time but it is beats mindless repetition and throwing one chip after another down the gaping maw.

188

Demeter the Fury

Demeter the Black wore funeral clothes while she went searching for her missing daughter. On the tenth day of her search she met Poseidon, who chased her lustily with no regard for her anxiety. Demeter took on the shape of a mare in a grazing herd but Poseidon turned into a stallion and raped her just as her own daughter was raped.

Demeter the Fury (*Erinyes*) is outrage. She embodies the collective horror at child molesters, torture, racism and other taboo behavior. She is the feeling of being betrayed by your own family. Demeter's outrage and suffering can be the price you pay for keeping the peace with the family. It is a normal part of the family self and its experiences.

Violated during her grief and panic, she cannot shake her rage until she washes it away in the nearby Ladon River. Her cult followers reenacted this fury and its cleansing ritual in the river. Demeter's animals, the dove and the mountain lion, reflect her two natures.

Every god has a downside, just like people. You can't just pick and choose, hoping for only the fun parts and avoiding all the pain. But mortals can balance one god against another to avoid the extremes of any single god. That is our advantage.

Every mood and point of view has its virtue, even though they may be unpleasant. Outrage can be cleansing because it stands up for basic human decency and dignity. A world without outrage would be worse than the world is already.

Poseidon shows a complete absence of personal feelings when he rapes the Goddess of Nurses and Mothers in her grief. This happens when your emotions rape your personal attachments, like a temper that destroys trust or words that sting forever. It happens when events or people treat you without any regard, violating your very existence.

Demeter is there when you ask why Zeus/God has betrayed you and how he can let such terrible things happen. The feelings are legitimate, but you don't have to identify with them or get stuck in them. It's

Demeter

how Demeter feels, and that's good enough. When her outrage is collective and strong enough, the politicians pass a law like Megan's Law or they start a program like food stamps.

Baubo and Iambe

Demeter is the Generous Nurse and her doubles are Baubo and Iambe, who cheer her up. Caring for someone is the Demeter side of medicine, distinct from Apollo's pharmaceuticals, operations, and doctors. Nurses generally pay more attention to a patient's comfort and emotions than do doctors, who like Apollo are busy with oracular diagnoses and prognoses.

Old Baubo makes Demeter laugh with a lewd pantomime, groaning with her legs open wide as if giving birth and then producing Demeter's own son, Iakchos, from beneath her skirts and revealing her wrinkled old legs. That breaks the ice and eases her depression. Iambe, Metaneira's lame youngest daughter, cheers Demeter up with jokes and gets her to smile, so that she finally accepts the drink of barley water.

The nurse is a variation of the Mother, but without the literal family ties. You can be sick around a nurse just like family.

Demeter may at some time press you into service for an old parent or relative. If you personify your new role as the Nurse, you don't have to take it as a personal burden. Rather than feeling trapped by it and even lashing out at the person you are trying to show love and helpfulness, you can be Baubo and Iambe, the loving caretakers, who have come to visit for a time. Let them run the show.

Studies show that when the nurse makes you smile, it improves your health. Smiling gets you outside of yourself when you are sick, so you don't identify so much with your illness. It's important for a sick person to remember that he is other people as well, so he doesn't feel trapped by that identity the way Demeter was trapped in her grief.

Kybele

Kybele is the Great Mother, worshipped throughout the

Mediterranean in prehistoric times. Her lover and son is Attis, who cheats on her and whom the gods punish by cutting off his genitals, though some say he cut them off himself out of remorse for infidelity. His self-mutilation, death and resurrection re-enact the life of vegetation, which dies in winter and resurrects with the spring.

Kybele mourns Attis until this annual resurrection. Her festival includes days of ritual mourning and celebration like Good Friday and Easter. Male followers castrated themselves in her parade hoping to join her priesthood.

The Great Mother and Earth Mother are materialism, because *Mater* is concerned with the physical side of your life—the *matter* of it. This point of view makes you connect all psychic phenomena to material events.

When a baby cries, the mother says it's tired or hungry or has a sick stomach—but she would never say it is depressed or pondering its mortality. Materialism sees dreams as personal messages and advice because it is so concerned with your own comfort that it can't imagine that anyone else could be involved and that dreams have their own life. Materialism tells you that the person you see in the mirror is always the same person looking back at you and that there's no one else to consider, even though a host of potential, unrealized selves dwell in dreams and fantasies.

Unchecked, the Great Mother can devour you through personalism and relatedness, overwhelming you with familiarity and obligations. You can hear this in up-speak, a kind of baby talk for adults that refuses to let Ares or Poseidon or any other unpleasantness enter the picture. By always asking a question and never asserting anything, up-speakers castrate themselves just as Attis did.

You can see the Great Mother in young people who fall so completely in love that they seem insipid and opaque. No mortal can promise to love someone forever because we don't live forever and the word *forever* tells you that an immortal god is talking through some unsuspecting human vessel. 'I'll always love you' acquires a funny echo the second or third or fourth time around.

191

Demeter

The Earth Mother's relatedness locks the soul in a grand cycle of birth and rebirth. The idea that you will be reborn again and again with the same people robs Eros of his freedom to wander in chaos and dark imaginings. Besides, if your mother reincarnates as your nephew, what's the difference anyway? The psyche contains very real impersonal feelings, including murderous impulses, inhuman intuitions and moods, and selves that precede our humanity. These must be imagined clearly. That's why the cozy and secure life in suburban Eden tunes in to car chases, crime sprees, and gossip for its nightly entertainment.

The Greeks rejected the life of safety and warmth. Their gods offered no guarantees and little hope of salvation from mortality. The cult of Demeter did not promise a heaven where you would go on living as yourself forever. It only granted a sense of identity beyond the personal and mortal selves. The Greeks did not seek rebirth in the bosom of the mother, at least until the cult of Isis in late Hellenism when similar faiths were erupting at the same time. The Greeks lived in the clear light of day where there is never any reason to presume that everything will be all right, and Mother cannot help you.

Gaia

Gaia or *Ge* is the Earth as 'the World'. This is especially true of your home turf, which acts like a person in your life—someone you have a relationship to and whom you can't help loving.

The Broad Bosomed One is the common mother and home of all human beings. The oldest of the gods appears in the creation stories, bearing the Sky, *Uranus,* and then bearing him children as the Sky covers the Earth. Ge bears the Mountains and the Sea without mating and without Love, *Eros.*

Uranus, fearing a rival among his children, prevents her from giving birth, causing her horrible cramps. His fear is realized when his son, Cronus, cuts off his genitals with a sickle and takes his place.

Ge is never fully personified like Zeus or Athena. She is more soil than mother. She is the planet we evolved on and our sense of

192

belonging to it. Today she is remembered with efforts against global warming and for sustainability, including Gaia Theory.

But she is seldom the entire planet. Ge is more a locale—any place within the horizon, distinct from others. She might be Vermont, the Northeast Kingdom, Bennington, or Bennington College--the sense of place that makes it a specific world. Ge is the customs and character of a place, its laws and local heroes--its geography in the broadest sense. She is Law and Order, *Thesmophoros,* especially peace, quiet, and the common good like respecting property, supporting the local animal shelter, and forming groups like Mothers Against Drunk Driving or the school committee. Earth is easy to honor because she is right here. She demands our attention.

The Greeks often swore by the Earth, grasping a handful of soil and proclaiming, "As Earth is my witness" like Scarlett O'Hara.

Ge is shown in artwork rising from the ground and often from a graveyard, for our bodies return to her soil. The old prayer declaims, *We are your incense.* In ritual, barley cakes were tossed into a chasm to honor her, but you can honor her in a host of ways: by making a mulch pile, avoiding pesticides, picking up litter, planting flowers on a traffic island, clearing wilderness trails, or taking part in local government. By doing so you will automatically feel a closer connection with Ge.

Rhea

Ge's daughter is *Rhea,* derived from *Era* or *Earth.* More human than Gaia, she is a lively older woman. She is spryness—a self who is active, brisk, and a scold for decency.

Rhea is the closest of the mother goddesses to the popular image of Mother Nature from the old margarine commercials. The Mountain Mother has a hand like the five-pointed oak leaf. Artwork shows her driving around in a chariot pulled by lions amid a ruckus of castanets, kettledrums, animal and bird cries, splashing water, and leaves rustling in the wind.

She is the mammalian brain, with its mixture of wildness and tameness.

Demeter

Rhea loves liveliness and hubbub, whether it's a baby's cry or the roar of a stadium. She leads you to seek freedom in noise, like driving a Harley, carrying a boom box, or partying all weekend. Earth Mothers love the power of sound like Dionysus, who was initiated into their cult. Rhea convinces you that you are quite a rebel during the weekends so that you can continue under the control of the mother—that is, living the safe life--during the rest of the week.

She has an obscene side as a goddess of fertility and was called *a virgin, a mother, a whore and a crone.* Rhea is the Mother of War who wants to rid the Earth of excess population.

She is a Scold who prefers to dwell away from the limelight and who speaks for common people and common sense, like Grandmother Spider in Native American mythology. Rhea makes you call out injustice even if it means going against everybody, and she tells you when to keep the peace even at your own expense. She is the voice of conscience that speaks truth out of the corner of the crowded town meeting, surprising everyone with its simple common sense.

But we cannot embrace nature naively. The grizzly bear doesn't want to hug you. Earth is wild and unpredictable, for the Deceitful Savior *tames every wilderness and makes wild every street.* She is the reason that it really is a jungle out there, that civilization is a thin veneer, and that there are no safe streets at 4 a.m.

Moving On

You know you are identifying too much with Demeter when family and personal relatedness take over your life. You might detect a phony ring to all the happiness and togetherness, telling you it's time to move on. Studies consistently show that raising children is an unhappy affair for parents despite all the pieties around the subject, and that the best part of childrearing is looking back at it or befriending your own adult children.

Turn to Athena, who is the citizen and the professional--selves that let you relate but not so personally. Or spend some time with Hermes the Friend, a god of free affiliations that have nothing to do with

194

relatives or obligation.

The other social goddesses, Hestia the Homebody and Hera the Social Self, are an easy transition as well. Stay home alone or get away with your partner or an old friend and leave the family behind. If you have spent time raising children it might be a great idea to seek some intellectual stimulation with Apollo by taking a course and setting aside your motherly persona.

Artemis and Hermes love doing things for their own sake rather than for love or loyalty. Try Artemis out with sports, hiking in the woods, or going somewhere no one knows your name. Or try Hermes by traveling or going out on the town—anywhere you can mingle with friends and strangers. These gods of freedom renew your soul with the fresh breeze of adventure that yields pleasures that are intimate but not personally related, like wanderlust, making deals, or competition and games, which take you outside the family system.

HESTIA

Gracious Hestia is who you are at home, especially when you are home alone. She is not your family self: that is Demeter.

Hestia is the sense of a psychological center, and another great unifier of experience. This calm Center is there even when you are all over the place or stretching yourself too thin. Hestia is a good anti-dote to the wild ways of Dionysus the Intoxicated, Hermes the Swinging Single, and Poseidon the Emotional Self, offering the safety and privacy of familiar surroundings with the bills paid, food in the fridge, and the pets on the couch.

You are like Hestia when you save and store for the future. She is the quiet satisfaction of taking care of yourself and your home and putting something aside for a rainy day.

Hestia

Hestia means *the Hearth.*

She is especially the kitchen, where everyone crowds around at parties even when there's plenty of space in the living room. *The Hestia* can be the den or the television, which some people leave on for comfort even when they aren't watching anything because it acts like a fireplace.

My uncle always had a ballgame on the radio with the volume down low—because no one was really paying attention to the game. It was comforting to hear the crack of the bat, the roar of the crowd, and the excited commentary of the sportscaster filling the house like the aroma of his cigars. That was his version of Hestia.

She is the warm oven baking food and the comfortable bed to sleep in. Greek soldiers set up camp by starting the fire and saying, *it's time for Hestia*, because she is the idea that wherever you sleep is where you live now. In ancient Greece, hearthstones were passed down like family silver and cleaned before and after sacrifices, which is why Hestia is mentioned at the beginning and the end of all ceremonies. All the gods like clean sacrifices, so most temples have a hearth called *the Hestia*. Her

196

mildly smiling and self-deprecating manner is good to bring to the worship of almost any god.

The hearth was the place to swear a solemn oath like promising to take care of your mother into old age. Children, brides and slaves adopted into the family were led around the hearth and showered with nuts and dried fruits as a welcoming ritual. Often the remains of dead ancestors were buried in the foundation or the walls so they would stay *at home.*

Hestia the Homebody

The Homebody lives an uneventful life and there are few stories connected with her—and that is the point. Hestia is your boring self.

Her gentle heart offers a quiet kind of love. You are like Hestia when you are home alone with the cat or the television or a book and don't need anyone else's attention. You are also like her when you can be 'alone together' with someone else who doesn't constantly demand your attention or require you to wear a certain face all the time. A Hestia friend lets you do your own thing and not interrupt each other.

I went to a wonderful party once where the company more or less took over the house. People were reading magazines, watching television, playing Frisbee out back and cooking in the kitchen. It was completely unsupervised and it was marvelous to feel at home in someone else's place.

You are more relaxed and natural at home because at home you are accepted as you are. Hestia is a part of you that doesn't need any special attention from others. She is why so many people like to work from home.

Hestia makes you feel perfectly happy to stay in at night and miss all the fun going on downtown. Hestia wants you to like comfort and safety, common sense, cleanliness, and an orderly life. You are like her when you actually enjoy doing housework and find that it clears your mind when you are dealing with difficulties, because all of the gods are fond of her.

Hestia

Hestia the Virgin

One time Aphrodite cast a spell that made Apollo, Poseidon, and Dionysus fall in love with Hestia at the same time. To keep the peace Hestia swore off sex and marriage forever, which pleased her father, Zeus, immensely because at least there would be one Olympian Ego who isn't causing constant trouble and complications.

She is Solitude. You are like Hestia when you don't need someone else in order to be happy.

She is not loneliness. Her love of solitude is not a cry for attention. That belongs to Hera the Personal Self, who runs away from Zeus and hides at her home in the mountains, hoping he will come get her.

Apollo wanted to marry Hestia, quite understandably. She doesn't need the big city or expensive things, she is not competitive, she would never cheat, and she doesn't mind playing second banana to a gigantic chauvinist. She refused him.

You are like Hestia saying 'no' to Apollo when you choose intuition over intellect and simple pleasures over refinement. Refusing Apollo means you choose neither to rise above things nor to let yourself be manipulated by others. Hestia keeps her Center to herself.

She also refuses Poseidon, the lusty God of Emotions. You repeat her *no* to Poseidon when you refuse to get carried away by emotions-- your own or anybody else's. Hestia's mood is even and low key. She is never foolish or impulsive like Poseidon and she doesn't want you to live entirely in feelings and appetites like him. She would never want to live with Poseidon's overwhelming physical needs and excess. He is far too sexual for her. Hestia keeps her own counsel and maintains a peaceful, respectful household.

She refuses Dionysus as well. You are like Hestia saying *no* to Dionysus when you stay sober and avoid passion for the sake of peace of mind. When Dionysus first shows up at the Olympian table the twelve seats are already taken so Hestia yields hers—which no other Olympian would do—because she is the self who can give things up for others and let them take the starring role in life.

When you're with Hestia you don't need to 'have it all' to be fulfilled. Hestia prefers to keep things running smoothly and quietly, even if it requires self-sacrifice. She wants you to learn to live vicariously and to share in others' victories and defeats so you don't have to literally do things to experience them. She makes you happy to sit in the audience rather than on stage in front of everybody else, far from the stress of the spotlight.

Goddess of the Center

The *hestia* was a circular fireplace at the center of the Greek home or temple and open to all sides--more like a campfire than a fireplace in the wall.

Hestia is the Center, the Circle, and the Sacred Fire.

She is the feeling of being centered. She is deeper than the stormy seas of Poseidon's emotions or Hera's social pretense. Her name can also mean *Essence*. You are with Hestia when someone listens to you as if you are the only person in the world.

People spend a lot of time and effort meditating in order to find their center. But in the Greek view, you don't need to find *your* center; you only have to find *the* Center because Hestia is always there and she belongs to everybody. She can be found so long as you aren't drunk, carried away by passion or emotions, or acting superior, because Hestia refuses to marry those particular gods. When something shakes you to the core, you honor Hestia by isolating in privacy--drawing the curtains, not answering the phone, and clinging to routines to keep the world out for a while.

This self is never needy and doesn't allow others to overwhelm her with their needs. With Hestia, you can be a reliable friend who can be taken for granted but not be taken advantage of. She is the unmoving center of the circle--and that is her dignity. No matter what happens, Hestia gives you the choice to remain calm and poised in any situation.

Of course, being centered has nothing to do with being the

Hestia

center of attention, self-centered, or self-absorbed. Leave that to Herakles and Hera. Being centered does not make you competitive or selfish, because Hestia has no desire to dislodge anyone else's center or to play king of the hill.

Hestia and Zeus

Statues of Hestia show a mature woman, usually seated with a full form covered in heavy drapery. Hestia is not about drama or sex appeal. She is about reliability and predictability.

The Helper enjoys the supporting role. She is the guest who clears the table and does the dishes without being asked and without making a fuss. Hestia makes you glad when everyone is comfortable and putting up his feet. You can see her in the simple smile that looks like fishhooks pulling up the corners of the mouth with lips sealed and teeth covered.

This meek goddess had only one temple in all of Greece— unless you count all the hearths in every home, temple and building. Hestia warms even cold gods like Apollo, whose temple had a hearth, because her humility makes it easy to deal with someone who thinks he's perfect. Her simple smile shows that your personal and authentic feelings do not always have to run the show.

In the artwork, Hestia often sits next to Zeus, who relies on this one Olympian who is so un-Hollywood and the complete opposite of his wife, Hera the Drama Queen, who makes such a fuss about everything. Hestia is the only Olympian who never argues with anybody.

Her mercy is so great that criminals only need to touch her hearthstones to be protected and cared for--though they still face justice in Athena's courts.

These are Hestia's glories and the reasons she was beloved by all the Greeks, rivaled in their affection only by Hermes, the god the Greeks called Friend.

Goddess of Homebuilding

200

The Greek Gods Among Us

Hestia is one of the most physical of the gods. She is the House where you live. It may seem strange to think of your home as both a person and a god, but anyone who has been homeless knows that the home is a god. Your house forces you to do things, so it is One of the Stronger Ones and it will be there when you're dead, so it is *immortal* compared to you.

People take care of the home just like foxes and orioles do. Hestia has a strong cult in America and is part of the American dream. The Goddess of the Foundation is your emotional and financial security because if you lose your home, you will probably be ruined.

Within, warm comfort reigns. Hestia's home is not the mansion of Hera the Queen who desires prestige of address and high-end finishes. Nor is it the masculine perch in towers of wealth and power that are home to Zeus and Apollo, gods of superiority. Apollo's fancy lighting and floor to ceiling windows are not for her. She finds impressive homes uninviting and seeks out cozy places to sit.

Hestia's home offers comfort and relaxation. She likes overstuffed chairs and treasured possessions in modest, sweet homes with charm, like the Old Woman Who Lived in a Shoe. She is the homey touch: curtains, Afghans on the sofa, and beds for the pets. Hestia's home can never be too clean but it can be too neat, because she dwells in the lived-in look of scattered pillows, half-made beds, and books everywhere.

When all the doors are closed and the outside world is shut out, Hestia is in full swing. She loves true privacy, so making sure your home or your room is private is a gift to her. Any Greek sacrificing to Hestia would say he was *on secret business.* She is a part of you that is nobody else's business. That is part of her virginity.

The Greek home had several layers of divine protection and privacy to protect this virginity. Four gods in particular aided Hestia as friends. A well-equipped courtyard had a little altar of Zeus of the Fence, *Herkeios,* facing outward to neighbors and standing for the fact of your ownership, because Zeus is the owner. There might be a statue by the door of Apollo Of the Street, *Agyieus,* or Apollo Averter of Evil, *Apotropaio.*

Hestia

Apollo is the law. He defends Hestia's virginity as her private property and her privacy. And Herakles is the alarm system and the locks on the doors that act with a Hero's strength and vigilance to keep out intruders.

There might be a stone phallus on the street for Hermes, the God of Good Luck, like a wishing well on the front lawn or a decorated mailbox ready to receive good news. The head of the family would thank the boundary gods every so often with a word or a small offering just to keep the good luck going, like walking your property lines once in a while.

Hestia the Spinster Aunt

The unmarried great aunt of the Olympians appears in the artwork as a stiff but dignified matron. She is the aunt or uncle who lives on the edge of the family and stands for cooperation and emotional evenness. 'Charity begins at home' is her motto but unlike a mother, she is under no obligation and can pick whomever she wishes to help.

Hestia will only offer an opinion if she's asked for it--and then she'll advise you as gently and tactfully as she can. She is not a scold or an outraged crone like Rhea, Demeter and Hera, goddesses of family obligations and morality. Hestia may be old fashioned but she never goes on a rampage or judges anyone—at least not out loud. She gives you homey virtues like humility, independence, and contentment.

The last of the gods to escape Cronus' belly after he swallowed them, Hestia spent the longest time in his dark bowels, although Hera claims the same distinction. She can handle being alone a lot, and prefers loneliness to a bad relationship. She is used to being overlooked or left behind to take care of things and pick up after everybody. She doesn't mind at all because it makes her feel useful.

She is the comfort of routine and predictability, even boredom. You please her by keeping a clean home and celebrating traditional meals and holidays that maintain the order of the year. Spend all of your time with her, however, and you will feel trapped by time and reluctant to try new things, as though you were swallowed up and kept inside too long.

Hestia complements Hermes: he stands for the world outside

while she stands for the home. He is the self who goes to work and on the town while she is the one who stays in. He is the salesman and she is the bookkeeper—or the salesman filling out his travel and expense reports.

Their friendship helps you balance these two sides of life. Stay in and put things in order if Hermes has you running around too much or get out and do something new if you're bored being a homebody—but without trying to change either one of them, because their contradiction is useful and gives you options.

Hestia of the Cupboards

Hestia of the Cupboards, *Tamias,* and Hestia Who Takes Care of the Reserves are friends of Zeus the Keeper of Wealth, *Ktesios,* whose symbol is a jar, since the ancient Greeks lived in agricultural times.

The Storer and Saver brings the homey contentment that comes with having enough. She is the pleasure of leftovers in Tupperware and food in the pantry that saves you from going to the store if you don't want to. Martha Stewart is a Hestia of the Cupboards with her virtuous can-do attitude--with a heavy dose of Hera the Socialite. Among my Syrian cousins it is considered a homey virtue to be able to whip up something in the kitchen at a moment's notice with whatever's available.

Hestia wants you to pay your bills and set aside savings every month. She is good for your credit. Her doubles are the women in television ads clutching mugs of International Coffees and reviewing their mutual funds.

Hestia Boulaias

The Goddess of the Council presides over the government, but she is not the government or the politicians. That is Zeus and Athena.

Hestia is the buildings and the institutions themselves that sit with quiet dignity as landmarks in our towns and cities. She is the hospital, the court, the library, the bank vault, and the community center--buildings that stand for continuity and the public trust.

Hestia *Prytaneias* is the Goddess of City Hall, which houses

Hestia

the Common Hearth, a flame available to anyone whose fire goes out that was kept going for years as a link to the past. She is not the fire itself; that is Hephaestus. She is the warm center and the sense of belonging. Hestia was honored on Founder's Day, like our 4th of July or President's Day. You share her civic virtue when you go to the local parade or take a tour of the oldest houses in the city, for example.

Hestia of the City is the square deal and the honesty that lets you do business with others without having to hold anyone ransom. She is the ideal of public service as a sacred trust. Hestia Boulaias was an honorary title bestowed on notable women, like someone who is *an institution* among the citizenry. Corruption and scandal offend her and are punished by the Hearth Abiding Spirits, *Daimones*—these days, in the form of investigations and media exposure.

Hestia and Priapus

One day while the gods were napping after a cookout, Priapus, the little garden god with a huge penis shaped like a backwards hoe, got drunk and jumped on Hestia as she snoozed in the hayfield. The braying of a donkey woke her up.

Hestia screamed to find the little monster on top of her and sent him scurrying, much to the amusement of the gods.

She is sexual modesty. Hestia sees sex as ludicrous and doesn't want anyone 'getting queer' with her. Even the ass—a symbol of lust--thinks Priapus is vulgar and outrageous to jump on someone like Hestia.

She makes you see other people's compulsions as ridiculous and disgusting. Although she is never vicious, Hestia loves juicy gossip that shows what happens to people who lose their Center, like Priapus, who got carried away with lust. Her idea of sex is both vulgar and cute, like couples that use nicknames for body parts and sex acts. Hestia uses childish voices to say what is too embarrassing for her normal voice. That way she keeps things friendly but modest.

204

Moving On

When you get bored with Hestia's quiet peace you can turn to her friend, Hermes, to get you out into the world and seek some adventure. Hermes leads to all the other gods because he's friendly and knows everybody.

The other social goddesses—Demeter the Family, Athena the Citizen and Hera the Personal Self—are easy transitions from this sensibility, because they emphasize respect and awareness of others. Greek art often showed these four goddesses hanging out together.

Aphrodite would be a complete change for this virgin, as would Dionysus the Crazy. When you turn to them, this goddess goes away because you have lost your center. No matter, the center isn't really lost. It has just stepped aside and is waiting for you somewhere, because Hestia is loyal and no trouble at all. She will calmly hold the center for you.

PART FIVE: GODS OF FREEDOM

These gods stand for freedom and enjoyment.

Pan is the body, personified. He is the freedom to be lazy, because sometimes that's what your body needs. Pan grants the ability to imagine things instead of actually doing them, as in masturbation. With Pan, you can watch a documentary about Antarctica instead of needing to go there, or watch a ballet without needing to take lessons. He is the vicarious function of culture, which allows us to learn through images and not only through experience.

Hermes is the freedom to change and to 'travel' through the psyche. He knows that almost anything can be pleasurable for a while and that 'this too shall pass'. He takes you from one god to another, changing moods and mental states with ease. Hermes is a sense of humor and the desire for new experiences, especially those that bring pleasure or profit. Hermes and Artemis are *the cure for boredom*.

Artemis is the animal self and physical purity. She leads you to follow authentic desires and instincts and frees you from dependence on others. You are like Artemis when you are absorbed in an activity for its own sake. She is often the indirect cause of events that you only realize later. Artemis likes you to be active and to maintain the good health that frees you to do what you want.

PAN

Pan is a satyr: a man on top and a goat on the bottom. This beloved satyr lives in Arcadia, a beautiful area in the south of Greece. He is an amusing, bohemian creature who likes nothing more than lying around a meadow or beside a stream, daydreaming.

Pan is the self who is a drop out. Pan lives the 'dolce far niente' attitude in life, which is a good break from hyperactive gods like Athena, Hera, and Herakles, gods of progress who always have some goal in mind. Pan wants you to forget about the future, to set aside being an admirable person, and just be a bum for a while. This self wants you to stop participating in social competition like those more civilized gods. The patron of children born out of wedlock draws you to the provisional life and alternative life styles.

In artwork, he carries a flute or a folk guitar like an old hippy. His landscape is never towns or tilled fields, always streams, grottos, woods and meadows. Woodstock suited him fine until it got too commercial.

Pan is a god of simple folk and of a mood that is not quite civilized or socialized. His only real vice is his perpetual horniness. He is always looking for a good time with some nymph or young man and he loves to boast about his sexual conquests. He is the rogue artist like Bono, Mick Jagger, or Picasso--all known for their unconventionality and their libidos. He is your rogue artist within.

Pan's *goat dance* is the source of our word, tragedy, so he is no stranger to depression and abandonment, but that is the price of his freedom from all ties. It's easy to get depressed if you have nothing to do all day. Following him can be dangerous. Pan may lead you to the boondocks, to the rock concert that turns into a stampede, or to the wrong side of the tracks and the wrong person's bedroom. If he takes over your life, you might end up like him, living on the edge.

But Pan takes being forgotten and overlooked in stride. He's okay on his own and doesn't want to fit in with society or build a resume or even think of life as some kind of progress.

Pan

Satyrs

The satyrs walk upright like people but on goat legs, sporting long, thick tails. They are not immortal and many are fat and bald in the artwork—a disgusting image to the body-conscious Greeks.

The *good for nothing, mischief-making satyrs* are gods of hedonism, chasing sex and drugs at all hours, even into old age. They move to the drums and disco beat, and make you measure your virility by how hard you can party and play, like their followers, the club kids chasing Xstasy.

But there's always a touch of despair in this, as if they are grasping after physical pleasure before it's too late like people often do after a bad diagnosis.

They are a dangerous crew. Their music has to be loud enough to prevent conversation. Mostly, they just want to be left alone with their counterculture on the riverfront or the bad side of town out of sight of socially upright gods and selves like Hera.

Their sexuality is anonymous and devoid of personal feelings. In fact, asking to meet for coffee beforehand kills this date, because he isn't interested in your personality. The satyrs love the leather fetish for its totemic power, because leather makes you half an animal and offends gods who want to minimize your animal aspects, especially Hera, who was counted among the satyrs' enemies. Of course, we're not talking about European leather with tailoring but we are talking about blue jeans, too, because they are classless.

God of Panic

Panic comes from Pan. He can make you thrust aside Athena's sense of normalcy and head for the hills. Pan makes you laugh after screaming at horror movies and feel relieved to wake up after a nightmare—which he sends to you in your sleep. So it was only a dream after all! It's dangerous to rouse him from his lazy sleep for he's likely to let loose his terrifying scream. To him, interrupting is a kind of psychological

208

violence. You interrupt Pan when you address someone with sudden urgency, shake someone out of sleep, talk during a movie, or rouse someone from a book.

Panic can happen alone or in a crowd. It can happen to a buyer or to an entire market. The Greeks said Pan panicked the Persian army at the Battle of Marathon, delivering victory to the greatly outnumbered Greeks.

Pan Nomios

Pan *Nomios,* the Shepherd, is a humble guy who guards flocks, herds and beehives. He is the Leader of the Herd. Pan Agreus is a God of Hunters. Boys used to beat his image with squills when game went scarce.

But shepherds don't spend all their time watching sheep.

Pan is fantasy. Alone among the major gods, he is an impossible being. You are like him when you can imagine things instead of actually doing them. He is culture as vicarious experience. He is also the god of masturbation.

With Pan as your friend, you don't have to live life to its fullest like Herakles the action hero. By fantasizing about things instead of actually doing them, you shepherd your own resources without limiting your freedom. That is Pan's virtue. It's easier on your budget and your health to watch a National Geographic Special than to actually go to Zaire or Antarctica to see it for yourself. Of course, the downside of too much Pan is procrastination and dreaming instead of actually doing things. Athena the Goddess of the Golden Mean can cure that because she wants you to live in proportion.

Fantasies and desires are nymphs to Pan. The souls of old trees, streams, mountains, and waterfalls are lovers to him. Pan's nymphs might be a fantasy of quitting your job, moving somewhere beautiful, or letting your hair grown long--anything to escape a rigid schedule and to follow your instincts.

209

Pan

One nymph he chased was Echo, who had a voice but no body, like someone you take for granted or who follows you slavishly.

He also went after Pitys, who prayed to the gods for help. When they turned her into a pine tree, Pan fashioned a hat out of a branch, which happens when you are satisfied with a taste of something and don't really want to plunge into it after all.

Another nymph, Syrinx rejected all suitors. Pan caught her by the river, and she cried for help. The gods turned her and her water nymph friends into reeds, each indistinguishable from the other. Pan grabbed a handful of the naiads and made a flute.

He got lucky with Selene the Moon by donning white fleece and cleaning himself up. Not realizing who he was, Selene rode on his back and gave him a good time.

Pan's love is anonymous and impersonal because it is based on fantasy, not on actual interaction with another person. He is the Internet profile and the other person as an image. Pan grabs at any reed, fondles the pine, and appears in disguise just to score. He is the need of the body, coupled with an image or fantasy that doesn't take the other person into consideration.

You honor Pan whenever you imagine doing something instead of actually doing it and then dedicate the experience to him, because he stands for the freedom to imagine. You please him when you allow yourself any fantasy, knowing that you don't have to act on it.

Aigipan

Aigipan nursed alongside the baby Zeus, his foster brother, in a cave in Crete. Their nurse was Amalthea, the goat-nymph.

Aigipan is the cure for thinking you are a spirit trapped inside the flesh. He is the body as a person and a friend for a lifetime—a point that becomes more obvious with age. The Greeks made him half an animal to get this point across.

When people tell you to listen to your body, they are telling you to take it easy and learn to be a little lazy like Pan. He is your shocking animality: the hair, the flesh, the smells and funny noises hidden beneath the clothes and manners of civilization. His monstrous shape is our monstrous shape. Never mind a hairy back, just look at how weird your hands and feet are!

Aigipan is *the oldest of the gods*, much older than the Olympians. Several gods claim this status, but in this case, *oldest* means 'primary', because to the Greeks the body comes first. You get a glimpse of Aigipan when you see someone scratch himself or adjust his underwear. Pan is everything that Hera's Society tries to hide about being a human animal.

At least twenty different gods, nymphs, and humans claim to be his parents, because you imagine your body differently when you are dancing, driving, or lying in bed asleep. Most sources agree that Hermes is Pan's father by the daughter of a farmer whose sheep Hermes was tending. The girl flees in terror when she sees the young monster which looks like Rosemary's baby.

But Pan is more comical than threatening, like the naked body, which is why Hermes the God of Humor sponsors him. He wraps the baby in a rabbit skin—because rabbits are horny—and brings him up to Olympus to delight the gods. They *all* adore him, for *Pan* means *All*, and the body is necessary to all experiences. MRI's show that even spiritual and out-of-body experiences occur in the amygdala, so all of the gods depend on him.

They take advantage of him freely. Apollo wheedles the art of prophecy out of him and Hermes copies the panpipe he drops and sells it to Apollo, just as these days, corporations buy tunes from rock and roll bands and play what was once edgy music to sell cars and financial services.

Many ancients puzzled over Socrates' prayer to him: *Oh dear Pan, grant me inner beauty of soul,* because that sounds more like a prayer to Apollo than to Pan. But the body is the source of symptoms and moods and if you listen to your body you will know what the gods want from you. Pan is around when you think of your body as a temple of metaphors, full of subtlety. With Pan, the gods are more than an intellectual exercise. They

Pan

are right there in your body, giving you self-regulation as an instinct and not just a top-down program telling you what to do.

Pan the Deliverer

Pan the Deliverer sent the Greeks a dream with the cure for a certain plague. He is the idea that dreaming is good for you and that the soul interacts with the gods and with the dead when you are asleep.

Pan offers a kind of prudence that keeps you from taking on more than you can handle. He wants you to sleep on it first because you and your body have limits. He lets you know when you're dead tired, you need to change your lifestyle, or you are uncomfortable with a situation. He provides the wisdom to know when you are not up to something, even if you could force yourself to do it. Mostly, he wants you to hang out doing nothing, watching television or watching people go by.

Sleep doesn't get much respect these days. Arianna Huffington has written about the sacrifice of sleep as a kind of business machismo. It comes from Herakles the Hero, who has a bad attitude towards Hades, the Underworld of dreams and images, and only understands literal actions. The 'quality time' of busy Athena the Goddess Who Never Sleeps, his patron, is a euphemism for 'very little time'.

Pan wants his afternoon nap and he doesn't want you to live only to work. He gives you the ability to leave the office at the office and he likes it when you lose track of time and act naturally.

God of Arcadia

Arcadia is an ideal landscape and a state of mind. It is Eden, the ideal of your favorite beautiful place, and the place you would ideally retire. Pan's world teems with other beings, like the art of the Minoans or Henri Rousseau, where animals, people, plants and landscape are presented as equals. It is the pastoral underworld of *The Tempest, The Odyssey* and *Midsummer Night's Dream*.

The God of Arcadia resides in a world where man belongs among the animals--not a place where he is an intruder. He is Middle Earth

212

before the Elves left and the wilderness of fairy tales with princes and fairies and talking animals. He is your childhood when you could easily make believe. You nourish this self when you read a fairy tale or myth before you go to sleep because it is more exciting to dream about a prince or a goddess than to dream about your job.

Danger is real here because fantasy is not only infantile. Pan takes you out of the city walls of your mind and into open country, his uncanny wilderness where adventure abounds and your success and survival are not guaranteed, just like real life.

He is the terror of the lonely cowboy and the driver on empty roads at night. He is the fear of the dark or of the woods. He is demonic possession, like gulping food in the middle of the night or smoking one cigarette after another without realizing it. Pan is around when you wonder what the hell you're doing or when you get a mood of childish behavior and pranks amid the grown up seriousness around you.

With Pan, stones are not only stones and trees are not only trees. Everything has its own poetic life and its right to exist beyond its usefulness to humans. In this mindset, the hooting owl isn't only a symbol of Athena, nor is the seashell only a symbol of Aphrodite—they actually are Athena and Aphrodite. Pan helps you see the gods in concrete forms in the here and now and not only conceptually.

From his point of view, we don't need more consciousness, more self-awareness, or more self-esteem. We need more of Pan's wildness—more familiarity with the wilder regions of the Psyche that do not want to be dominated or suburbanized by the idea of a single self that 'life's about'. We need less logic and progress and clearing of the forests because material things can never satisfy us if they have no meaning. Respecting Pan means you can never really figure out death, love, money, or even losing weight. These things are mysteries that cannot be explained away without losing their meaning, but they can be related to as people. The social brain hypothesis states that our brains got bigger so that we could keep track of people. With Pan, this extends to the people dwelling within.

213

Pan

With the rise of Christianity, rumors circulated that Pan died at the moment Christ ascended the cross. The cry was heard from a ship sailing off the coast, *The great god, Pan, is dead!* The Church gave Satan his ears and hooves.

What died with Pan was the animistic view of the world—the idea that there is soul everywhere and in everything, not just in humans. The god whose name means *All* represents *all* the gods and his death signaled the loss of that luminous view. Pan's death meant that we forgot that we are animals that belong on earth and that our behavior is made up of instincts or 'gods'. The monotheist paradigm that replaced the old, pagan order insists on a single self and declares that the soul ends at the edge of the human body. That makes the rest of the world dead and soul-less, even demonic, as in horror movies, where things seem haunted and threatening simply because other selves dwell within them.

Silenus

Greek actors performed satyr plays as comic relief between their tragedies, which were performed one after another during the festivals. The satyr plays mocked the preceding tragedy and turned the human woes in the story into one big campy joke.

The chief of the tribe of satyrs is Silenus, an old, fat and bald satyr with thick lips and semi-human legs--a repulsive figure to the Greeks.

Silenus is the cynical self. Silenus is around when you cry in your beer. His most famous saying is that *the best thing is for a man never to be born, and the second best is to die young.*

If you follow Silenus, nothing is worth the trouble. He's the reason to keep on drinking, as in the song, *Is That All There Is?* But Silenus is a good reality check for busy gods like Athena the Normal Self and Herakles the Hero, because in a hundred years you will be dead and so will everyone who knew you and all the things you worry so much about today won't matter a bit.

Silenus tutored Dionysus, who *followed him in his madness*— meaning he taught the drunk all about drinking. This nihilistic teller of tall

214

tales claims that his donkey's braying scared the giants away during the battle of the gods against the Titans, but he's always so pickled he can't tell truth from fiction.

The gang of Sileni hang around with the Satyrs and Maenads, crazed followers of Dionysus. You join them when you get moon-sickness and act weird every now and then or once you get your paycheck. But you are most like him when you have something bad to say about everything.

Centaurs

The earliest Centaurs were joined together at the waist like a Push Me Pull You. They hailed from a paradise in the far west, like San Francisco, Key West, Provincetown, and other coastal refuges for those who need to get as far away as possible from the prying eyes of mainland Hera the Church Lady.

These peaceful country bumpkins memorably attended the marriage of Cadmus and Harmony with all the gods, wearing adorable caps of grass and holding fir branches and predicting good times ahead, like multi-cultural ambassadors. Later, they are shown in the artwork with only one head and looking more dangerous, especially after a few drinks. Vases depict them with brazen erections raiding villages and raping the women and boys.

The Centaur is the rowdy self. They are the outsider, the motorcycle gang, the leather crowd, S&M, and any group behavior devoid of personal feelings. Their way of life offends Hera the Personal Self, Demeter the Family Self, and Athena the Normal Self. They are Hell's Angels roaring down Main Street, scaring everybody and calling out sexual adventure and booze like Marlon Brando in *The Wild One*. The motorcycles correspond to their lower, animal parts. Centaurs personify all the antisocial things you are capable of doing which don't fit the personality everybody expects you to have—which is why they don't live in town.

You don't have to act like a centaur to be like one, you just have to recognize feelings that aren't personal or acceptable. These days, television shows about prison life can give you a feel for these psychotic

215

Pan

selves who hide in the quiet man next door whom no one ever suspects of being a serial killer.

Chiron

Chiron, or *Hand*, is the most famous of a noble line of Centaurs. He is a cousin of Zeus with no relation to the other Centaurs.

He is the mentor. You are like him when you teach someone, sponsor someone, or heal someone. Chiron is the wisdom of kindness, a virtue Zeus promotes. He is wise, sober, and civilized. He embodies the instinct to cooperate and help others who are not like you—not for personal or social reasons but because that is your nature.

Chiron's expertise is medicine. These days, he runs a vitamin or organic food store, or practices massage, acupuncture, and chiropractic. He tutors all the best heroes because he stands for ancient wisdom, the liberal arts and the great books.

You know Chiron when you find advice and direction in the least expected places like an old, uneducated relative or the surprisingly thoughtful and insightful mailman. You are also like him when you are the one advising. Pan gives you the wisdom to pay attention to the 'little people' that Hera the Goddess of Society may overlook because they aren't socially prominent.

One time, Chiron accidentally pricked himself on one of Herakles' poisonous arrows and begged to die to escape the pain--but he couldn't because he was immortal. This is what you experience when your body fails and your mind does not. Zeus let him trade his life with Prometheus, who helped mankind in a more heroic fashion, and set aside the constellation Centaurus in his honor.

Moving On

Turn away from Pan when you have had enough of being lazy and wild and are well rested.

216

Athena can help you get things done and Hestia can get your house in order. Going to restaurants or the theater can get you into more sociable selves like Hera, Dionysus, Aphrodite, or Hermes.

Hermes is the easiest transition, as he is with so many other gods. Pan's father and sponsor lets you change the subject and do something else with no judgment of what you were doing before. Hermes lets you laugh at your body and behavior and gain perspective on it, for he knows that no single god can define you.

Athena the Waking Goddess may fret about the time you 'wasted' and get you back to your list. And Hera the Goddess of Society who worries about your reputation may want to get you to act more respectable.

HERMES

Hermes is the Messenger of the Gods, the one with the winged feet. He is the God of Travelers through places both physical and psychological. The God of Twists and Turns is the ability to change persona, like when you fall asleep.

For Hermes, experience is not a continuous novel about *me*. It's an archipelago of different selves in different places: who you are at the office, at the gym, or driving. This self makes you feel at home anywhere because he isn't tied to any one place. He gives you the feeling that you never left when you find yourself back at work, with an old friend, or visiting a place you knew years ago.

He's so used to moving around that he can get you out of any identification just by holding up the image of whoever you are being and poking some fun of it, because once you can laugh at yourself, you have already taken one step away from the person you were identifying with a moment ago. He is the mindset that knows that nothing lasts forever.

Hermes is amoral and hedonistic, but he is so cosmopolitan and charming that you can't hold it against him. He is the fascinating and gregarious man about town seeking pleasure. Even when he's a thief he is more like Zorro than a ruffian. Most of the stories about Hermes concern his two favorite things: sex and money.

These days, the God of Messengers has us obsessed with our devices and checking our messages constantly. We are completely under his spell when we are 'anywhere but here', like couples at dinner texting their friends and people talking on the phone in elevators. He likes to keep you jumping around and never identifying with the here and now. He is a great one for sending you in twenty directions at once and starting more things than you can finish.

This complex and fascinating god seeks out a crowd--at the movies, at the market, or at the bar, and yet he is also a loner who sees life as a solitary venture. He travels solo and even if he gets married his marriage it's more likely to be an arrangement than a sense of finding a

218

soul mate. To Hermes, we each die alone and our lives are measured by profit and pleasure. Memories are to be collected and cherished.

You may know Hermes as a friend or acquaintance whom you only know in one scenario, like someone you meet while traveling, only know from the gym or from a class, or only see when you're out walking your dog.

Hermes doesn't seek fulfillment from other people because he knows he can't count on them, just as he cannot be counted on. He makes you see yourself as a person, capable of good or bad, and not as a 'good' person like Hera or Herakles.

Spend time with him when you take yourself too seriously or you get bored or stuck in any one self because Hermes sees change as fun, especially if there's something in it for him.

God of Thieves

As soon as he ss born, Hermes wanders out of his cave looking for adventure and trouble. He wants to taste meat for the first time.

Meat was a sign of wealth in ancient times. Hermes is the one talking when you want a bite of the Apple--and as easily as possible, working smart rather than working hard. He wants you to end up with the pot of gold. Hermes the Opportunist is around when you want things—love, money, or an education—and you just can't sit still about it.

On his doorstep, Hermes finds a turtle he dubs Beautiful Dancer in mockery of its awkward shape—because Hermes is jaded and sarcastic. He picks the creature up gently and warns it of the dangers of going out alone at night. Then he takes it into his cave and mercilessly kills it, scooping out its insides with a knife and making the first lyre out of its shell. He then accompanies himself to brazen songs about his mother's affair with Zeus and other colorful stories about the gods, sparing no sordid detail.

Hermes is a complex god--both amusing and ruthless. You are like him when you use things or use others, whether you're making a purchase in a store, charging someone for services, or charming a table for

Hermes

a tip. This doesn't have to be cynical, because most deals are fair deals, not bad deals. You generally get what you order in a restaurant.

When he spies the cattle of his brother, Apollo, grazing in a field, he decides to steal them by tying rackets to their hooves to make it look as though they are walking backwards-- the first racket, literally.

The old vine worker, *Battos,* Chatterbox, sees Hermes leading the cattle away but sells his silence for a bribe, because this self doesn't mind greasing a palm or two to help things run smoothly. Battos the bribe-taker is another Hermes, because all of the details of a myth are parts of the persona of the myth.

Hermes then slaughters two of the cattle and performs a ritual of thanks to the gods for his new riches—the first ritual to the gods. When he finishes, he creeps home—the way he may have you do sometimes—tucks himself in and puts on his innocent babe face, but his mother, Maia, isn't buying it. She scolds him for going out at night, a mere baby, but he answers that he can take care of himself and improve their lot as well, telling her they can do better than living in a cave in the boondocks and that he is going to make sure it happens.

Apollo easily gets the truth out of the old vine worker and drags Hermes before their father, Zeus. Although he pretends not even to know what a cow is, Zeus sees through his lies and tells him to return the cattle, whereupon Hermes hands Apollo the bow and arrows that he just lifted from his pocket with an obliging smile.

While Apollo is wondering how he had been pick-pocketed so easily, Hermes produces the lyre, which so enchants Apollo that he begins to admire his half-brother's inventive and nimble mind. When Hermes next hands him a shepherd's pipe--which he either invented or stole from Pan-- he wins Apollo's frank admiration and friendship.

Apollo offers to teach Hermes fortune telling through dice and cards while Zeus gives him power over all roads and travelers, commerce and heraldry. These days he is the media and the Internet as well.

Hermes later goes back to visit old Battos in disguise and easily gets the story out of him, so he changes him into a rock. Battos is a

220

dumb version of Hermes who is opportunistic but not quick like the god; he is the stupid criminal who looks into the surveillance camera he's turning off.

Hermes is no common thief because he has the fine art of living: eloquence, charm, and a fascinating complexity. Artwork shows a handsome young man of style and verve, often wearing the hat of a traveler. There are elderly versions of Hermes as well and some that are bearded, but his build is always wiry and agile to indicate he is quick in both physique and mind.

The Helper of Mankind

Hermes shows mankind how to befriend the gods through ritual. A ritual can simply involve putting on the right clothes and face to match the mood of the occasion, as long as you hold an image of the persona you are going to be.

Hermes is the only god who gives gifts to other gods because the God of Messengers and Friends connects them all. You are with the God of Feasts and Banquets when you play the master of ceremonies, make a toast, ease introductions, give a eulogy, or act like the life of the party.

In his ritual, Hermes cuts the two head of cattle he stole from Apollo into twelve pieces, one for each of the gods, including one for himself. Although he cut the meat haphazardly, once he had actually made the cut, he handled each piece reverently as if it was tailor-made for each god. This is an important detail.

You cut up the meat and distribute it among the gods whenever you perceive a different self within an experience. That experience then becomes a gift to that god as a taste of mortal life through you. A ritual can be any action in honor of a god as long as it is meant sincerely, like any gift to a friend. It is never manipulation or a pay-off, and it doesn't require belief. This sincerity is Hermes' reverence.

You can wave a feather around the house in honor of a god or do whatever you were going to do anyway and *give it* to the god. You make

221

Hermes

a gift of an experience just by dedicating it to a god rather than keeping the experience to yourself. If you hold a clear image of the god while you act, the image can guide your actions and shape your persona to the god.

For instance, you can go into a meeting like Zeus, acting like you own the room. Others will sense this authority and respond to it. You can go into a date with your lover as Aphrodite or her hot boyfriend, Ares, and your date will go better than if you went in just as yourself, or whatever random mood you were in at the moment. People want the gods *through* each other.

This becomes automatic as you practice it. Friendships with the gods take time just like friendships with people. Some require years of ritual practice like gymnastics or speaking another language.

The Friendly God

The God of Friends makes it easy to like everyone and to be liked in return--and he's perfectly happy for people to think he likes them more than he does. Hermes makes you easy in your skin and happy to see others.

You are like him when you smile and act friendly. He is the very impulse to engage others as equals instead of ignoring them, including the other selves in your psyche. Hermes inspires you to do favors knowing that someday you might call in that favor, and to flatter or find ways to get on someone's good side as a kind of investment in the future.

He knows full well that you don't have to like someone to be his friend. How much do you really have to like your tennis partner or your business partner anyway? The Friend to All is the customer service rep who is friendly but professional and not really your friend.

Hermes is the friendliness itself—delivered in just the right tone and tact to say just about anything and get away with it. He is the soul of diplomacy who knows that if you are free with compliments and turn on the charms, you can engage a Cyclops or an angry drunk and still act like everyone's cool.

When Apollo's mother, Leto, readies to engage him in the

battle of the gods, Hermes offers to skip the fight and she can tell everyone she beat him—not because he is a coward but because he seeks the easy way out and sees no profit in fighting. He makes you care only about results and not about glory.

The Friendliest of Gods to Men sends you anywhere people congregate: to a mall, a theater, or a political rally. He is the urge to go downtown to see what's happening. Hermes is especially the friend you have known for a long time but really know little about. That's because his friendliness is personal but it is not human, for it comes from a god. The Giver of Good Things is a gregarious loner who keeps his own counsel but is blessed with *the gift of friendliness*. With him, life is an adventure for one and everywhere you go, there will friends to be made there, too.

You bring your best manners and mien to a Hermes friendship because they include plenty of absences and no guarantees. Hermes stays single and doesn't want you to settle down either, but he is okay with an arrangement like when he is paired with Hestia and she plays the quiet type at home while he goes out looking for fun and trouble. He has a longstanding affair with Aphrodite, whom he calls whenever he's in town with a delightful idea of how to spend an evening. The theme in Hermes' friendships is always fun and mutual benefit.

Hermes the Traveler

Hermes On the Road, *Enodios,* is the traveller. He is the entire experience of travel, including the roads and the airports and the strangers you meet along the way. Artwork shows him with winged sandals, a broad hat for the sun and the rain, and the clothes and overnight bag of a tourist.

When you travel you are like Hermes, more open than usual to meeting people and trying new experiences.

He is the Stranger who shows up suddenly and magically, perhaps at the hotel or at the museum, with whom you strike up a conversation and suddenly find yourself spending a lot of time with. The Running Escort is the Leader of Men—not a political leader, more like a tour

Hermes

operator, trainer, or cabbie.

Hermes makes you welcome change as an adventure instead of dreading it. With him around, you can feel at home anywhere, in any crowd, and in any mood. He wants you to be interested in everything and in everyone, because there is always money to make and erotic possibilities to explore. You can sense Hermes in your own free spirit, exploring a new city with winged feet and a credit card. He is your ability to quickly size up a person or a situation, slip adeptly along a busy sidewalk, or change persona as easily as dropping off to sleep.

Traveling gives you the sense that no place or situation is so awful that it can't afford some small pleasure. For Hermes, every mindset is a place to visit so there's never a sense of being trapped and it's easy to pick up where you left off with an old friend or a skill. In fact, it's as if you were never apart.

The God of Searchers will have you searching for a lover, a career, or a meaning in life—because searching brings you into new territory in experience. But this has nothing to do with the longing of Apollo the Perfect who holds out for something better. Hermes would rather you grab the opportunity at hand than be tragic and superior and go without.

Hermes the Messenger

The Herald of the Gods is the news and the talking heads and anyone with something important to say. The patron of reporters and ambassadors can go anywhere and park anywhere with diplomatic impunity. His daughter, Tidings, *Angelia* is the news itself.

You are with Hermes the Messenger, *Diaktoros,* when you spread the news. It can be gossip, a sales pitch, or the latest joke. It's fun to be the Bearer of Good News, but it's also exhilarating to spread the bad news, because being the first person to tell someone something matters more to this self than the news itself.

Hermes delivers messages from the gods through dreams, symptoms, suspicions, longings, and ideas.

In the Greek view, *you* don't have ideas. Ideas *occur to you* of their own accord. That's why they can occur to several people at the same time. Hermes is the god of Eureka moments, when the solution to something wells up from some other part of the mind that is busy working without your conscious help. Hermes thinks *as fast as death* because he is your ability to think in ideas instead of in words. Because of Hermes, you see the implications of an idea as soon as it appears—because he spreads the news to all of the gods.

You might think of stealing a candy bar and even have some rationale straight from Hermes like 'this store rips me off all the time'. But by the time Hermes tells the other gods what's happening, in come Zeus, Athena and Apollo--gods of property, self-restraint and limits—to stop you dead in your tracks.

The Running God of Luck

The Running God of Luck, *Eriounios* entices gamblers to his table with the adrenalin rush and the spectacular reversals of gaming.

He is the God of Luck, *Tychon,* and his female companion is Tyche. His winning manner makes friends everywhere, because this self knows that good luck sometimes takes a little help and ingenuity, like pretending to accidentally bump into someone you want to meet or sending in a job application to a company that just posted good earnings.

His gift is the lucky find, the *hermaion*, which pops up out of nowhere like a twenty-dollar bill on the sidewalk. However, when someone stupid has great luck like winning the lottery, the Greeks would call him *a rich friend of Herakles the Hero*, not of Hermes. Feeling lucky with Hermes has to do with helping your luck along like a card shark, not entitled like Herakles, the egomaniac.

To Hermes, life is a series of ups and downs-- windfalls, swift moves, and strokes of fortune, good or bad--rather than the heroic narrative that Herakles wants to make out of your life. Playing cards and board games are great avenues into this adaptable mentality, and they give you a chance to exercise your Game Self which can be quite different from your usual selves. In games, you can let loose your aggression towards beloved

Hermes

others and experience their betrayal without hurting anyone's feelings.

Master of Animals

Hermes the Leader of the Herd and the Master of Animals is often shown in the artwork with a dog. He is the god of caretakers. You are like him when you care for your pets and for other things.

Hermes Protector of the Flock, *Nomios,* watches over sheep and goats, but you are like him as a scout leader or an attentive tax accountant. The Keeper of the Flock, *Epimelius* knows good business practice and the God of Animal Husbandry can grow your business, keeping your focus on the bottom line. The Guardian of Wealth hedges and saves so that the Goodly Giver, *Eudorus,* the business itself, can provide income for years. He's a self that unabashedly loves money.

At his festival, the best looking young man was chosen to carry a ram on his shoulders around the city walls to ward off disease and bad luck. Images show Hermes holding the ram under his arm or standing next to it with his hand on its head—a touching picture of the good shepherd caring for the flock that was later adopted by Christianity.

Hermes belongs to simple people who are used to being told what to do, especially in service jobs like waiting, assisting and attending. He gives you the ability to pay attention to subtle changes before they become problems, whether it's a diner who seems ready for the next course or a patient who needs some attention.

The same goes with moods. Hermes Protector of the Flock would rather you manage your moods with respect and care than to own them or identify with them. He never owns the livestock he tends; they always belong to someone else. He is your ability to care for other people's property and for your own moods and ideas with genuine concern. His mentality lets you herd your various selves so they don't linger too long or disappear altogether, extracting you from tricky situations easily--because Hermes always knows where the other moods can be found, like straying sheep, and he's an expert at acting innocent or coming up with excuses for getting out of obligations and doing what he really wants.

226

Hermes of the Market

Hermes *Agoraios* is the God of the Market, the God of the Mall and the God of Downtown where the stores are.

The god of entrepreneurs embodies buying and selling and all aspects of dealmaking. Hermes Profit, *Kerdos,* and Hermes Trade, *Empolaios,* are gods of small business owners and tradesmen and anyone who lives on a commission. He knows how to carve up a company as easily as a roast, repackaging it and selling it back to the market. You know him through success and fame, or *kudos,* in business. His Roman cousin is Mercury.

Hermes gives you a good attitude and a cheerful mood at the office that makes work enjoyable.

His strength is his resourcefulness. The Cleverest of Gods is a great one for rediscovering things like antiques, fashion, or music and putting them back into circulation. He is the impulse among artists and thinkers to plumb the culture for old images and ideas that can be re-worked in a new way, instead of making everything up from scratch. He is the god of this book, which presents the Greek gods as ideal selves, informed by Evolutionary Psychology.

Hermes wants you to work so you can be independent and he's willing to have you take a job you don't love if the money is good enough. To him, a bird in the hand beats two in the bush, whether it's a job or a partner, so that you can live on the better side of town and be happy. He is the reason the French word *miserable* actually means *poor.* Hermes isn't one hundred percent honest but he will help you survive and not resign yourself to some lesser fate.

Hermes the Whisperer

Hermes shares the name, Whisperer, with Aphrodite and Eros, especially Persuasive Aphrodite and Aphrodite Weaver of Tricks. Hermes knows that getting what you want in love and business takes cunning. He helps lovers find the object of their desire, but his idea of

Hermes

romance centers on fun and pleasure. He doesn't want to stare into your eyes like Hera's daughter Hebe, the fiancée, to find true love like Eros and Psyche, or to spend his time longing like his brother, Apollo. Hermes is the god of 'getting lucky.'

He is sex appeal, which the Greeks considered a gift of the gods and a tremendous advantage in life.

Sex appeal is more than good looks. Few aerobics instructors are sexy even though they have perfect bodies. They represent Artemis the Perfect, admirable but untouchable, more healthy than naughty. Hermes Giver of Joy, *Charidotes,* is the luck of being appealing to others. He's the clothes you wear and the way you wear them and everything that makes you intriguing.

Whispered words are magic words. Pillow talk is not normal conversation and it usually doesn't need an answer, because it speaks directly to a god, not a person. Those seductive words are Hermes himself.

For this mindset, sex is adventure and recreation, not procreation. Hermes never marries because he likes having fun too much. He can laugh and still be manly. He is a god of affairs, booty calls, and romantic interludes. Hermes likes to sleep with his friends and with strangers.

He is always on the lookout. Vases show the Friend of Lovers leading a young man out of the bedroom from his sleeping wife without waking her, as quiet as *a breeze through a keyhole,* because sneaking out is an art of Hermes. It helps not to look at the sleeping person if you want to pull this off successfully, because Hermes is a god of misdirection.

This tremendous flirt doesn't really care about your feelings, but he isn't cynical either. He gets a rush out of being outrageous and charming his way through life. Sexual fidelity never occurs to him. His affair with Aphrodite produces several children but it is an open relationship with no jealousy, questions, or expectations, only lots of fun.

But he is not one to cross. When he loves Herse, her jealous sister stands in the way, and he not only turns the sister to stone but makes her pregnant as a statue. Hermes can make you a cheat in love who

228

disappears when the test comes back positive, the money runs out, or the spouse suspects something.

Hermes and Apollo

These brothers round each other out like humor and intellect. As a child, Hermes lures Apollo out of his ivory tower with his inventiveness, his street smarts, and his frank offer of friendship--something the imperious god isn't used to since Apollo is never just 'one of the guys'.

Out of admiration he puts Hermes in charge of his cattle and teaches him how to read fortunes through dice and the movement of bees.

Apollo is facts while Hermes is interpretation. Apollo is logic and insight while Hermes is speculation and application. Apollo is science while Hermes is interpretive fortune telling like astrology, economics, and technical analysis in stocks.

The power of *hermeneutics*, the art of interpretation, is almost magical, because the meaning of something changes when the understanding of it does, as if its very reality changes. Seeing experience in terms of multiple selves instead of a single self changes the nature of experience.

The Greeks used to say that both gods *compete for the Muses*—for the Arts. Hermes is more interested in success than in the purity of art, the way a bestseller competes with Apollo's 'literary novel'. Apollo says that *I, too, am a companion to the Muses* when the intellectual envies a pop culture phenomenon. His job is to keep Hermes from playing all the time and to keep him within the law—at least literally. Apollo and Zeus allow Hermes to mislead and omit so long as he doesn't outright lie, just as I was encouraged as a stockbroker to tell the client that a stock is going up even though that was only a hope. Apollo and Zeus are civilizing gods who stand for the world of order. They counter Hermes' tendency to make you quit and move on to the next thing before finishing. Their sense of right and wrong checks Hermes with questions like, *is this legal? are you leaving a trail of broken hearts?* Or *do you really think that's funny?*

Hermes gives you a friendly but guarded attitude towards the

229

Hermes

world. Hermes the Protector often has a statue in the courtyard of the ancient Greek home—and even in the bedroom. His dog companion is a guard dog and friend—and a lure for strangers. In Japan, single people rent dogs to walk in order to meet dates.

Property lines in ancient Greece were marked by *herms*, or rock piles and stone pillars carved on one or more sides with a smile and an erection. The herm at the boundary was the site of trade between ancient cities, because it was neutral ground. It often consisted of a mere pile of stones. Passing travelers would leave a rock on the top the same way today's hikers do or they left some food for the ghosts of the crossroads—a way to get on the good side of any would-be thieves.

Hermes shares crossroads with Hekate the Witch Goddess, who has similar pillars with faces pointing in several directions, but while Hekate is concerned with your fate, Hermes is more interested in your next adventure.

Lord of the Gymnasia

Gymnazein means to exercise naked, as men did in ancient Greece.

The three Lords of the Gymnasia are Hermes, Eros and Herakles, each with his own approach to athletics. Some go to feel and look good like Eros—and maybe to meet someone romantically or at least to gawk at the bodies. Eros loves the spa. Others go to the gym to get bigger and stronger than everyone else like Herakles. You can find him proving himself in the free weights section and the Ironman competition. Herkales likes weightlifting because it lets him measure his progress in numbers.

Hermes goes to the gym to be around people and to be active. He would never run on a treadmill at home. Hermes brings a friendly, sporting attitude to competition and likes chatting between sets. The Lord of Contests likes all sports and games. His physique is trim and flexible, the kind of wiry body that comes from agile sports. The God of Twists and Turns specifically loves boxing and gymnastics, where his agility

230

can be tested. Hermes' agility, which is awareness in movement, extends to facility in speech, ease with new circumstances, and the easy ability to change persona to deal with others.

Castor and Pollux

The twin sons of Zeus and Leda hatched from an egg after Zeus took Leda as a swan. The Sons of God, *Dioscuri,* handsome and strong Horsemen, *Hippios,* whom the Greeks saw as superheroes. Castor is a boxer and Pollux is an equestrian gymnast.

The Saviors of Saviors always save the day at the last minute. They protect travelers like heroic pilots, off-duty police officers, and everyday citizens who direct traffic when the lights go out. They are the salvation that comes at the last minute, while Hekate the Witch is the miraculous reversal.

The Dioscuri combine Hermes' friendship with the courage and fellow feeling of Ares the War God, the kind of guy who can put his arm over your shoulder without feeling goofy. They are the friends you would die for and who would die for you, as in war movies. They are buddies— the twin, the partner, and any friendship that has loyalty without domination. You are like them when you and a friend share in each other's success and in the hard times as well. As Achilles tells his beloved friend and partner-in-arms, Patroclus, *we must share it all.*

Tyndareus is their legal father but Zeus is their actual father. You have two fathers when you are *born* to something, the way a great baseball player is born to baseball, or someone is a born teacher, or born to run a business.

Hermes coached them in sports. The Twins stand for sportsmanship—a kind of civic attitude at the gym and in sports. We are in sore need of this virtue today.

These superheroes didn't escape the pain of mortality. A rival set of twins—their shadows as Bullies, including the strongest man on earth--kidnapped the brothers' brides on their wedding day. Everyone died in that fight except Pollux.

Hermes

He begged Zeus to bring his brother back to life or to allow him to die so he could join him in Hades, but Zeus decided to allow them to take turns living one day in Hades and the next on Olympus. They see each other in passing, like friends who take turns being strong for one another. They are heroism as a brother or sister in the psyche.

You can also imagine the Twins as your waking self and your dream self. It's one thing to not be able to remember dreams, but it's another to say you don't dream at all and to assert that the dream self doesn't even exist. That insults Hades, who is both a person and the Underworld of dreams and images.

Simply imagining that someone else comes alive when you are asleep gives that self some recognition and respect, even if you only glimpse it remotely and in passing. That may be all that it wants from you, because that person has his own priorities and purposes that may have nothing to do with the selves of your waking life. Not all of the gods seek our friendship, but none of them likes to be snubbed or ignored.

The Greeks believed the Twins could take messages to and from the dead, because they were always on that Underworld escalator. Common folk used to leave out little snacks for them with messages to the dead like a cookie for Santa or the wooden troll my Norwegian grandmother used to leave out for the *little people.*

The Dioscuri are Sky Gods like Zeus, with whom they are closely identified, for they are always on the side of justice and dignity. The Gemini Twins are demi-gods of the stars and stargazing and the inspiration behind our fantasies about living in Outer Space.

God of Persuasion

Conversation is a living form of Hermes, which is why you respect the conversation by letting it go where it wants to rather than forcing it or thinking about what you want to say while the other person is talking. Hermes of Persuasion, *Peitho,* has the skill of directing an innocent conversation to a topic he wants to address with diplomacy and tact and a

232

little premeditation, all the while allowing the words to flow freely.

The God of Speakers, *Logios,* is who you are when you speak to a group. The Great Persuader of Men gives you quick retorts and eloquence on the spot, like when Lloyd Bentsen told Dan Quayle, *You're no John Kennedy.*

The God of Persuaders and Seducers might address a voter, a client, or a lover, but not as merely Athena the Normal Self. This self has more style than that Plain Jane, though he knows how to put on that act as well.

His friends among the Muses include the sisters Persuasion *(Peitho),* Adornment *(Aglaia),* and Cheerfulness (*Euphrosyne)*—as well as the goddess Coaxing. Hermes knows that how you say something is as important as what you actually say, and that you can say almost anything if you say it well and diplomatically

He is in advertisements designed to part you from your money. The God of Guile can con you into anything because he knows how *to maze the mind of humans*—as he does every night when you wander off to sleep.

One strange sibling of Persuasion is the dread goddess, Compulsion, *Ananke,* who is around when you are compelled to believe something like North Koreans and people who bought into the Housing Bubble. She can be spotted shopping at the mall for the latest fads or foods.

All of the gods of persuasion are amoral because to them, the persuasion matters more than the thing they're promoting. These gods can land you in a bad mutual fund, a wrong relationship, or a dress that doesn't really fit even if the clerk insists it does. I had a friend who was such a natural salesperson that she'd try to convince me to do anything at all, like using a hot sauce at a restaurant or painting my apartment a different color just for the satisfaction of it.

These days, our rhetoric has become so impoverished that the only tools of persuasion we have left are repetition and name-calling. Even the hooks in popular music are disappearing. Hermes' playful

233

Hermes

impulse may be genetic but the art of convincing requires learned refinement.

God of Tongues

Hermes was often shown with a tongue on his forehead. The herald was traditionally given the tongue at Greek banquets.

The God of Tongues personifies language, especially refined language and multilingualism. He is why accents are so contagious. He is the reason you seldom find yourself stuck in the middle of the sentence and often don't even know what you are going to say until you hear yourself say it, because your sentences have a mind of their own.

MRIs confirm that your personality changes when you speak another language. When I studied French, I made up a French name and personal history because I didn't want to play an American speaking French. I wanted to sound like a Frenchman speaking French. I gestured and made the faces the French do, pursing my lips during a pause and letting my mouth feel different than in English. I imagined my English-speaking self as someone else and put on a French persona through the ritual drinking of a glass or two of wine.

It helped immensely. My accent improved, I dreamed in French, and I stopped translating in my head, which is like trying to swim while holding on to the sides of the pool.

Learning a language requires a lot of memorization--another specialty of Hermes, thanks to his close friendship with Goddess Memory, *Mnemosyne,* who lives in the Underworld of images. Hermes is said to have a perfect memory, like a merchant who remembers what he paid for every last item.

Hermes Slayer of Argus, *Argeiphontes*

Argus was a hundred eyed giant who could stay awake constantly by letting only some of his eyes sleep at a time, a gift from Hera the Personal Self.

234

He is the too self-conscious self—a cross between Hermes' fast thinking mind and Hera's feeling that all eyes are upon her.

When Zeus tries to hide his lover, Io, by turning her into a cow—Hera's animal--Hera has her captured and sets Argus to watch over her. Zeus sends Hermes God of Schemes, *Dolios*, to get rid of Argus.

Hermes uses his charms--friendly conversation, music and a drink--to lull Argus to sleep and then smashes his head with a stone, earning the name Slayer of Argus, *Argeiphontes*. Hera remembers Argus for his service by putting his hundred eyes on the peacock, her very self-conscious bird that symbolizes living in the eyes of others.

Argus is the racing mind that keeps you up at night and the self-consciousness that distorts your instincts. The problem with being too self-conscious is that most things are best done unconsciously, like making love or looking before you cross the street. Being conscious about something is best when you need to make an adjustment and then do it unconsciously again, as in choreography. Keep going with Argus and you will be so manic you'll need to remind yourself to step right and left so you don't trip over your own feet.

The way to handle the self-conscious self is to see it as a separate person, as Argus, instead of identifying with it and feeling trapped by it. The stealth of Hermes can distract that racing mind by focusing it on something else, like changing the subject.

When I took a few dance classes, I was awkward and self-conscious, so the teacher advised me to give all my attention to the music and to what I was doing so there would be nothing left over to be self-conscious with, creating a distraction the way Hermes did with Argus. It did help me with not feeling so self-conscious, but I was still awkward, because the gods of dance weren't particularly fond of me.

Autolycus

Hermes' son, Autolycus, is the God of Thieves and Trickery.

He is hard-edged with his father's treachery but none of his charm and culture. Autolycus is what you get when Hermes denies Zeus

Hermes

and Apollo, who are Good Will and the Law personified, as well as Aphrodite, who is Charm.

Autolycus gives the ability to deceive without lying. You are like him when you mislead, mince words, answer partially, omit, or answer literally what is meant metaphorically. For instance, when asked, 'Do you know him', Autolycus answers, 'How could I know a man I haven't met?' which is a true statement even if he knows the man in question.

He is what happens to the bill that goes through Congress and comes out completely unrecognizable, as in 'Look what they've done to my song, ma'. He is the flatterer who wants to get something out of you, whether it's the aura of success, the use of your vacation house, or your connections. He knows how to make things unrecognizable like a plagiarist, a money launderer, or an affair.

You are like Autolycus when you evade responsibility, because he simply dons his hat and becomes invisible like so many embezzlers. On a smaller scale, he's the one who prompts you to leave the parking lot after you dent someone's car, to take an overly generous deduction for charitable donations, or to sample a few too many grapes at the grocery store.

Literary doubles include Moll Flanders, Butch Cassidy, and a host of literary and cinematic thieves and cowboys. Autolycus is a model of the independent life: amoral, on the edge and a bit seedy.

Fellow of the Night

Hermes is a friend of Night, *Nyx*, an ancient goddess whom the Greeks called a *Friend of All* and *Helper.* They prayed to Nyx to calm fear and terror-- which is very Greek since the Night is often the very thing feared.

The Friend of the Night makes you safe by making you invisible, because the killer in the woods is more likely to see you if you carry a flashlight. The Fellow of the Night makes you blend in with the night or with a nightclub full of strangers by making you act less innocent and sunny than daytime selves like Athena, Hera, or Apollo, who bask in the approval, admiration, and envy of others. His friends are the children of Night: Friendship, *Philotes,* and Deceit, *Apate,* because both look the same in the shadows.

Hermes brings you into a peculiar twilight mode, full of intrigue and mystery. You can know him in a glittering evening, the fascinating light of a cut gem, or a bold remark that catches you off guard, because it seems to fly in from the shadows.

He lurks in the sideways look, the backwards glance, and the reflection, like when a salesman mirrors your mood, you do a double take, or a motel owner gives you and your 'spouse' the fish eye. Hermes dwells in the sudden shift of position, the enigmatic smile, and the gesture that you spy out of the corner of your eye that tells you that someone is gesturing behind your back.

He can send you napping during the day to break from the waking self or keep you up and out at all hours. Hermes is the double life and the dark secret and the love of covering it and uncovering it. He is always ready to gossip but not everything he says is true.

The Spy of the Night, *Nyktes Epopoeter,* helps anyone who does business at night and the Good Look Out, *Euskopos,* can break into a house without a sound, help you walk down the street without being noticed, or slip out of a questionable situation without a trace.

Hermes Guide of Souls

Hermes the Guide of Souls, *Psychopompos,* is a courteous and understated young man who leads dying souls down to the Underworld, more like a handsome tour guide than a Grim Reaper. He is a friend of Hekate, the witch who lives in a cave on the edge of Hades, with whom he shares the grim humor of horrific situations like emergency rooms and battlefields.

The God Who Descends is the underworld guide who helps you easily fall asleep, get absorbed in a movie or novel, or daydream about a conversation. All it takes is a nod from Hermes or a touch of his magic wand, the caduceus, *kerykeion,* on the forehead and you forget what you're

Hermes

doing. He is said to tap on the forehead for a gentle death as well.
Archetypal psychologists like Thomas Moore now use magic wands in their
therapy to help people 'snap out of it'.

In ancient Greece, when a silence paused a dinner party that
a moment before was engaged in lively conversation, the Greeks said that
Hermes has entered the room. He is the last toast of the evening for good
dreams and a safe trip home. In some homes his image was placed facing
the bed to grant passage through the dream world without nightmares.

Hermes is one of Hades' few friends because he loves
images, which is what Hades is all about. He has a lyrical presence that
softens the world and makes death seem less frightening. He is the fairy
tale atmosphere of *The Odyssey* as opposed to the violent realism of *The
Iliad.*

In later times, Hermes became the god of alchemy and magic
arts. The old alchemists mixed one chemical with another to metaphorically
add a new persona to a psyche too dominated by one state. Their work
was psychological. You do the same when you feel you have been in one
mood long enough and need to do something completely unrelated in order
to refresh your mind. The god of change can help you then, perhaps first
with some magic like a cup of coffee or doing some exercise.

Maia

The Greeks called any wise old woman Maia like calling her
Auntie.

Maia lives in a cave in Arcadia, not in the palace on Olympus,
because she is a Titaness, a member of the race that precedes the gods
and is, therefore, a second-class citizen. The Modest Nymph doesn't hide
her poverty but she isn't proud either. She makes you not care about other
people's opinions, and to do so without a chip on your shoulder. Maia is
cool.

She just wants you to do your own thing for the fun of it. Maia
makes you happy to live on the fringe so long as you answer only to
yourself, not to others.

238

Homer mentions her *awesome hair*. She is a hippy and a true free spirit who is independent in a peaceful way, without having to rebel or to shock anyone.

Maia is Hermes' mother and also his friend. She gives him plenty of freedom growing up as a child--the opposite of Apollo's mother, Lordly Leto, whose son is a brilliant doctor. When Hermes steals Maia's clothes while she is taking a bath in the river, she tells him that his father, *Zeus, created him to be a headache* to everybody, but this is only play-acting because she loves the good-natured teasing.

It is said that Zeus' mind *found completion* in Maia because she and Hermes are all about enjoyment, as opposed to impressive gods like Athena and Apollo with their important duties and accomplishments. Zeus' affair with Maia is fun for both of them; she stands for enjoyment itself and the fun of life. You honor her when you do what pleases you without worrying about what everyone else thinks about you, yet in a peaceful and pleasant way, not as rebellion or rejection.

Moving On

Hermes doesn't like to stay in any one place too long or with any one mood.

He can get you caught up in always being in the next place, looking at your messages, and playing with your gadgets so much that you are never *here*. The god of superficial friendships on the Internet can leave you feeling lonely and empty. Like Artemis, his love of play can wear on the heart.

More sincere gods like Demeter the Family and Hera the Old Friend can fix this, because they get you to think about other people beside yourself. Loving people by remembering they are only human brings in Psyche with her depth and patience, which roots you in reality by reminding you that we are all mortal and life is not just a game. You are not Hermes. He is a god.

The God of Friends was the most popular god in Greece along with Hestia the Goddess of the Home. You can give Hermes a safe

239

Hermes

home base by keeping the house clean and stocked and staying in once in a while with Hestia the Homebody.

Or you can turn to Apollo and Zeus to keep Hermes within limits if you are becoming greedy or using people too much. They are the law and respect for other people and their property, and they will straighten you out quickly if you've gone too far with this god.

ARTEMIS

Artemis is a particularly complex and elusive god. Linguists cannot explain her name because Artemis cannot be reduced to a formula or an easy description. She embodies everything you cannot fully know or grasp, like instincts and skills. Artemis is whatever escapes you all the more, the more intensely you pursue it. She is anything that has its own being and can't be reduced to 'a part of me'. Artemis is a way of relating to the gods as elusive creatures, wild in their unpredictability.

Artemis the Hunter

The Greeks prayed to Artemis to *give us the skill of the hunter*, a skill that applies to a lot more than just hunting. Anthropologists see hunting as the basis of science, for it requires conjecturing about animal behaviors. You use the skill of the hunter when you hunt for bargains, for a career, or for a partner. Sometimes you need to look directly and at other times you have to wait to see what shows up. A rabbit might show up when you're looking for deer and a partner might show up who is kind but doesn't look like the one you envisioned. Artemis helps you spot opportunities and adjust plans to obtain the maximum of fun and freedom.

Goddess of Authentic Desires

When Artemis is born on Quail Island, *Ortygia*, she helps her mother, Leto, swim across the strait to Delos, fated to be Apollo's island. She is self-reliance as a person in the psyche, even in those who have little of it.

At three years old, Artemis sits on her father, Zeus', knee and tells him exactly what she wants: eternal virginity, as many names as Apollo, a bow and arrow like him, the job of bringing moonlight—Apollo has the sun--a practical outfit for hunting, sixty ocean nymphs, twenty mountain nymphs, all the mountaintops in the world and one city. Zeus is pleased at how specific Artemis's desires are, telling her that *if all my children were like you, I'd have no problems with Hera.*

241

Artemis

Artemis is authentic desire. She doesn't desire things of status and prestige intended to impress others like Hera. She doesn't really care what other people think, though she is beautiful and graceful. Artemis sees through pretense and has no time for Hera's worries about other people's opinions. She is authenticity and you know her through authentic desires and needs. Artemis knows what you really want and she wants you to go after it like a hunter.

Zeus grants her wish and throws in thirty cities to boot. Since she was born with such ease, he puts her in charge of childbirth and of all young things, human and animal, duties Artemis would not freely choose but to which she resigns herself as part of the deal. You're like Artemis when you can hold a job you don't really want in order to afford the life you really want. With Artemis, you're never confused about what you want and what you have to do, but she's a realist who let's you deal with situations without fooling yourself. Artemis is behind a lot of marriages where the money, the children, or the convenience glues it all together.

She picks a group of nine years olds to hunt and play with whose mothers are thrilled to see them go off with a goddess. Then she visits Hephaestus' factory to pick up her bow and arrows, boldly ordering the old Cyclops, Brontes, to stop working on a horse trough for his father, Poseidon, and offering to pay him with her first kill. When Old Brontes tries to get a little too cute with her she yanks a fistful of hair out of his chest and pushes him away, because Artemis doesn't want you to do anything you don't want to do unless it's necessary and she doesn't care if you hurt other people's feelings. She gladly leaves that loud and unpleasant place, because factories and parking lots are not her scene. The Goddess of Nature prefers wild surroundings, including places of repose within the city like cemeteries, small parks, and empty churches.

She then visits Pan who is cutting up an animal to feed to his dogs. He gives her ten hounds to fulfill Zeus' promise.

Artemis relates to others indirectly, especially through groups. She's the friend on the sales team, in the baseball league, or on the line dance. She dwells in friendships that are intimate but not personal.

242

Artemis Virgin

Virginity has a different meaning for each of the three virgin goddesses: Artemis, Athena and Hestia. Athena's virginity is the asexuality of the normal self or Ego, because you don't want to act overtly sexual in front of your neighbors and co-workers. Hestia's virginity is the sanctity of the Home, where you are loved for yourself and not for your money or sex appeal.

For Artemis 'virgin' means 'bachelor'. Her virginity denotes a self that stays single no matter how married you get. Artemis never wants you to be half of a couple or to act as if you're joined at the hip. She is the wisdom of not sharing your every thought with your spouse and the appeal of someone who still retains some mystery in marriage.

Her admirable self-possession has nothing to do with showing off or withholding. It's the real thing. Artemis lets you put aside worry and leave the office at the office. The Greeks prayed to her to *wipe away the wrinkles of worry.* They turned to her for a smooth face, unfazed by the concerns of life. When my mother died her face smoothed out remarkably as all the years of worry disappeared.

Artemis is the ability to concentrate by blocking out everything else so that you can read in a noisy train or meditate on a park bench. She is complete absorption in an activity. You are like her when you act unconsciously and naturally, especially when no one else is watching. Artemis' virginity is at heart the very privacy of experience. No matter how empathetic your friends are, they can never know your pain.

Artemis guards this privacy fiercely, because instincts do not like to be interrupted or spied on. When the hunter, Actaon, catches her bathing in a river she turns him into a stag that his own hounds tear apart. When Sipriotes sees her bathing she turns him into a woman. You feel Artemis' anger when someone interrupts your reading, wakes you up suddenly, or walks into the bathroom while you're on the toilet. That momentary desire to either flee or kill that person is Artemis reacting through you.

243

Artemis

Artemis and Hera

Artemis of Authentic Desires and Hera the Goddess of Society have issues. Your authentic desires may not really want you to go to that family cookout or to a friend's baby shower.

The Greeks called Artemis *the cure for boredom* because she leads you to new and fun things instead of things other people want you to do. She makes you incapable of sleeping with someone you aren't attracted to, even your spouse, unless there's something else in it for you like money and independence.

When you follow Artemis you may seem selfish and cut off from others from Hera's eyes. *The Goddess of the Yoke* of society, marriage, and responsibility doesn't prioritize your fun over everything else. Even when Artemis loves someone, it is because they have something in common, like a hobby, an attraction, or money and not because she wants you to be there in sickness and in health. She lives in friendships based on common circumstances like being on the same team or working in the same office. Artemis is the self that secretly knows you are not really going to keep in touch with your departing co-workers. Hera stands for bonds that last *forever*. And unlike Hera, Artemis doesn't need to be seen in prestigious places or made a fuss over.

At one point during the battle of the gods, Hera whacks Artemis on the nose with her slipper like a bad puppy, saying *take that Missy* and sending her back to Olympus in tears. To Hera, Artemis' emotional distance leaves a lot of hurt feelings in its wake. When you don't uphold social obligations, Hera sees you as a user or a snob.

Artemis has a cult following in men who are 'bears'--who dress down, avoid fragrances, and sport potbellies and facial hair—all to reject Hera's social restraints in favor of less formal connections.

Artemis Hagne

The glorious twin of Apollo matches his intellectual perfection with her physical perfection. Artemis *Hagne* or 'Pure and Holy' is the

244

purified, idealized version of *me* in perfect health and youthfulness. She is good health, beauty, and animal grace.

Like her brother Apollo, Artemis shoots arrows that can send or cure illness or cause sudden, painless death. She tries out her bow four times: twice on trees, once on a wild beast and last on a city of unjust men. Her gentle shafts swiftly punish anyone who insults her from afar, like people who abuse animals or who poison the environment, which is her abode.

Hagne is a particular kind of purity distinct from the spiritual purity of Apollo. Artemis Hagne is the physical purity of clean water, untouched snowfall, and youthful skin. She is unblemished health and the body's ability to cure itself with clean living, fresh air, clean water, and plenty of sleep. Her love of sports and outdoor activities brings youth and positive energy. Artemis' followers carry refillable water bottles and are very careful about what they eat, about getting too much sun, and so on. She is a goddess of teenagers with their cruel perfection, as depicted in many teen movies.

Artemis Hagne is your good health. Your relationship to your health is your relationship to Artemis. When you abuse your health by smoking cigarettes you offend the goddess. When you are friends, Artemis makes you want to jump out of bed in the morning and go 'play outside.' Artemis Hagne differs from Athena Health in that she personifies Health while Athena stands for hygiene and healthy habits.

Only Persephone the Queen of the Dead shares the title, *Hagne* or *Pure and Holy* because these gods see through pretense and know what really matters.

The ancient Greeks asked Artemis to *purify us from evil* like bad habits and laziness. She can help you confront addictions with a savage attack like dogs attacking a hunted animal. If Artemis gets you to quit smoking, she will make you hate all smokers in your vicinity—at least for a while--and even resent the smell of cigarettes on the street.
You can't fool her by running and eating yogurt while continuing to smoke. To her, that's like a friend who is nice except that he keeps poking you in

245

Artemis

the ribs in the middle of every sentence. Though her punishment is merciless, many Greeks prayed to sway it as in *Artemis, I have smoked, forgive me goddess.*

The Goddess Who Slays

Artemis' arrows, like her brother's, send illness, pain and death. The Greeks prayed to the Gods' Executioner for an easy death.

Artemis is the Mirror of Pain. She is your pain as if it was happening to someone else. *The Helper in pain whom no pain touches* is the self who observes your pain. She is the animal cry of childbirth.

Animals feel pain but they don't feel wronged by it like Hera the Personal Self who asks God, *why me?* Animals try to hide their pain so that other animals son't take advantage of them. We admire this quality in humans especially as they approach death because it reveals the dignity and courage of the goddess herself.

The Queen of Women and the Sovereign Goddess of Women is *a lion among them, killing as she pleases* through childbirth, women's diseases, and accidents. But to her followers, being singled out for death by Artemis is not a punishment. It is an election and an honor. Artemis kills the ones she loves the same way she picks her playmates to run off with her.

When my mother got lung cancer, we moved the birdfeeder close to the window so that the birds zoomed right towards her chair in the kitchen. We visited the pond down the street to feed the geese—as long as she was able--especially one goose with a big red spot which stood apart from the others.

My mother was already a friend of Artemis. She loved feeding the birds and spent many happy times golfing with her elderly girlfriends like Artemis and her team of playmates. She was able to put the Demeter Mom persona aside for a while without loving us any less.

Every so often, a deer came to the birdfeeder and emptied it by tilting it back with its snout. "I don't mind it eating all the bird food," she said, "I love seeing the deer."

One time as it scooped out the birdseed, the deer stopped and looked directly at mom, holding her gaze for a moment from a few feet away. We looked at each other afterwards but said nothing, and then I went to my room and wept out of sight, for I knew then that her death was near and that the goddess had chosen her as one of her own.

Artemis has a darkness that hearkens back to ancient human sacrifice. She is the god of martyrs for a cause and innocent victims of war, who are as tragic as the innocent hunted doe. Artemis kills the same animals she suckles, just as you love your pets but come home from the supermarket with a pound of 'meat'.

At her festival in Sparta, young boys tried to steal cheeses from the altar while their friends whipped them severely--sometimes killing them—just to show they were able to separate themselves from the physical pain. Mohawk tribes used to torture enemy warriors who would mock their tormentors and pretend they felt nothing. After their death they were honored as gods and protectors. Submitting to extreme pain is a form of Artemis. In her name, human sacrifice was symbolically re-enacted with goats dressed up in clothes and called *my daughter*.

Her most grisly ritual was at Patras, which began with a procession led by a virgin priestess on a chariot drawn by stags. The next day, the celebrants drove these same living animals into a bonfire along with wild boar, deer, wolf and bear cubs, and other adult animals, beating them back mercilessly when they tried to escape. Such is the cruelty of Artemis—and of nature, in which animals eat each other alive.

Artemis Grace

When Artemis has her fill of sports, she puts away her sneakers and gear and dons her most beautiful dress to dance on Olympus with the Muses and the Graces for the entertainment of the gods.

Artemis is a goddess of posture and grace. Her many cults include yoga, Pilates, Alexander, and Feldenkreis--teachings that seek health and illumination through posture. Limberness is freedom to Artemis

Artemis

because she likes moving around a lot. Sports promote good posture and agility, bringing the Artemis persona more fully into display.

Posture is where sports and good health meet society. People with excellent posture seem more intelligent and capable than people who slouch. Good posture is classy like Audrey Hepburn, Ingrid Berman, and Lauren Bacall.

But good posture takes work just like charm. It only looks easy and natural when it's done well. Animals move gracefully as part of their natural athleticism, but that doesn't mean they're not working at it. They just don't want others to know they are weak or vulnerable.

Artemis helps you display like a regal animal, ready to move in any direction. You perform a ritual gesture to her whenever you sit up or stand up straight, looking relaxed while you do because posture is a direct way of knowing Artemis. Just mention bad posture and watch how everyone around you reacts instinctively to defend himself.

Hippolytus

The son of Theseus, the king of Athens, was the original gym fanatic and friend of Artemis the Pure, for whom he built a small temple.

Hippolytus is perfectionism. He is the love of health and physical perfection that becomes yet another unhealthy obsession. He is the idea of food as only medicine instead of as also delicious and a way of sharing.

Hippolytus would have been fine pursuing physical perfection and devoting himself exclusively to Artemis. The gods don't mind if you love one of them more than another. The problem arose from his hostile attitude towards Aphrodite. Of the Goddess of Sex, he says, *I worship her, but from a long way off, for I am chaste* and swears to remain celibate forever.

Aphrodite might overlook this but she draws the line when Hippolytus refuses to even greet anyone who isn't in his league. Hippolytus pretends not even to see his physical inferiors, snubbing them without any pretense at politeness. This infuriates Aphrodite, who requires you to at

248

least be friendly to everyone and to mingle freely.

She makes Phaedra, his stepmother, fall in love with him when they go to the yearly festival up at Eleusis, where Hippolytus looks *admirably stern* in his white linen suit with flowers in his hair and a brooding expression on his face. Phaedra watches him exercise naked—as the Greeks did--from behind a small temple she dedicates to Peeping Aphrodite. Soon she is following him everywhere and refusing food and sleep.

Her nurse guesses the problem and tells her to write him a letter, a plan that backfires when Hippolytus burns the letter and rants against Phaedra, unaware that she is hiding behind a screen listening. Broken hearted, she hangs herself from a doorjamb, leaving behind a letter accusing him of rape. His father, Theseus, bereft and enraged, uses one of the three wishes granted him by his father, Poseidon, to kill Hippolytus.

While the young man rides his chariot along a narrow ledge of road by the sea, a giant wave sweeps a sea monster onto the road, making the chariot veer and the reins catch on an olive branch, smashing the car into a pile of rocks, throwing Hippolytus against a tree, and dragging him to his death. His soul becomes the constellation, Charioteer.

I see many men like Hippolytus at Chelsea Piers, one of the top gyms in New York City, who pretend not to see each other. One New Year's Day I ran into one of them at the water fountain. We were the only people in that giant space and yet he avoided my gaze, moving his eyes in every direction except towards me. I called him on it.

"I do not have to greet you," he said, offended that I addressed him.

"Yes, but you do have to see me".

I fondly recall the Rules of Safety posted at the YMCA in Attleboro, Massachusetts, a blue-collar city where I grew up. Rule Number One was to 'make eye contact with those around you'. That is sportsmanship, a lost art that respects Artemis and Hermes, gods of competition, and honors Aphrodite as well.

Hippolytus is anyone who thinks he or she is too good looking

Artemis

to be friendly with the 'likes of you'. Instead of being grateful to Aphrodite for his beauty, he holds it against everybody else. People naturally despise arrogance and therefore, so do the gods.

Anyone who has had an injury will tell you how easily the athletic self can desert you, even if you were an Olympic athlete. Christopher Reeve was Superman and then he wound up living in a tube. Hippolytus learned this when Artemis left his broken body lying on the road, saying to her, *Farewell to you, oh holy maiden. Go in peace. You can lightly leave a long companionship.*

Artemis and Hermes

Both gods sat on Zeus' knee as children and dazzled him with their precocity.

To them, life is a challenge and a game. They are gods of adventure: enthusiastic, with an innate trust in life and great ease in dealing with its ups and downs.

Both are opportunists. Hermes relies on his wits and Artemis uses her hunting skills to navigate the world. These two demonstrate a hard clarity that allows you to handle uncertainty, unlike gods who require guarantees like Herakles the Hero and Hera the Personal Self. Both make terrific salespeople because they are good at improvising, mix easily with others, and can live on straight commission. You know these two are around when you start hearing nicknames. Calling someone Skip or Chip instead of a real name keeps things intimate but not personal, because it is all about the game not the person.

In ancient times, Hermes was shown as a pillar of stone with a smile and an erection, imagined to be looking at the naked Artemis or Persephone like a groom on his wedding night. Hermes and Artemis see sex as sport and are good at keeping secrets. They could have you easily manage an affair. Hermes is the god behind the honeymooner's old joke about 'the elephant' a man makes when he pulls his pockets out of his pants and pulls out his penis while making a trumpeting noise.

The Greeks called Artemis and Hermes *the cure for boredom*

250

because they are gods of fun and freedom—since nothing is a pleasure if you have to do it all the time. You are like them when you welcome change, especially variety for its own sake.

This ancient Greek prayer to Artemis comes from the play, *Hippolytus*:

> *This is the lot in life I seek, and I pray that god may grant it me, luck and prosperity and a heart untroubled by anguish. And a mind that is neither false clipped coin nor too clear eyed in sincerity, that I may lightly change my ways of today when tomorrow comes, and so be happy all my life long.*

Atalanta

Exposed as an infant and raised by bears, Atalanta was a tomboy who refused to marry anyone who couldn't outrun her, and she would only give them the chance to do so on one condition: she gets to kill the losers.

Soon there was a small graveyard of would-be lovers but Atalanta's beauty kept them coming. One young man, Melanion, asked Aphrodite for help. He was exceedingly handsome, so Aphrodite gave him three golden apples to help fulfill his wishes. He tossed the golden apples in front of Atalanta as they raced alongside each other. She couldn't resist scooping them up one by one and lost the race. Atalanta willingly wed her victor and they lived happily for a while.

The trouble came when they forgot to thank Aphrodite and then had sex in Zeus' temple—a double offense. Aphrodite turned them into lions, which were believed to mate only with leopards, so she made them sexually incompatible.

Atalanta is the opportunist in love who is attracted to your qualities and strengths but has no time for human weaknesses. Melanion wins Atalanta because of his golden apples, his virtues but not his person. When love comes with conditions and you can only love a winner then the love is not human, because we are all subject to disease, bad luck, and failings.

Artemis

Atalanta is a mix of Artemis and Aphrodite. She is the beautiful and unattainable Lady of the Lake, the Lady of the Marsh, and La Belle Dame Sans Merci. She works in the personality to keep others at bay, like a woman who says she is too strong for men but never encourages them in their masculinity or a man who keeps a little black book and treats his dates like numbers, not people. She wants you to rule people out for whatever fault you can find, as if you were scoring a game. This kind of love fades fast when someone gets sick, gains weight, or loses his career.

Aphrodite sleeps with you because she wants you, not for the sake of your job or your golden apples. She wants charm and pleasure on both sides and only likes to go with someone when the feeling is mutual.

Orion

An old farmer who was a son of Poseidon once held a feast of freshly slaughtered bull for three of the gods: Poseidon, Hermes and Zeus. They were so pleased they promised him a son. Then they urinated on the dead bull's skin and told him to bury it for nine months.

That how's Orion—from *urion*, 'to urinate'-- was born.

Others say that Orion killed a man when he was young and sacrificed a bull to satisfy the gods and that they ordered him to drink their urine and cover himself in the bull skin. At any rate, he grew to gigantic size and became a mighty hunter, endowed with the qualities of all three gods.

Orion is big living. He is the desire to revel in hearty appetites and physical challenges. He wants you to chase pleasure, especially the physically demanding kinds. He's the guy who has a snowmobile, a watercraft, and a parasail in the garage, and probably works for himself so there's no boss to slow him down. Orion is the sports legend, the hedonist, and the mood that says *too much ain't enough*. He is your inner Falstaff. This sexy mix of arrogance, mania, and talent is around when you glut yourself on physicality like sports, food, and sex.

The Handsomest Man Alive has many adventures and a long

list of lovers who can't keep up with him. Among them was Eos, the Dawn, who snatches him up to be her lover because he can keep you up till dawn. To Orion everything is a game, including love. He sends his wife, *Side*, or Pomegranate, to the Underworld because she tried to compete in beauty and charm with Hera, which probably means that she clung to him as a wife and he killed her. This overly confident persona is a sadist, sexually and otherwise.

Artemis comes to know Orion through hunting and grows to love him, but not everyone is happy with this situation. Mother Earth is annoyed at their wildlife killing sprees. Apollo doesn't like his divine sister hanging out with a mere mortal, especially one who violates his mantra of *nothing in excess.* He challenges his sister by daring her to shoot at a *scoundrel* swimming off in the distance. Not realizing that *Candaon*, or Scoundrel, is one of Orion's nicknames, Artemis shoots and kills her lover. In grief she sets his image in the stars alongside his faithful dog, Sirius the Dog Star.

Orion's passionate high living can be bad for your health. It's no accident that he was killed in an accident.

Artemis the Savage

Artemis the Savage, *Agrotera,* is the wilderness as a person in your psyche. She is yelping dogs in the distance, long views, evergreen laurels hidden in the woods, and songbirds at dawn. She is the beauty of the wilderness, the light of the crescent moon, and the serenity of craggy scenes battered by winds and untouched by humankind.

The Goddess of the Woodland Clearing can appear as a deer, fox, bear, or any local wild animal, elusive and wary at the edge of the woods. You are with her when you spend a lot of time outside, especially in natural settings. The Queen of Serenity loves unfenced wilderness and makes you long to get away from civilization and run through the woods or to go any place *where no one can call your name.* She appears in uncanny instincts like the way you know that someone is looking at you in the car next to you at the stoplight. Artemis loves the dawn and dusk when the

253

Artemis

light is diffuse and the wildlife venture out.

Hers is a starlit beauty, fleeting and miraculous, a beauty that is longed for but never attained like the perfect work of art, the perfect body, or perfect happiness. Artemis dwells in uncharted gorges and forests and in the dark, crystalline wilderness battered by winds and half lit by the crescent moon where the calls of wild animals pierce the night. She is the danger of life in the elements and northern expanses of wilderness. She is mountain preserves that we set aside to honor her just as the Greeks did. Her virginity is the sanctity of our national parks.

She is not Mother Earth. The landscape of tilled fields, skating ponds, apple trees and pumpkin patches belongs to kindly Demeter, the Goddess of Food and Family, who lives on the farm eating unprocessed whole grain cereals and dropping her g's.

Artemis embodies a kind of twilight consciousness, crystal clear yet rooted in dark nature. She is in the way you must not think too much when you're doing a lay-up, playing the piano, or making love. She does not need your supervisory selves running everything and making you too self-conscious. Artemis' world is dangerous and exciting and it requires being wary like a hunter and ready to change plans on a moment's notice. She brings you calmly into the moment, making you quiet and observant and ever alert to the senses. She is the excitement and wariness you feel when you know there are bear or wild cats on the trail you're hiking. She is the thrill of walking in the woods at night, far from houses, far from your civilized life.

You can honor Artemis by simply disconnecting the phone, turning off your devices, and listening to the birds and the wind or talking to the people around you.

Artemis Friend of Children

While Apollo is in charge of teens and especially boys, Artemis is in charge of the very young, and especially of young girls. To her, children are animals that love pleasure and have to be taught how to play and what is proper to do in public. Like other small animals, they need

254

to run around outside, eat well, and get plenty of sleep. The goddess of babies, tomboys, and summers off wants you to be *like a boy* in strength and fitness, according to the old prayer. Artemis is for women's fitness and those who fight for it fight on her behalf.

The Greeks didn't have only one Inner Child like we do with our monotheism. They imagined numerous gods as children including Athena, Hermes, Zeus, Ares and others. Young Hermes is a lot of clever trouble, like when he hides his mother's clothes while she is bathing in the river like Dennis the Menace. Young Ares is kidnapped by the Titans, stripped of his leg sinews and closed up in a jar—a very different childhood experience. Young Athena accidentally kills her friend, Pallas, while playing with the javelin and makes amends to her friend as best she can. The baby Zeus shares a nurse with baby Pan, the satyr, so he is raised with a goat-boy as a brother and without prejudices. Apollo is the young genius.

Artemis Kourotrophos, the Nurturer of Boys, watches children like a concerned pet owner. Her bands of young women, the *Arktoi* or 'little female bears' are our Brownies, Girl Scouts and Camp Fire Girls. An old prayer declares that *She holds freedom's key while we learn its use.* Kourotrophos is the negotiated personal and sexual freedom of the growing child and early adolescent—and any negotiated access or freedom like being admitted to the inner circle at work after proving yourself.

Childhood used to be a dangerous time and it was quite an achievement in ancient times to live into old age. When Greek boys came of age, they would toss their hair cuttings into the local river and pray to Artemis Friend of Boys to *lead me straight into the season of old men,* free of disease or accident. Girls did the same when they were ready to settle down in thanks to the goddess for raising them wisely.

You honor Artemis Kourotrophos when you see childhood as a kind of animal rearing and help to protect the vulnerability and innocence of children. Artemis wants you to treat children and even your own instincts not as a mother but as an alpha dog, wise and protective. You can be with Artemis the Child at any age if you are young at heart or delight in protecting children. She demands you be open to change.

Artemis

Leto

Leto, the mother of Artemis and Apollo, has *lovely white ankles*. This gracious lady breaks the ice when Apollo arrives at the Olympian table like an intimidating superstar, helping everyone relax in his imposing presence. He may be perfect but even Apollo has a mother.

Leto is the parent of grown children.

She is no mothering Demeter. Leto relates to Apollo as an equal at the table. You might know her as the mother in high school whom all the kids love because she talks to them like an adult. Leto has children who are gods but she is fair-minded and considerate.

You don't have to be a mother to understand her. Your accomplishments in life can be your 'children', but you are like Leto when you don't identify with them and only hold them close like family.

One time, a mortal woman, Niobe, foolishly boasted that her children were better than Leto's, incurring her wrath. Apollo and Artemis dutifully killed her three sons and three daughters, probably through a series of freak accidents and illnesses. When they were done they turned Niobe into a stone, destined to weep forever. You are like Niobe when you live through your children—a dangerous idea to the Greeks because mortals can't be counted on and there's no guarantee that your children will grow up to be your friends.

The Mistress of Beasts

Artemis Mistress of Beasts, *Potnia Theron,* loves does, wolves, steer, boar, and fish—and all the wildlife in your area. She is fond of dogs as outdoor pets but not as pampered children. The other domesticated animal she likes is goats, which were sacrificed to her and called *the Maiden* or *My Daughter.*

The Goddess of Wild Animals presents an interiority that is personal but not human. Our brain retains the mammalian and reptilian brains so a lot of consciousness presents in forms that precede what we think of as our humanity. Animals in dreams are particularly significant and can be remembered as companions during the day if you want to befriend them and find out what they want or have to say.

Before Artemis, religion in the Mediterranean was dominated by Cybele, the Lady of Ephesus, an ancient Mother Goddess shown with animals clinging to her many hanging breasts. The festivals of the Mistress of Beasts featured dances with phalli and men wearing antlers. The animals in her groves were said to be tame like those in the Galapagos.

Our attitude towards animals is changing as brain research reveals their emotional life. Not long ago, it was debated whether they even felt pain, though some Christian groups still claim they do not. Now we know that animals are not animalistic only, not beastly only. Animals try very much to choose whom they mate with and are mostly peaceful and cooperative. They try to stay out of each other's way.

Not all instincts are murderous or selfish. Animals get a bad rap from people who act like animals--usually Dionysus and his *Girls Gone Wild* or Poseidon's frat brothers—but not Artemis. Life is tough enough for animals already. They display themselves with particular calls and behavior as if announcing their natures. You can hear human birdsong when you hear the voices of people talking in the distance just far enough away that you can't make out the words.

Like any wild animal, Artemis has a cruel and unpredictable side. She can make you enjoy competition with an animal's killing instinct that makes everything a game until someone gets hurt. Those cubs frolicking in the documentary are practicing hunting after all.

Goddess of the Crescent Moon

In ancient artwork, Artemis drives around in a chariot pulled by stags and lit by pine torches cut from trees struck by lightning. She wears a tunic and carries a bow and arrows and may sport a diadem with the crescent moon. The Goddess of the Moon, like the Roman Diana, is especially the crescent and half-moons that give just enough light to make things visible, more or less. This light brings out wildlife that do not dare venture out in broad daylight—and the wilder, less civilized parts of the

257

Artemis

psyche which you only glimpse fleetingly or during the wee hours of the night.

Artemis personifies the dim corners of awareness that lie beyond consciousness. She is your secret life, the kind of double of yourself who can do things naturally and easily.

She is instinct personified. Artemis Goddess of the Moon helps you relate to instincts that you cannot understand or know directly, because your instincts do not want Athena the Conscious Mind to spy on them, by definition.

Artemis is there when you do something perfectly the first time—singing, throwing a ball, or having sex--but then you can't replicate the performance because the wrong self takes credit for it. Her keen eyes are splendid with starlight and her glance is the half moon and the uncanny moonlit woods at night. She is whatever you cannot know directly, and you honor her when you don't interrupt your actions by thinking too much at the same time.

She is often the indirect cause of things, the thing you will look back on later and say, 'it all started after we saw that dead deer on the side of the road', or 'he just wasn't the same after he sold that house'. She is the explanation for seemingly random events. Artemis starts and ends things but she is seldom involved in the middle of things. That is part of her purity.

When Agamemnon hunts a stag in her grove, Artemis holds back the winds from the Greek navy heading to Troy and it takes them a long time to figure out what is going on. When he readies to sacrifice his daughter on board. Artemis snatches her up at the last moment and substitutes a deer. Who would have connected the dead winds with an offense against Artemis?

When I was hitchhiking across France, I told a fellow student how much fun I was having and he did the same thing, but he was killed in a car accident. I didn't kill him but I was the indirect cause of his death. I was Artemis to him.

She is there when you bring the wrong set of keys, leave your wallet in the other jacket, or leave the phone off the hook when you're expecting an important call--especially when there are consequences. Looking back, a part of you knew all along what you were doing and just wanted to see what would happen—an indirect action of Artemis.

Artemis and Hekate

Artemis and Hekate the Goddess of Witches are shown together as friends in Greek artwork, sometimes alongside Demeter and her daughter, Persephone, the Queen of the Underworld. A combination goddess Artemis Hekate personifies their mystery. Both stood as pillars at crossroads with three heads facing in different directions, signaling the different paths that life takes or different selves acting independently. They are gods of portals and gates, because Artemis stands for freedom and change while Hekate stands for being under a spell like a compulsion.

Artemis Hekate is a god of automatic action. She presents life as a kind of whammy. *Hekate* means *Distant*. She is the feeling that you are watching someone else in the midst of your experience and that every mood is a kind of spell or whammy over you. She makes life feel like a movie in slow motion, like the strangely elongated moments during a car accident. This self seems detached, observing events with fascination even while Hera the Personal Self panics and Athena the Normal Self looks for a way out. You can glimpse Artemis Hekate if you imagine looking back at your life now from twenty years in the future, as though you were looking at an old photograph of someone else.

In honor of Artemis, men wore grotesque masks of old women in ritual, as distant an image as possible from their actual appearance, perhaps to signify the selves that cannot be known. You can experience the mysterious power of masks just by putting one on and letting yourself go. That will give you a glimpse of Artemis Hekate.

Moving On

You identify with Artemis when you take your health for granted or when your health becomes an obsession. She is there when

259

Artemis

you feel threatened by impurity, whether it's drinking water or disease, or look down on those who are not perfect or fit. You can befriend Artemis by encouraging others in sports and exercise, spreading her cult. You can show thanks to Artemis for your good health by taking care of it and feeling lucky to have it.

You know you've gone too far with her when the fun and play start to feel selfish and lonely and you are leaving a trail of hurt feelings in your wake. Then you can follow Artemis' example to escape her isolation by getting dressed up and joining society, just as she occasionally dons her elegant dress and dances for the gods. The myth shows you a way out of the god, an escape hatch from her solitary nature.

Sociable gods like Aphrodite and Hermes provide a friendlier attitude towards others. Aphrodite wants you to get close to someone while Hermes likes the excitement of crowds and of the city. Demeter the Family Self can give you the sense of being loved unconditionally and not for your brilliance, your body, or your superiority.

Or turn to Artemis' father, Zeus, by doing something to make the world a better place, especially anything to do with conservation like volunteering at the animal adoption center or picking up beer cans by the roadside. That way you honor her nature while acting in unselfish ways to improve the world.

The best way to imitate Artemis and to limit her at the same time is to be open to change, because she is a self who likes uncertainty like a hunter or a deer, and who is liable to change direction without any notice.

PART SIX: GODS OF INSIGHT

All of the gods provide images to understand experience, but some gods show how to relate to images themselves.

Apollo gives you the ability to see through the surface of things to the person or image lurking behind them. The god of *know thyself* wants you to see through motivations and styles to discover the god hiding there—the self who possesses you at the moment. To be like Apollo is to know what you are doing.

Hephaestus is the god of skills, which are the ability to immerse in working material, whether it's an oil painting, computer programming, or welding. Hephaestus adds interiority to work like the active ingredient in a medication. He is any skill as if it had a mind of its own, which is the very nature of skills.

Hades personifies images and the imagination, including the dream world with its many actors. That's why he's both a person and a place. He constitutes a third of your life, not counting his invisible presence during your waking life. Hades also includes culture, the repository of images left to the world by people who are largely dead.

261

APOLLO

Apollo is the quintessential Greek god: lofty, superior, and beautiful. In the words of Guthrie, the English classicist, "He is the very embodiment of the Hellenic spirit. Everything that marks off the Greek outlook from that of other peoples, and in particular from the barbarians who surrounded them—beauty of every sort, whether of art, music, poetry or youth, sanity and moderation—all are summed up in Apollo."

Apollo is the higher self of New Age religion, including the affinity for music and healing.

He is the intellect, the spirit, and the true self—the one you come into contact with during the meditation at the end of yoga class. He is law, music, and medicine, and the ability to understand things by rising above them and seeing the bigger picture. You know him through comprehension.

His most famous motto is *metron ariston,* or 'nothing in excess'. Apollo wants you to reflect on what you are doing and to live a conscious life in which emotions and impulses are kept under control. *Metron ariston* also translates as *excellence in measure,* meaning that everything has its proper proportion. A similar motto, *sophresyne,* describes excellence in character.

Apollo's other famous saying is, *Gnothi seauton,* or 'know thyself'. Apollo brings the awareness of which self has you in its grips while remembering that you are only human—the opposite of identifying with a god and blindly acting out. His piercing intellect sees through situations to the god hiding behind them. Apollo's oracle at Delphi was consulted for all manner of advice from how to succeed in business to how to cure a disease. Mostly, his function is to see *through,* as Hillman terms it, to whichever god is informing your actions, especially any god you may have offended or ignored.

His encounters with the proud and mighty symbolize the vulnerability and weakness of human beings before the gods. Anyone who thinks he is above others is fair game for this god, who relishes cutting the proud down to size, whether through some accident, illness, failure, or through the inevitable humility of old age.

Apollo the Glorious

Apollo cannot be imagined making an appearance without demonstrating his superiority, even grandiosity. You may meet him at school as a brilliant student, at work as the star performer, or at the gym as the most perfect physique, either through yourself or through some other lucky person.

Apollo the Glorious is more admired than liked. He makes you need to stand out from the group as more brilliant, more talented, more beautiful, or wealthier than others. Apollo is a star, a prince, and a mother's boy accustomed to privilege and entitlement, and he's around whenever you feel that way. His name shows his singularity: *A*, 'against', and *polu*, 'the many'. Apollo is the sense of being an individual and authentic, rather than contradictory or part of a group. When you spend a lot of time with him you seem aloof and superior, because Apollo is a loner who rejects others as inferiors.

To him, *men's lives are like the leaves on the trees, growing full in summer then falling in winter*, to be followed by another generation in the spring. Apollo epitomizes the chasm between humans and the gods, because he fully identifies with consciousness and life and never suffers illness or old age. He can make you think you are above human existence and not like the masses, especially while you have youth and intellect at your disposal.

That is what makes him so dangerous. Apollo is tough on those who identify with him and cuts down anyone who takes the gifts of the gods for granted. It is one thing to befriend a god and quite another to try to take his place. Apollo makes fools of the proud and mighty and humiliates fair-haired individuals who take their advantages for granted.

When his mother, Leto, gets pregnant by Zeus, jealous Hera forbids all the cities and islands to let her deliver on their soil. Finally, the poor, floating island of Delos is coaxed with the promise of a temple and

263

Apollo

vast wealth, along with reassurances that its mighty son won't take one look at it and kick it into the ocean—because Apollo makes you dismiss things and people once you find any faults with them and has sadistic tendencies.

In the *Voyage of the Argosy*, the sailors notice a handsome, blond man with beautiful eyes walking along the shore. Rather than rushing down to get his autograph, they avoid looking directly into his eyes and sail on quietly, celebrating that evening farther down the coast—because Apollo is the intimidating side of perfection and genius and not the kind to reassure you or meet you on an equal footing.

Statues show an ideal male form, nicely muscled, perfectly proportioned, youthful and supple. Usually he stands or walks with a bow or lyre while exuding virile strength and sublime clarity. The Golden One has a noble brow and a handsome beardless face with flowing blond hair. His wide eyes command a look of superiority. His mouth is relaxed with a touch of melancholy or a slight smile as he gazes off in the distance, lost in some brilliant thought.

In Greek literature, Apollo's voice is said to carry across the room *with the majesty of thunder.* We all know that big, gay theater voice with its devastating sarcasm. The God of the Sun is the living embodiment of intellectual and physical superiority.

The Far Shooter

Apollo the Far Shooter, *Ekeboulos* is the archer, but his talents go far beyond shooting arrows. He is your ability to think long term and to aim at goals.

Apollo gives you the big picture, not the immediate picture. He wants you to contemplate the world from great heights and mountaintops—literal or intellectual—and he lives in moments when you see everything and understand. His temple at Delphi looks down from a cleft in the mountains across a valley and to the sea. Apollo is the detached and objective point of view. He is comprehension.

Apollo is in charge when thinking rules feeling and tomorrow takes priority over today. Apollo can make you feel that your life lies always in the future and never in the present. He can make you think you are so brilliant that the talent agent should find you and not the other way around.

Apollo gives the impulse to work indirectly and away from the action, because he prefers doling out advice through oracles, dreams, and signs—and not direct instructions. To him, it's not worth getting involved. He is not a good prospect as a date or partner, because he will tell you to move on at the first hint of trouble or complications. His first impulse is for you to avoid involvement and entanglement and to be true to yourself. When things get uncomfortable, he wants you to leave the room rather than get bogged down in a relationship, an argument, or the gory details.

He is New Age spirituality that aims to maintain the peace rather than confront things and work with the mess at hand. I remember a dinner party in California where everyone left after the hosts exchanged a few hostile words, something that wouldn't faze anybody in New York City, where Ares' hostility is a normal part of life.

Apollo Phanes

Apollo and Eros are *Phanes*, or White Light, but they are not identical. The light of Eros is Love which shines in the darkness without illuminating it, because when you love someone, you don't try to change her.

In contrast, the white light of Apollo is the brilliant light of the Sun. The *brightness which shines among men* makes life sweet for a time in perfect moments when everything flows and life is a giant work of art with a layer of glass over everything.

Apollo Phanes is the truth. The Revealer seems so true that everything else seems like an illusion, which is how people get trapped in spirituality and forsake other adaptive behaviors.

When my mother was dying of brain cancer, she lost this sense of authenticity. She was convinced she was living in an imitation of her house and that I was a double of myself. 'Go get Michael', she'd say, and there was no convincing her otherwise.

Apollo

The problem with the true self is that it is not the only self. It is just the one that feels *true*. That is its nature and function, just as Zeus is the King of the Gods but he is not mightier than all of them together. You cannot swim, drive, or go shopping as the true self, and there's no money in contemplation.

Apollo wants you to choose only the best parts of life and not to bother with the rest. He can convince you that you have an exclusive hold on the truth, because he is the only god who can read the mind of Zeus. His New Age followers claim to create their own reality and even take credit for their own good luck and health so that, like Apollo, they owe nothing to others.

In Greek minds, that is no way for mere mortals to talk. Creating reality is Apollo's fantasy, because living as the True Self all the time is no life for mere humans who sicken and die and need each other to get along.

Phoebus Apollo

Phoebus means 'holy, pure, and shining light'. It derives from *Phos* or 'light' and *bios* or 'life'.

Apollo is unencumbered, luminous, and penetrating divinity. He is the Genius within, imagined as an independent person. Ideas well up seemingly out of nowhere. Understanding just happens and cannot be forced. Answers surface after other, more brilliant selves have worked on it for days below the surface.

Phoebus Apollo is brilliance imagined as a young man. You call upon him when you dial up your intelligence before an important exam or meeting. *You* don't have to be brilliant. Let Apollo be brilliant for you. Just by imagining him you raise the level of your thinking, like people who 'act smart'.

Apollo *Mousagetes* is the Leader of the Muses and his stamp is the Classical style. Apollonic art *imitates all mankind* and his sons are the luminaries of any age—the likes of Mozart, Einstein, Picasso, and Balanchine, who are more than mere artisans. The degree to which his clarity and purity are present in a work of art determines its universality. When Apollonic art depicts war and suffering it creates a kind of aesthetic separation from experience--aesthetics as anesthetic. Sometimes this takes time; we weren't ready for a movie about 9/11 until years after the event.

The French identify with Glorious Apollo as the God of the Enlightenment, the Sun King, and the Dolphin—all various incarnations of the god. He is the reason the French are such self-conscious perfectionists and why they sit in cafes with chairs pointed at the street commenting on passers-by. Naturally, they are most drawn to people who seem most un-self-conscious, because Apollo is always longing for some nymph or perfect young man whom he can lift up and mold into his own image. He has no time for posers and phonies.

Delphinus

Apollo announced his purpose: *I will reveal to mankind the exact will of Zeus.* And then he set out to recruit followers.

He took on the form of a dolphin and flopped onto a Cretan merchant ship, which began to steer itself towards Delphi following a star that shone by day and night. On the docks at port, Apollo appeared as a beautiful young man with long hair and wide shoulders, asking the sailors, *Who are you men and what are you doing with your lives?* He told them that he was a god and that they would be wealthy if they chose to serve him at Delphi.

Delphinus is meaningful work. Human beings have an inborn need for meaning and purpose in life. We need to feel a connection to something bigger than ourselves. You can hear Apollo's voice in the bull sessions of college sophomores trying to steer a course in life and in your own voice when you wonder how to best spend your short time on earth.

Apollo warned the sailors against becoming arrogant: *Guard this in your hearts and avoid idle words, carelessness, incidence,*

267

Apollo

arrogance, or else other men will become your masters. The men danced all day and night on the ship without getting tired, like a big gay party. They gladly obeyed the god and set up his oracle at Delphi, the navel of the world.

Oracle of Delphi

Apollo does not decide events. He only predicts and interprets what Zeus decides, because thinking cannot determine Reality—which is Zeus--it can only change how you understand it, which can seem to alter reality without actually doing so. Seeing life as a set of relationships with the gods instead of as a lonely tale of one changes your perception of reality, but *you* are multiple already, like a traveling band of players.

Apollo's other most famous command is *gnothi seauton,* which translates as *know thyself* or *self-knowledge.* Individuals consulted the oracle to figure out which gods were affecting their lives, whether helpful or harmful, so that they could adjust their actions. He is self-knowledge as a companion in your life. You are like Apollo when you have a clear image of whatever god is acting through you so that you can contemplate an experience in the very midst of it. He is transparency, and to know him is to know what you are doing.

Apollo *Loxias,* the Oblique One, is the counselor who changes your perspective rather than telling you what to do. He is the meaning of events and symptoms, because even the slightest muscle tension comes from somewhere. After all, when you have tension, just who is gripping whom? Obviously, some other person in the psyche is trying to get your attention. Apollo identifies the gods hiding behind an experience so that you can relate to them more directly.

The Greeks went to the Oracle for advice on everything from disease to marriage to business decisions. Apollo's temples, like Zeus', offered every kind of fortune telling. The supplicant might be told to drink a potion or perform a ritual to get in the proper mood before sleeping in the temple and telling his dreams to the priest in the morning, a process called incubation that is akin to modern dream interpretation. The supplicant might ponder a cryptic message from the Oracle or be told to record the very first words he hears at the market upon leaving the temple for interpretation later.

When the question was psychological—like how to deal with a neurosis—the Oracle would try to find out which god was angry with the supplicant. This must have involved a lot of intuition, like when you want to tell someone who looks like she spends all her time at the library to get to the gym or out on the town once in a while. Apollo would cleanse people of their neuroses or crimes by having them perform some community service—a good cure for any problem that springs from too much self-involvement.

Asklepios

Apollo's arrows are *like flying snakes* that bring or cure illness or accidents.

The doctor's office is his holy precinct with its special furniture, rituals and costumes, and the doctor is his priest. Apollo the Helper, *Epikourios,* is the nurse, the health aid, and the pharmacist.

His son and double, Asklepios, is the God of Doctors. Asklepios personifies the entire medical experience: the diagnosis, the doctors, the drugs, and the recuperation. Once you become a patient, you acquire an additional self or identity as a votary of Asklepius. Your doctor, in turn, is only human, a fact that some doctors can forget because Apollo invites identification more than other gods do. The doctor holds the office of the god, a fact driven home by a diagnosis. Your doctor will probably play a major role in the drama of your death.

Asklepius was such a good doctor that he raised Hippolytus from the dead, but Zeus struck him with a thunderbolt for thereby violating the Fates. The Greeks lived in Reality, which is Zeus himself.

They prayed to various gods for good health, for there are many kinds of healing. Poseidon *Iatros,* the Healer, is hydrotherapy, Jacuzzis, and hot springs. He is the wellbeing that comes from pleasurable

Apollo

physical sensation. Chiron the wise centaur is alternative medicine. He is the retailer selling herbs and supplements at the vitamin store. Artemis the Athlete heals through exercise, hydration, and physical therapy, especially postural therapies like Feldenkreis and Alexander technique. Dionysus is healing passion, and Eros is the love that heals and massage.

Athena Hygiene takes care of sanitary conditions and prevention, because many deadly infections are acquired at the hospital. You can maximize your chances of survival by calling on many gods at the same time when you are sick. But any god can be called upon for any reason, and it was common to call upon one's favorite god or local hero for all manner of favors, including good health.

Apollo and Zeus

Zeus is Civilization, Order, and the World. He is Reality as person in your life. Zeus stands for human dignity and its pillars like private property and the right to justice. He is the facts, including the ones you don't know yet.

Apollo is science and law, disciplines which seek to understand and frame reality and order. You feel his power when the real world puts boundaries on your behavior, like having to show up for work in the morning or to obey the speed limit.

Together Zeus and Apollo create prudence. Apollo's *nothing in excess* works in the personality to limit other gods who want you to act spontaneously and to break limits, like Dionysus of Intoxication, Ares of Fighting Rage, and Poseidon of Emotions.

Apollo is the voice in your head that tells you the brutal truth. The god of self-knowledge would rather you go to an AA meeting, a shrink, or a doctor than mindlessly act out some love affair, addiction, or passing anger, because his priority is for you to know what you are doing and to *remember that you are not a god*—another of his famous maxims.

Apollo sees through arrogant selves like Hera and Herakles, who tell you 'it's all about me' despite the billions of other humans living on the planet. When Herakles shows up sick and bloodstained at Delphi

270

seeking purification, Apollo refuses to cleanse him because he knows he isn't sorry for a violent murder; he's just pretending for the sake of purification. Herakles then steals the holy tripod and rapes the priestess, proving his point. Thereafter, the priestess was an old hag.

Apollo's intellect sees Herakles' take-action approach to everything as simple minded and literalistic. To him, Herakles never tries to understand what it is doing and doesn't realize his impact on others. Apollo is the voice within, urging you to be cautious and not to follow Herakles into unremediated action.

Apollo is caution and prevention in all endeavors. You follow him when you fix problems before you have them. He is the Averter of Mischief.

Apollo Smintheus is the protector from mice—and from the slow erosion of your savings and your health from unwise practices. He is the Protector of Corn, the Averter of Grasshoppers, and the Protector from Hail. These days, the Protector of Private and Public Places, *Agyieus,* is the alarm system in your home and the cameras monitoring the streets. Apollo *Nomios* is a shepherd's god who wards off evil the way you avoid everyday disasters all the time: by complying with your medical regime, avoiding a dangerous driver, or washing fruit before you eat it. His foresight shepherds your life and keeps you from wandering from sanity and safety.

Apollo Karneios, wears ram's horns, ancient symbols of prosperity and strength. He guards your prosperity through insurance, paying down your mortgage, and paying your bills on time. He builds evergreen wealth, taking only dividends and not the principle and investing the maximum in a matching savings plan. He is a master at a mathematical medium like money and you honor him by doing the numbers.

It's easy to identify with Apollo when you get lucky in the real estate or stock markets, when everyone thinks he's a genius. Apollo is a constant corrector of those who mistake their good fortune for proof that they are smarter than everyone else and like him, standing on top of the world.

271

Apollo

Admetus

By killing the Cyclops in revenge for Zeus' killing his son Asklepios, who dared to raise a dead man back to life, Apollo made it possible that one day a rival could obtain a greater weapon than Zeus' thunderbolt, the Cyclops' invention. For this crime Zeus sentenced him to nine years of slavery to the kindly King Admetus, a double of the god.

This was no tragic or humiliating experience for Apollo, as it was for Herakles. The lordly Apollo is adept at serving because he lets you rise above circumstances. He can even help you admire your boss, unlike Herakles, who sees the boss as only a rival and enemy. Admetus quickly recognized Apollo's talent and knew he was no ordinary guest because his herds started to increase as soon as he showed up. Some say they were lovers.

He is the loyal employee. To Apollo, having a job is better than no job because for him, the worst thing is to owe money or to run into the law. He wants you to respect and care for the person or the company you work for out of honor and principles.

Admetus lets you play the company man and to do so sincerely. He naturally respects authority and welcomes guidance from superiors because he believes in superiors. Apollo wants you to root for the boss and for the company's success instead of being resentful like Herakles, who is jealous of other people's success.

You are like him when you *don't overlook the happiness of the poor man* or of the slacker who slips through life unnoticed. Apollo knows that the common peasant can be happier than a CEO if he can rise intellectually and spiritually above his lot and be true to himself. He encourages you to see your job as a necessity while you float above it and your real life resides in some other area like art, intellect, or spirituality.

To him, any job is an educational experience and a part of a long-term plan, even if it has nothing to do with your goals. When you can rise above things like Apollo, you can be somewhere else when you're at work and let the time fly by. Although he is superiority itself, Apollo can be known by submission to superiority, because you can know a god when you play his role in someone's life or when someone plays his role in yours.

Aristaeus

Aristaeus, or *The Best of All* was called A Second Zeus. He is the guy who is good at everything, like your hero in high school.

He is Excellence personified. He gives you a way to obtain Excellence without identifying with it and thereby provoking the *envy of the gods*, meaning 'other people'.

Aristaeus invented bee keeping, cheese, the oil press, and animal traps—improving the world and thereby pleasing Zeus, who is the World. He is the pillar of the community who knows when to make the right sacrifices, like enforcing a water ban during a drought or paying down municipal debt during years of surplus.

You honor him when you can have success without identifying with it. Success and Excellence are gifts from the gods, whether they arise from genetic gifts, good choices, or proper motivation. You can have all of those things and still fail, because success and Excellence are ultimately *for the gods to decide*.

Some people let their heads swell because of fame and become victims of their own personas. Donald Trump is a bully with his success. In contrast, I remember seeing Ella Fitzgerald at a dinner theater where she spoke between sets as mildly as if she was just 'ordinary folks'. I felt I could ask her over for dinner, but once she began to sing it was clear that she was a friend of some god and no ordinary woman.

Aristaeus lets your success take on a life of its own without interference or a need to own it, because the Greeks did not believe that you can have your cake and eat it, too. Instead, you can have cake but the cake is still on loan from the gods.

Apollo and Hera

These are gods of superiority. Apollo makes you think you're smarter or more spiritual than everyone else while Hera makes you think

273

Apollo

you're special just for being *you*. Remember: the wife of Zeus is the self who's married to God.

They are gods of exclusiveness. They make you think you're irreplaceable or that the world might as well end when you die. They are the reason that 40% of Americans believe that we are in the End Times—because that's how special their lives are.

They are gods of class snobs: Hera through social position and Apollo through intellectual superiority. Apollo's snubs occur through *not-seeing* other people, which was a separate word in ancient Greek distinct from the negative construction, *not seeing*. When you *not-see*, you deliberately pretend not to see someone--on the sidewalk, at a party, or at the gym. There are people at my gym who have *not-seen* me for years.

These two make you overlook the 'little people' who make life run smoothly, like the dry cleaner whom you don't recognize on the sidewalk because he's out of context, or the dog walker you forget to pay on time even though it's a big deal to her.

Personifying your feelings of importance helps give it back to the gods where they belong. Hera is the aristocrat and Apollo is the brilliant genius. Humans are only Psyche the Mortal. The rest is owed to the gods and can be taken back by them at any time.

Of course, if you find you are arrogant you can cure it quickly by turning Apollo's critical gaze upon yourself. His cruel honesty knows all your faults, like the fact that you're getting older by the minute just like all those inferiors in 'the great unwashed'.

Apollo and Eros

In matters of Love and Eros, Apollo is a state of longing.

You are with him when you fall in love with the idea of a person or a thing rather than with the actual person or thing with all its faults and complications.

Apollo can make you think you've found 'The One' the same way he can convince you that all you have to do is go down to Wall Street and you'll make a million dollars. He sees so far into the future that he can

274

make you forget that there are steps along the way. But then he makes you back off as soon as you see that the very possibility you seek may require commitment or involvement.

It all started when he sneered at Eros' power, calling the God of Love a lowly god. In revenge, the Eros shot an arrow right into his leaden heart, filling him with longing and obsession.

The first victim was Daphne. Eros shot arrows of love into Apollo and arrows of disgust into Daphne, which only deepened after Apollo murdered her lover before making his move. Daphne fled, calling out to Zeus and Artemis who turned her into a laurel tree. Apollo grasped the tree tenderly and cut a few sprays to make a wreath for his lovely head.

When Apollo is involved in your love affair, you reach for perfection. Daphne is an idea--a laurel wreath—and not a person. She is a trophy to prove his worth.

To Cassandra he gave the gift of prophecy, but when she still wouldn't love him he made sure that no one would believe her. He loved Sibyl so much he granted her one wish. Eagerly, she grasped a handful of sand and wished to live as many years as there were grains in her hand, but she forgot to ask for eternal youth as well, so she wound up a shriveled old grasshopper kept in a jar, like someone long forgotten in a nursing home staring straight ahead.

'What do you want, Sibyl?' the children ask in a Greek nursery rhyme. *'I want to die,'* she answers.

To Apollo, sex and love are just one more chance to prove how exceptional you are. His busy brain cuts you off from the other person and makes you need to be adored so much that he sabotages the whole enterprise. You're like him when you bring a script with you to bed and when breaking that script breaks the mood entirely. After all, it's not easy to be endearing when you feel superior to others. For Apollo, love is about the high, so it's always best at the beginning before you realize the other person has faults. Once the beloved shows the slightest imperfection the attraction fizzles, because Apollo's perfectionism can only lead to disappointment.

Apollo

What he seeks in love is spiritual purification. He wants you to rise above life by aiming upwards in love and refusing your inferiors—and to get a kick out of refusing them, too. Apollo gives you the crush that makes it difficult to take action or to make a real connection because the other person is no longer human.

Marpessa rejects him wisely, realizing that he can never be happy with a mere mortal. She marries the human, Idas, and they live happily ever after. You act like her when you see past the projection to the mortal human or real situation and stop kidding yourself.

I projected perfection onto a guy at the gym who seemed too beautiful for words. I stared at him awkwardly and felt extremely self-conscious, even though he was friendly and seemed genuinely interested for a while. Every time I saw him I stammered out the same few words, so taken aback was I by his looks. Eventually I came across as a stalker and he started acting like Apollo, glorying in his perfection. "I know, 'you look amazing'," he flung back act me in scorn before I could say the words.

Longing gets a bad rap these days but it beats constantly acting out, which is another kind of slavery. Anticipation combines the two, when longing has an end date. That way you can satisfy Eros and Apollo at the same time.

Alternatively, when you see someone or something that is your ideal of perfection, you befriend Apollo by enjoying the obsession and doing nothing about it, so that you are left with the longing and not its object, like Apollo holding the wreath.

Hyacinth

Apollo hates all weakness and tells his followers to *keep the woman under rule*--meaning all vulnerability and emotions. He is male exclusivity, whether in sports or in banking—and in either men or women, so long as the concern is about keeping feelings at bay.

One time, Apollo falls in love with Hyacinth, a handsome young prince from Sparta, and teaches him liberal arts and athletics, molding him in his own image. You can see these two in mentor/student relationships or in couples who mirror each other by dressing and acting the same, often without realizing it.

One day when they are out practicing the discus, Zephyrus the West Wind—out of sheer jealousy--knocks Apollo's discus into Hyacinth's head and kills him. Where his blood spills, a flower grows bearing his name.

Hyacinth is the perfectionist, a shadow of the Superior Self—and the one who's always worried. He is beautiful and a prince but he is no match for Apollo who is a god and likely to dump him at the first sign of weakness.

You are like Apollo in this relationship when you want someone for the perfection of his looks, fame, or talent--but not for himself. Apollo makes you want someone who makes you look good.

You are like Hyacinth when you feel inferior for no good reason and constantly need approval. You can also be like Hyacinth to your own high standards if your standards are Apollo in the equation. You can share Hyacinth's experience in feelings of inferiority and insecurity.

Hyacinth is an Underworld god with his own cult of gloomy sacrifices. He has a twin sister, Polyboia, for his feelings apply to both sexes. Hyacinth is always associated with the flower but he is not a god of vegetation.

He is Another Dionysus, paired with Apollo as Nietzsche described them: the individual against the powers of nature and instinct. Like Dionysus, the inferiority of Hyacinth allows you to access fantasies, dreams, and your body in a way that Apollo never can, because vulnerability creates openness and receptivity. The ability to see flaws helps in many endeavors.

Of course, you might know Hyacinth just by getting older and seeing your fantasy of perfection slip away. You can sense him when you don't identify with the young people anymore or when you realize that your success in life might be a lot smaller than you hoped—the accomplishment of a human and not of a god.

Apollo

Kyparrisus

Apollo loves Kyparissus—one of his many doubles as a young man--and gives him a pet stag that he dresses in wreaths and rides like a pony through the forest.

One hot afternoon while out hunting, Kyparrisus spots a wild animal in the woods and shoots it with his arrow, only to discover that he has killed his beloved pet. His heart broken, he begs the gods to take his own life as well, but Apollo turns him into the mournful cypress tree that bears his name.

Kyparrisus personifies the love of a pet.

Animals live in fantasy experience like the gods because they do not question their own nature. They act upon their instincts and are not divorced from their images the way humans are.

You are Kyparissus when a pet becomes the love of your life. Your pet's shorter lifespan usually ensures that you will go through what he did when your pet ultimately dies, at least momentarily. You are Apollo to your loving dog or cat because you control their lives, produce the food, and know how to switch the lights on and off like the God of the Sun. As Apollo, you outlive your pets and they, in turn, need your constant approval and reassurance.

Kyparrisus shows there's a place in your soul for a pet who means everything to you--and that's nothing to be ashamed about because no less than Apollo sanctions this love.

Marsyas

Marsyas, the satyr, was a talented musician who dared to challenge Apollo the God of Music to a contest, with the winner naming the stakes. While Marsyas played the pipes beautifully, Apollo played and sang while drinking ambrosia at the same time, easily winning.

All smiles and friendly, Apollo tied Marsyas to a stake and slowly skinned him alive with a razor, ignoring his desperate screams. Every so often he'd interrupt this torture to fetch his new wreath and asked

278

Marsyas if he should wear it this way or that, posing coquettishly while Marsyas wept in pain.

Marsyas is the suffering artist who strives for the perfection of Apollo in art or in any field of pursuit. He can make even the greatest craftsman doubt his own abilities. Michelangelo died thinking himself a failure because he left so many unfinished works.

Marsyas was popular in the Renaissance, which saw him as the Artist shedding his skin like a snake and creating images released from the soul. Marsyas is the psychology of first novels, in which writers write their way out of their personal history so they can write about other things.

Lykios

Some say that Apollo's mother, Leto, was a wolf when she gave birth to him. Others say Apollo can turn into a wolf or that he hunts wolves. At any rate, wolves are sacred to him and sacrificed at the temple of Apollo *Lykios,* the Wolf, in the market at Argos.

They are not sacrificed in the countryside, however, because this self is not really concerned with animals. Apollo Lykios wants you to be a wolf among people—to act with cunning intelligence and a cold heart. He is greed personified.

Greed is Hermes' profit motive turned against others, prospering at their expense, like a stockbroker who churns accounts or a friend who only wants you for your pool or your connections. You are like him when you have selfish friendships, which are friendships nonetheless.

Hermes once remarks that Apollo's sheepdogs *think like people.* Lykios is the wolf on Wall Street, the Lehman shark and the young Turk in the bond pit--hungry for green pastures and devouring other people's sheep in order to become the next shepherds. The goal of the broker is to become the client.

Wolf Apollo is Warrior Apollo, a cruel and calculating god of blitzkrieg and drones for whom war is a video game to be conducted from afar and without passion. He is the predatory corporation acting like a wolf and destroying the competition's sheep through any and all means. His

279

Apollo

cruelty is born of his superiority, because when you think you're better than others you don't feel the need to treat them with any consideration. He is a god of ambition who doesn't let anything stand in his way, like auditioning on the casting couch or tailoring your persona to get in with the right crowd—like a wolf in sheep's clothing.

Orpheus

The son of Apollo and Calliope, the muse of epic poetry, invents writing but is most famous for his music, which can settle quarrels, calm wild beasts, and even move rocks and trees.

Famous Orpheus is the spiritual artist. He makes you care about art with the passion of Dionysus. He weds Hephaestus' art with Apollo's universal ideals. He is Art with a capital A—like a movement that changes the world: Cubism, Surrealism, or Serial music. Orpheus is a Dionysian revolutionary who stands for the power of Art and its controversies, including its *enfants terribles*.

He has many adventures but is most remembered for going down to Hades to fetch his wife, Eurydice, who dies after stepping on a poisonous snake. His music charms the begging shades that crowd around him and even sways Persephone to let Eurydice leave the Underworld, provided he not look back at her until she walks into the daylight behind him.

Once he reaches the upper world however, he turns in joy to his beloved, only to see her slip away forever, for she has not yet come out of the shadows of the cave.

The backward glance becomes familiar with age. Orpheus longs for what is lost and rues the day. Eurydice can be the dream you never pursued or the novel you never wrote, which disappear into the realm of images. Or she can be the work of art that fails to live up to the artist's ideals and is never fully realized. Turning back towards the Underworld also happens when you access the Unconscious through art and dreams or find deep or hidden meaning in art like Orpheus.

The Greek Gods Among Us

Once he loses Eurydice, Orpheus becomes militantly gay and starts preaching homosexuality as a religion, which leads the men to abandon their wives. Dionysus makes the wives insane—perhaps by getting them very drunk—and they tear Orpheus to pieces with their bare hands.

One of them throws his head into the river, where it sings as it floats along for days without putrefying until it is rescued it and placed on a pedestal, where it continues to tell oracles. This can be any writer or artist who is long dead but who still speaks to the soul. Resenting the competition to his own oracle, Apollo sends a plague that can only be cured by burying the head and erecting a temple of Dionysus on the site, which was then declared off limits to women out of deference to Orpheus.

Orphic cults began quite early in Greece and continued into the Hellenistic Age through Neo-Platonism. Orphism considers the body the prison of the soul and has rules for food, sex, and clothing meant to purge the *ancient woe* of physical existence—a very Apollonic view of human life. Today, Orpheus' cult continues in diet crazes that promise to transform you by burning off the mortal fat and leaving behind only the immortal celebrity, the *fabulous you.*

Orphic priests sold cheap magic spells to bind people. Nowadays they sell aromatherapy and essential oils that promise purification.

You are like Orpheus when you have an artistic message or point of view. He is the artist as revolutionary. However, unless you let the work take on its own life and allow the Muse to lead you where she will, you are like Orpheus looking back at Eurydice. Michelangelo claimed that he didn't sculpt, only that he removed the parts of the marble that didn't belong to the statue.

This is a personified way of thinking. The Greeks personified the work of art as a Muse and a person in its own right who tells you what to do--and not the other way around.

Moving On

281

Apollo

You break the identification with Apollo by noticing brilliance wherever it occurs, especially in others. You honor the god when you remember that your 'own' brilliance is on loan from him, because Alzheimer's or a brain injury can quickly put an end to that friendship.

You know you have gone too far with Apollo when you immerse in the intellect, spirituality, or art so much that you seem out of touch with the world. Unchecked by kinder gods, Apollo makes you hard and removed from life. The antidote is to turn to those feminine virtues he tries so hard to suppress.

When he intimidates the gods at the dinner table his mother, Leto, breaks the ice by getting his chair and speaking softly to him. Leto is a variation of Demeter the Family Self and a welcome change from Apollo: it turns out that even the genius has a mother. Some warm, family time can bring you back down to earth, because your family doesn't care how perfect you are.

Hermes is one of Apollo's few friends. He can lighten things up by getting you to laugh at yourself. Or he can inspire you to sway others with charm instead of intimidating intellect, adding his magical *peitho* or persuasion. Hermes wants your artistic ideals to go out in the world and make some money.

Dionysus is Apollo's true opposite. Doing something as if you were possessed balances out Apollo's calm and quiet peace. Dionysus replaced Apollo in Delphi every summer, like college towns with summer theaters. You can tune into him with a few drinks or by going to the edge in any activity.

Ares' courage can get you involved and up close with someone or something. His physicality cures intellectual removal. You can please both gods by exercising with close attention to form.

Hephaestus the Artist can help you put Apollo's lofty ideas into an artistic medium, creating art instead of theorizing about it. It's easy to set Apollo aside if you remember that the true self and the spirit will be there, waiting for you when you come back to them.

The Greek Gods Among Us

HEPHAESTUS

Hera bore Hephaestus by herself as revenge on Zeus for bearing glorious Athena without her help.

The God of Skill projects the interiority of Hera into an artistic medium, creating artistic individuality. Hephaestus personifies the skill of the artist, the tradesman, or the computer programmer. He is the ability to project psyche into working material like the active ingredient in a medication.

There is an art to plumbing, to baking, and to customer service. Hephaestus is not limited to the fine arts. He is the second nature of any skill that you learn until it becomes second nature to you.

Born with his feet on backwards, Hephaestus is the unnaturalness of any artist. He is the inadequacy that lives in each of us and which causes even great artists to struggle with self-doubt and questions of identity.

Work matters most. Hephaestus is 'disabled' because your normal self is disabled when you immerse in work--creating something, turning out a product or service, or donning a persona. He stands in stark contrast to his brother, Ares the Jock, who is a natural at everything but is never an artist.

You can see Hephaestus in the way that a carpenter handles a hammer, an accountant types on an adding machine, or an artist paints with a brush. He is the secret to *Arete* or Excellence in work, whether it's in art or in mechanics, because a skill that takes on a life of its own shows that a god is guiding your work.

God of Craft, Skill and Art

Hephaestus the Artisan can work in any medium so long as it is close and absorbing work. When you practice a skill, the world recedes to the size of the cubicle, the sculpture, or the screen in front of you, like Hephaestus passing the hours alone in his underground forge. Even ballet dancers live in their own narrow world apart, like Hephaestus at work.

284

The Greek Gods Among Us

The Greeks didn't make the distinction between art and craft that we do. Their concept of art was not as grandiose as ours, because ours is tainted with the specialness of Hera the Personal Self and Jesus as the exceptional person chosen by God. Yet if you ask an Italian about Michelangelo, he will not say 'he was a genius of the ages'; he will say that 'he was a most excellent sculptor'.

This is true of all personal qualities. Where we describe 'possession' of a skill, the Greek say only that the person 'knows' that skill. Rather than some glorified idea of the artist, Hephaestus personifies the very process of art. At his forge he is the fire itself as a transforming agent. His crippled legs are its wavering flames and his laughter is the crackling wood. When the Greek cooked meat, he *held it over Hephaestus.* When you are absorbed in close work like programming or painting, your brain acts like fire, permeating the medium and transforming it through your acquired skill.

Hephaistos *Techne,* is Skill and Technique. A highly skilled person seems to work spontaneously and inevitably at the same time, like the late doodles of Matisse. Hephaestus is a way of knowing the world intimately but impersonally. He is the very quality in art that makes it ingenious, marvelous, and complex. He is the inner working of craft, whether in a novel or a factory. He is the beauty of industrial landscapes with their smokestacks and highways. He likes you to be alone in the office early in the morning and late at night when no one can interrupt you. *Without Hephaestus, men would still live in caves,* according to the Greek proverb. Because of him, *life is easy the whole year long.* Thanks to Hephaistos we have heat and running water, the Internet, and apples in July--gifts from the gods that our ancestors could never have imagined.

Hephaestus brings excellence in any field and the personal wealth that comes with it, because his skill is unmatched. The best way to know him is to improve your skill in your specialty, but you can also visit his mindset along with Hestia the Homebody just by tinkering around the house and the yard, because small projects absorb you in their own details.

285

Hades

When you imagine your skill as belonging to someone else, it can take on its own life. That's why a pianist is a different person when she's performing than when she's picking out her clothes in the morning. It's also why that same pianist must not stop and think about what she's doing or how her fingers are moving. The artistic self is distinct from one's personal life, and great art can be produced by someone who's unhappy or suffering or downright nasty—because the personal life has nothing to do with the artistic life. This is the opposite of our conception of art as self expression.

Hephaestus is a friend you can honor with practice and dedication. His broad shoulders can handle anything.

The Crippled God

When Hera saw the crippled baby she bore after Zeus brought forth glorious Athena, she pushed it off Olympus in shame. Hephaestus fell spinning for an entire day before landing in the sea, his legs hopelessly broken. Artwork shows him hobbling around with golden crutches or with his feet on backwards.

The disabled self feels inferior to others in more than just physical ways. Hephaestus is the only Olympian god who isn't perfect, because his perfection is in his skill not in his person. He is your inner monologue about why you just aren't good enough, which is useful when it separates you from your work so you can improve it. Geniuses have been shown in studies to be people who are just never satisfied with 'good enough'. Work narrows you because it focuses the brain on a specific task while the rest of the body and personality is 'disabled' or turned off. Hephaestus can't walk, but look what else he can do.

He doesn't even try to compete in the normal world of men like his backslapping brother, Ares the God of War, his polar opposite. Gregarious and handsome, Ares thrives in physicality and has no skills but fighting, dancing and lovemaking. He seems to have it easy in life. He even sleeps with Hephaestus' wife, Aphrodite.

286

The Greek Gods Among Us

Happiness for 'the Artist' is hard to attain because artists want more out of life than physical pleasures. If you have an actual physical disability, you can counter it by cultivating some skill and putting everything you've got into it. Better yet, you can imagine it as Hephaestus instead of identifying with it all the time, which frees up your imagination to be other people as well. As the Greeks said, *you do not have only one fate.*

The Laughter of the Gods

Hephaestus brings on the fabled *laughter of the gods* when he scurries around on his backwards feet, busily serving them nectar and urging his parents to get along. He makes a fool of himself like any artist who takes risks. When the gods laugh at him like cruel teenagers, he laughs right along with them.

He is the clown, because going out on a limb risks the derision of others. Hephaestus has a deep interiority that knows that you lose no advantage by laughing at yourself, especially if it makes others feel comfortable around you. In fact, it is charming when someone talented is also humble and human. Laughing at yourself makes you open to new things, because learning a new skill requires looking foolish at first. Hephaestus differs from Hermes the Comic because he acts in earnest and not ironically.

I met a dance instructor in Paris whose tango studio was faltering because the French don't like to make fools of themselves in public. They are possessed by Apollo the Perfect and mock each other mercilessly. She told me that the typical Frenchman would show up for class after a few private lessons, whereas Americans, who had no Sun King and are not obsessed with Apollo's superiority, eagerly put themselves out there, as in cruise ship entertainment.

Hephaestus only cares about his art, not other people's opinions. He is a peacekeeper who puts the world of competition in perspective. When Zeus and Hera bicker at dinner, he urges them to calm down. *Let's not all fight over mere mortals,* he says, handing Hera a golden cup and telling her to speak sweetly to Zeus. The golden cup is Art, which

Hades

is a salve and a sweet drink to help Hera's personal self submit to Reality, which is Zeus, by putting life in perspective and seeing its beauty.

Hephaistus and Aphrodite

Hephaestus can't believe his luck when Aphrodite agrees to marry him, because the Goddess of Beauty doesn't have to settle for someone who looks like him. He builds her a fabulous palace and lavishes her with jewelry and marvelous gifts of his own creation, including a golden girdle embroidered with love spells that makes its wearer irresistible.

Most importantly to their marriage, he lets her come and go as she pleases. These two are the model of being alone with someone, with each pursuing his own interests.

Hephaestus is as deep as Aphrodite is shallow. He turns everyone and everything into symbols while she dwells in beauty that is skin deep. Aphrodite is his Muse and inspiration. Theirs is the marriage of Beauty and Craft that distinguishes great art. The marriage is never consummated because Aphrodite is an ideal to Hephaestus, not a physical person as she is for Ares, with whom she has a longstanding affair.

Hephaestus is the idealizer who sees things symbolically.

His emotional reactions are always a bit off, for he isn't wired like the rest of us. Small gestures matter a lot to him—probably too much. Hephaestus can convince you that you have a relationship with someone with whom you exchanged a few words years ago or who nods at you every now and then. He makes you read too much into things, as artists tend to do, for their task is to instill rich patterns into their medium. Hephaestus goes so deeply into his art that he can make you feel outside of life and lost in your own little world, like when you absorb yourself in a project and emerge to the world of daylight as if you were just waking up. He turns his mother's ability to substitute one thing for another, like Haagen Dazs for sex, into the ability to sublimate restless energy into work and skill.

When Helios the Sun, who sees everything from his position in the sky, tells Hephaestus about the affair between Aphrodite and Ares, he pretends to go out of town and she quickly sends for her lover.

288

Hephaestus snares them *in flagrante delicto* under an invisible net as fine as a cobweb and as strong as steel. Then he calls upon all the gods and goddesses to witness his betrayal, demanding a divorce and his dowry back.

Poseidon, playing the kindly uncle, offers to pay the dowry and marry Aphrodite to restore her honor--the old letch—but in the end nothing changes and Hephaestus looks foolish once again. He loves Aphrodite too much to ever leave her, and without her ideal of beauty, he wouldn't be much of an artist.

Hephaestus and Hera

Hera disowns Hephaestus when she sees his deformity and throws him off of Olympus' heights. Many artists go through Hephaestus' fall from Olympus into the existential abyss of identity crises and separation from reality.

Hephaestus the Artist is born from Hera's personal self by projecting that self into a medium. These two must be distinct for the sake of both the art and the person. Many who would be artists are simply acting out Hera's need to feel special—which makes the art take a back seat to their egos. Hera can only see art as self-expression—as proof of her exceptionality—a Modernist view of art that privileges the artist and is not necessary to all art. Michelangelo did not only express himself when he painted the Sistine Chapel.

Hephaestus soon begins making jewelry for Thetis and Eurynome, the kind sea goddesses who take him in and raise him as one of their own. When Hera gets a peek at some of the marvelous work she asks after its maker, and when Thetis hesitates she forces it out of her. Hera summons Hephaestus to Olympus at once, makes a great fuss over him, and sets him up in a fabulous workshop with twenty bellows working day and night. But she still won't admit she is his mother because of his looks.

The first thing he creates for this new benefactor is a gorgeous throne encrusted with jewels, but when Hera sits upon it, ready to be envied and admired, invisible chains tie her to the chair as it lifts ten feet off the ground. She demands Hephaestus release her, and then she begs him, and all the gods join in: *Free your mother.*

I have no mother, he answers and goes back to his adopted family in the sea.

Ares tries to convince him to come back but is blasted away by the heat of his furnace, because force seldom works on artists. Dionysus eventually wins the day by getting him drunk on wine and hauling him back to Olympus on the back of an ass, an allusion to the addictions which commonly plague artists. This is an iconic image in Greek mythology showing the artist making an ass of himself.

Hephaestus agrees to release Hera on one condition: she must find him a wife. When she chooses Aphrodite, he delightedly sets her free.

Hera the Queen is not really interested in artists, who are often poor, unpredictable, or embarrassing creatures, because originality requires doing something no one has done before and which has not yet been socially accepted. Hera would prefer you to know the artists who are famous already so you can share in their prestige like any namedropper. That's why most people with high status would choose other professions besides the arts for their children, but love to have artists around their decor.

Hera makes you think that knowing fabulous people makes you fabulous, too. After all, she is who she is only because she is married to Zeus. You are like Thetis when you recognize talent before everyone else does—because it's easy and safe to admire the Rembrandt in the museum.

Hephaestus and Athena

Both Hephaistus the Craftsman and Athena the Normal Self are *polymetis*, 'of many counsels', like Zeus. They entertain many points of view and multiple angles before deciding what to do.

The Greek Gods Among Us

One time, Athena asks Hephaestus to make a new set of arms for the war at Troy and he gladly agrees, saying coyly that he would do it for love. Poseidon had convinced him that Athena wanted him to make violent love to her—because the emotional self likes to convince the artistic self that success is just around the corner.

When she arrives at the workshop, Hephaestus chases her and spills his semen on her clothing. Athena wipes it away in disgust with a bit of wool and lets it fall on the ground, which impregnates Mother Earth, who is now angry at them both.

Athena loves the arts as an educated spectator but she is no artist, because the rational self is not crazy enough to be an artist. The Waking Goddess wants you to love art but not to risk a life of poverty or to act self-absorbed. Athena would rather you recognize artists by fitting them into a tradition or movement and helping us understand their significance. The Goddess of Culture is the reason you don't esteem a photograph the way you do a Leonardo.

Prometheus

Prometheus is from the race of Titans, the giants who preceded the gods. His name means Forethought and his brother, *Epimetheus*, is Afterthought.

Once humans were fashioned out of clay along with the other animals, the two brothers were assigned to hand out gifts. They did so very eagerly so that by the time they came to mankind, Epimetheus has already given all the useful gifts to the animals, like excellent hearing, sight and smell, so there was nothing left to save people from utter helplessness.

To save mankind, Prometheus stole fire from Olympus and began the march of technology. This infuriated Zeus, who had his henchmen Strength, *Kratos* and Force, *Bias* chain him to a mountaintop, where an eagle ate his liver every day and it grew back every night to prolong the torment.

Eventually, Herakles freed Prometheus, because the hero can serve the social good in revolutions or heroic legislation. Prometheus

291

Hades

makes peace with Zeus and warns him not to marry Thetis, whose son will replace his father.

Prometheus is the crusader, whether an artist or a political leader, who works for social progress. One of the few gods to ever help mankind, he is a cross between Athena, Hephaestus, and Herakles.

Nations honor him with national projects like passing infrastructure and jobs bills. The hero of the working class wears the iron neck ring of the slave to remember his suffering at the hands of Zeus— because you are not truly free when you are bound to work or to a cause.

Prometheus mixes Athena's Good Citizen and Hephaistus' know-how. Like his father Zeus and Zeus' father, Kronos, he is *ankylometis:* sneaky, cunning and good at ambushes, like coming out with a revolutionary product or a disruptor technology that changes the entire economic landscape.

Pandora

Hephaestus' distant relation is the crafted persona. Pandora is the personality you create deliberately like a work of art by cultivating an accent, embellishing your personal history, or putting on airs. Some celebrities wear hats, giant glasses, or moustaches to create their brand.

Prometheus makes Pandora, the first woman, out of clay. *Pandora* means 'All Gifts' or 'All Giving' because each of the gods gives her some talent or quality. Aphrodite gives her charm but also guile, Hermes gives her lies and treachery, and Athena gives her life and clothing.

Pandora is Zeus' revenge on mankind for obtaining fire against his will. He sends the fully loaded Pandora to *Epimetheus.* His brother, *Prometheus,* warns him not to accept any gifts from Zeus but Pandora's charms prove too great to resist. She brings with her a lovely box that she opens, loosing all the evils upon the world including death, illness and injury.

Only *Elpis,* Expectation or Hope, remains beneath the lid. Hope is a virtue that the Greeks, with their tragic view of life, held at an

292

ambivalent distance. Hope keeps people from committing suicide so they can go on with their suffering, the way Prometheus suffers under Zeus.

Cultivating a persona was as common in the Renaissance as it is in Hollywood today. Greatness of character was worked on like a piece of art. An artificial persona serves social climbers and entertainers and can be a boon if you are not naturally charming or sociable. By working on various virtues, you are like the gods giving Pandora her various gifts. In the Greek and Renaissance views, 'cultivated' doesn't mean 'phony'. It means 'cultured'.

My mother assumed an artificial persona while she was dying, pretending to be hopeful and calling the wheelchair her motorcycle to spare us her pain.

Helpers

Hephaestus has a set of golden female robots in his workshop that can think, talk and work without cease like an automated factory. He also has golden stools that move on their legs and a variety of gnomes who work magic in their specialties.

They are productivity personified as one-dimensional automatons. Work focuses you into narrowly defined functions, because throwing yourself completely into a task requires repressing or at least setting aside other selves. The automatons show how impersonal work is and the gnomes show how the job shapes you, like the customer service rep with a crooked neck from bracing the phone on his shoulder or the executive with a heart problem.

When you work, you are a stunted version of yourself with no sensuality or personal intimacy. You honor the workplace by remembering how little you actually know the people who work with you.

Not all workers are happy and sweet. The Fingers, *Daktyloi* are magicians who cast spells and counter spells, like lawyers pointing fingers at each other. The Telchines are evil gnomes who jealously guard their secrets like the AMA, the CPA and any profession eager to keep others out.

293

Hades

Pygmalion

Pygmalion, or 'Dwarf', carved an ivory statue of Aphrodite and fell in love with it. He ate with it, slept with it, and prayed for it to come to life. Aphrodite granted his lover's wish and Pygmalion married the statue woman come to life.

Pygmalion is the love of work. He is married to his job. Work is the Muse to this self—an inspiration and the thing that keeps it going. As my father used to tell me, 'when you love your job, life is easy'.

Daedalus

Daedalus, or Cunning Worker, is a double of Hephaestus as the patron of inventors. He created the famous labyrinth for King Minos of Crete. His type lives in the cloistered world of scientists, designers and highly technical professions. You are like him when you take courses, apprentice, or read the trade magazines, even if your business is hair design.

He is technique and technology. If you don't think technology is a god, just consider how many times a day you check your messages.

One day, Poseidon sent a white bull to King Minos to sacrifice to him, but Minos kept the beautiful creature for himself. In revenge, Poseidon made the King's wife, Pasiphae, lust after the bull—a lust that Daedelus satisfied by building a wooden contraption to allow her to have intercourse with it. Pasiphae bore the hideous Minotaur, a monster that is half man and half bull and eats human flesh.

When Daedelus completed the labyrinth, Minos shut him and his son, Icarus, in to keep his wife's secret safe, but Daedelus escaped with wings of feather and wax. Icarus got carried away with the thrill of flying and ignored his father's warnings about flying too close to the sun. His wings melted and he plunged to his death in the sea that bears his name. Icarus is anyone who can't handle success yet, like so many rock stars.

Minos then became obsessed with finding and punishing Daedelus. He traveled all over Greece until he came to King Cocalus, whom he suspected of harboring him. He gave the king a spiral seashell and challenged him to thread it. Daedelus ingeniously tied a thread to an ant and put a drop of honey at the end. Minos found his man.

Cocalus promised to surrender Daedelus after Minos takes a nice bath. His daughters then mercilessly plunged him into boiling water and scalded him to death. You feel the same pain psychologically when revenge boils your blood.

Later in life, Daedelus became so envious of his brilliant nephew, Perdix, that he pushed him off a tower. The gods turned him into a partridge, which nests low--far from any towers. This is professional jealousy, which you can see when a new technology displaces an old one or some new genius comes along, supplanting the old one.

Moving On

You identify with Hephaestus when you think you're a great artist, competing not to be like him but to take his place. Those feelings belong to the god, not to you, and you put them in perspective when you appreciate great art and recognize the talent of others—or get a medium and work at it until Hephaestus is satisfied.

When I was an undergrad at Williams, I was so serious and obsessed with being a writer that one of my professors took me aside and told me, 'you don't have to be a writer all the time'. She was trying to do me a favor, because humans are subject to all of the gods and I missed out on my social life by being so grave all the time.

The soul needs oxygen and doesn't want anyone to be any one thing all the time. Stepping away from a project or from your usual activity for a while lets the other selves go to work while you do something else, like taking a nap while you're studying for a test. Think of it as letting Hephaestus work on it while you pay attention to someone else.

Hermes is a good break from Hephaestus, because he likes being around other people. Hephaestus' brother, Ares, offers a stark

Hades

contrast because he's so natural, so you can try him on for size by going to the gym and sweating instead of staying at work like a shut in.

Aphrodite's sensuality gets you out of work mode, but something as simple as cleaning the house like Hestia the Homebody can absorb you in simpler tasks that don't require so much concentration.

Going out is a challenge for this introverted type, so you may have to design your persona beforehand and decide how you are going to act. This can be fun. I used to enjoy pretending to be French in a crowd. You can put on a created personality like Pandora—who can be any of the gods—and wear it until it takes on a life of its own.

HADES

Hades is both a god and a place. He is not the Devil and his abode is not Hell. On the contrary, the Greeks imagined him as a quiet, kindly, and wise god, if a bit grim.

The Greeks had no word for evil, only for *crimes*. They never split the world into Good and Evil. Instead, they talked about *the Beautiful* and *the Ugly*--the Beautiful most closely resembling the gods in nature and quality, including human talents and traits. The Greeks found a place for all impulses and sensibilities and idealized them to make them beautiful through the gods.

Hades is the brother of Zeus and Poseidon and the realm he was allocated includes the Dream World, the Imagination, and Memory. He is the realm of images.

He is a deep and mysterious god. There is nothing like death to bring depth to your outlook and imagination to give perspective to your life. Hades is the god to turn to if you are shallow or caught in a superficial life and need some depth and understanding.

The Invisible One

Hades is a strange god.

He is absence. Hades is the Self Who Is Nobody.

You are like him when you feel as though you are invisible, like a shadow, or don't know who you are—not in the sense of confusion or amnesia but in the little daily moments of non-recognition when suddenly you realize you are driving on an errand or staring at the wall and you don't know how you got there, what you're looking at, or even what you are. He is the negative capability described by Keats. His void and his depth is your ability to see yourself as an image, granting this image its own spontaneous life while you simply disappear like Joyce's dramatic artist.

Artwork shows a bearded man like Zeus but with his face averted or left completely blank. Hades is a borderline autistic self who comes across as deeply out of touch and can make everyone around him

297

Hades

feel rejected or misunderstood like Hamlet brooding around the castle. You can see Hades behind the total dead pan, which is much more disturbing than a relaxed face. This face disturbs and casts a pall on feelings and relationships like Bill Murray in *Broken Flowers*.

Hades means 'Hidden' or 'You Hide Us'. The Invisible One wears a helmet of invisibility and is more concerned with your dream life and unknown experience than with your conscious daily reality. When you are close to him, he can bring so much absence and self-doubt that it becomes hard to act normal and you have to put deliberate thought into how you dress, speak, and act in front of others. Nothing comes naturally to him because Hades is foreign to natural consciousness.

The Greeks called him the Gate Fastener and the Hateful One because they viewed death as final. Despite their several cults of immortality, the Greeks focused on reality and the present life and held out few hopes for an afterlife. Hades has many names, including the name of anyone who is dead.

The Mighty Corrector of Mortals records every image and memory of your life, including all crimes and lies, including the lies you tell yourself. He is stern but never cruel or vengeful. He doesn't seek to punish or to tempt like the monotheist Satan. Hades is grim and inevitable but mild in character. Mostly he stays in his Underworld and only hears what is happening on earth from the newly arriving dead and whenever people strike the ground and curse.

Death

Hades' double, Death, or *Thanatos*, is more despicable. He has a heart of bronze and is *hateful to men and to the gods* yet even he is not one-dimensional. Homer shows him and his brother, Sleep, *Hypnos*, removing the body of a dead soldier from the battlefield with moving tenderness, like a squad recovering one of their own.

Most people meet Death involuntarily and then say it comes too soon, even if they wished for it earlier. The Greeks felt there was no preparing for death and that when it does finally come, it is always against the will of the individual who then feels that age and illness are not such a burden any more.

They saw death more as a falling apart than as a culmination or summing up as in Hollywood movies. Death is a slow parting from the gods, and you are more likely to be fiddling with pills or with the toilet paper at the moment of death than imparting some great wisdom to loved ones or watching your life flash before your eyes. Usually, the gods leave you one at a time. Perhaps the athletic and sexual selves go first, then the working self, the healthy self, and so on—before Psyche the Mortal Self actually dies.

The Greeks believed that the gods love you most when you are near death because that is when your true character displays its nobility. We remember people for how they died, especially if they died with courage or doing something 'just like them'. These 'typical' behaviors were depicted on Greek gravestones showing the departed as 'Another' Eros, Demeter, or other god.

Contemporary American culture sees death as some shocking scandal or unusual event. This is a vestige of Christianity, which is based on the denial of death and of facts. We identify so much with the innocence of young Persephone and the personal feelings of Hera and her Facebook images that we forget the basic fact of human life. We even encase our dead in concrete as if that will save them from rotting like so much meat.

The Underworld

Hades' abode is in the far west with the setting sun, but there are many *ploutonia*, direct entrances to the Underworld, and *psychopompeia*, cliffs and ravines where souls can peek out at the upper world—and where people committed suicide.

Hades is the Dream World. You spend a great deal of your time in Hades even if Athena the Waking Self doesn't remember it. People who say they don't dream are correct in one sense: the self that dreams is not the one giving the report.

The waking world and the dream world are two sides of

Hades

existence, which is why Hades and *Zeus* are brothers. The two gods live largely separate existences, though they are also considered to be doubles. This means that you don't necessarily have to remember your dreams because they live in an entirely different place than waking gods. Nevertheless, it's a good idea to at least imagine that there is such a person as the dream self and such a place as the dream world. That is at least a polite gesture to Hades and to the other people down there.

He's always listening, even when you're awake. The Greeks imagined Hades the way we imagine the Unconscious. Hades is always in the background like a word on the tip of your tongue. From his point of view your waking life is the raw material for more dreams and not the other way around.

The Underworld is where the images of your loved ones and your memories seek permanence and rest, because the shadow of the living world is where all things lose their mortal aspect and become images. There is a joy in this 'dying' from the real world, a joy of permanence and of things revealing their essence. Often gifts to Hades were broken— *cancelled* or *killed* in Greek terms--because his realm is imaginary, not real.

You know Hades when an actual relationship or way of life 'dies' from lived experience into memory and the imagination. You might remember someone you were once close to, a place you used to live, or the person you used to be--as if you were remembering someone else, like someone from a novel or a movie. Things 'die' when they become images, so finding the god or gods in an experience 'kills' the identification with it by letting it go its own way and be its own self instead of owning it or treating it as a part of *me*.

In Hades, the souls of the dead are mere gusts of wind or flitting bats with squeaky voices or hums, because death is *voice robbing*. The dead cannot speak for themselves and they cannot speak with the living. To the Greeks, the separation of worlds was absolute, so they spent very little time worrying about ghosts.

Once the soul leaves the body, it becomes a fixed image--an *eidelon*—that dwells in Hades because it only exists in the imagination and

300

in memory. Your eidelon is the idea of you, often identified with your face, but it is also your character and reputation, including how you died.

The Greek idea of character has nothing to do with today's cult of celebrity, because we would never ask Madonna for a few wise words before the meteor crashes into the Earth. Your eidelon is your greatness of soul and style, like the Renaissance obsession with reputation, or *fama*. It shows the lasting worth of your soul, your dignity, quirks, and excellence. You give it status when you show others how to face death by dying with courage and character.

James Hillman noted that when someone beloved dies and becomes only an image or memory, an amazing transformation takes place, beginning in the eulogies. All the person's quirks, faults, and dark spots become like the rubies and emeralds in a stained glass window, so that you love him for the very things that made him seem impossible to live with. These images of character are frozen forever in Hades as the *eidelon,* the image of who that person was and the essence of his character.

Morpheus

Morpheus is the Leader of the Dreams, the *Oneiroi,* of which there are countless millions. The God of Dreams is the leader of that underworld crowd. The Greek did not *have* a dream. Instead, he *saw* a dream or said that *a dream came to me.* Dreams were imagined taking human shape with wings and appearing at the foot of the dreamer's bed and spilling their contents.

You know intuitively that dreams are good for you, even nightmares, because they get you under your daylight consciousness and everything you hold dear. Hades is *Trophonios* or Nourishing--his limitless world of images relieves the soul from the slavery of identification with the waking self and its personal life.

Dreams are independent of the dreamer and can appear to several people at the same time. They can visit you once and disappear forever or come back years later with every detail intact. They may have no

Hades

link to reality, which is why you can't be angry at your sister for something she did to you in your dream. They may appear only to reveal themselves and have nothing more to do with you, like a passing stranger.

Some dreams may be messages, but to think they are all directives from below gives them to Herakles the Hero, his self-importance and love of utility, instead of respecting dreams for themselves. The Greeks weren't naïve about dreams. They knew that the gods could send them to help or to deceive, like when Zeus misleads Agamemnon by sending him a dream full of false hopes of victory at Troy.

Sometimes the dream reminds you that you are asleep, as in *you are asleep, Achilles.* Lucid dreams are common, but most dreams do not need your conscious attention or assistance. They can manage on their own.

Your attitude towards dreams and sleep is what really matters. There are ways to act friendly towards the images below. You can stop chasing away the dream world first thing in the morning with Athena the Waking Goddess' ritual of television and coffee. You can wait a moment to feel the effect of the dream or write whatever snippets you can remember as you lie in bed. You don't need to remember everything but Jung has shown that carrying the dream around and playing it back as though you were re-reading a poem or re-examining a piece of art is almost always a productive source of insights.

James Hillman suggests inviting a single image from a dream into your waking life by simply bearing it in mind as you go about your business. Bring the black dog from your dream to the office and it will add another dimension and perhaps surprise you—and take you deeper into Hades.

You can go farther than that. You can offer the dream image gifts. These can be anything from drinking a glass of water while thinking about the black dog or going for a walk and imagining the black dog enjoying it with you. The Greeks used to pour wine and blood into graves as *offerings to the shades* because they, too, wish to taste life through you like the gods.

The Greek Gods Among Us

Animals, friends, and gifts are especially important images, and it is especially important to show thanks for a gift, just like with people. There are no rules. Guidebooks to dream symbolism need to be taken with a grain of salt. And attributing your images to some kind of collective unconscious like Jung defies belief. Dreams don't want you to pin them down or to be squeezed into a single meaning or function. They like to be discussed, engaged, and remembered but not to be explained away, just like people. Homer shows on numerous occasions his characters discussing their dreams as they wake in bed.

How you behave towards the people and animals in Hades the Dream World shows how you relate to the gods. Some may be willing to be your friend and improve your life through the almost magical powers of the 'unconscious'. If you are spending all your nights fighting monsters or running from the bogeyman, you probably need to learn to become friendlier towards people who aren't like you. You may be the one who needs to be chased down and fought, not them.

Besides, the boogeyman might be hot.

Mnemosyne

Mnemosyne, or Goddess Memory, lives in Hades because your memory is made of images. The Greeks considered Memory a goddess because memories have a life of their own and change over the years. If you try too hard and shine a light into her eyes you can't even remember things that are normally at your disposal, like the name of an actor or a password.

Memory has a spring near Hades' palace right alongside the spring of the River *Lethe,* or Forgetfulness. Uninitiated souls, destined to forget who they are, drink from the spring of Lethe, while those who drink from the cool water of the pool of Memory remember everything. You have this experience when you have a dream many times with all the details intact but still can't remember a thing when you wake up.

Remembering past events takes you out of the present, as if you are visiting the dead or going back to younger days that are lost

303

Hades

forever. As you age and lose loved ones, it's as though you have one foot planted in Hades and the other on Earth because your relationships increasingly inhabit the realm of images.

Memory was a valuable art to the ancients, who didn't have books or the Internet. Many could recite hours of Homer starting from anywhere in the story. In the Renaissance, the art of memory used exaggerated images or placed each idea in a familiar location in a house so that walking through the corridor and seeing the blue vase, for example, brought forth the images of a speech in the right order.

You can sense Memory in the midst of an experience as the sense of meaning, because Memory is about the meaning of what happened, not about the literal details of the event. It's not difficult to get into this person's mindset, because all you need to do is to hold a memory and walk around with it for a while as if it was a friend hanging out with you.

Persephone, Queen of the Underworld

Hades kidnapped and raped the daughter of Demeter the Family Self when she was just an innocent teenager, dragging her down to the Underworld to be his queen. Eventually a deal was worked out where she spent half the year with Hades and the other half with her mother in the upper world, but the experience forever changed her, as a close brush with death always does.

When Persephone returned from the Underworld with an inner depth and strangeness to life, she was called *a wonder to gods and to men.* She had become a person who no longer 'plays at being ordinary', to paraphrase the anthropologist Harvey Sacks. Persephone inevitably grew to love her husband, Hades, because death is a part of human consciousness and it is the best measure of what matters.

She is the self who is in love with death, because she's married to him.

Persephone has two aspects, like the two sides of Judy Garland. *Kore* is the innocent Maiden. She's your inner Dorothy. And then

304

The Greek Gods Among Us

there's the mesmerizing drug addict of the Carnegie Hall concerts.

The Bringer of Destruction likes to clear the air by sending stock market crashes, plagues, and ruin. Artwork shows her with a gorgon's fangs and monstrous eyes and at other times looking like a mild and gracious lady. Persephone makes you want to tear everything down or throw everything away just to clear the air and to be free of the person you think you are.

It's common to feel an adrenaline high when terrible things occur, even if you are personally devastated by the news. You may sometimes find yourself rooting for the hurricane. That is Persephone welcoming in the fresh air that comes with destruction and death, because at least something is happening and life is real again. Persephone makes you secretly glad when some beloved old object breaks, because that thing has been cluttering up your mind for years.

The Mother of the Furies, the Beautiful Avenger, and the Venerable and Awesome is often shown holding a scepter and a little coffin-shaped box full of the cream of Invisible Beauty, or the Beauty That Cannot Be Seen. This mysterious beauty belongs to the perspective of Persephone, who sees life from the viewpoint of death. She gives some to the girl, Psyche, who is your mortal Soul, but to no others. It can only be conferred upon those who truly see themselves—including Psyche the Mortal—as personified. It is the beauty of seeing yourself as someone else.

Persephone is the Star in the Apple, which is only revealed when the apple is cut in half. She makes you dead in life, which you do when you give your experiences to the gods instead of identifying with them. Persephone knows *the secret pattern*, the plan that Zeus has for you, and she reveals your hidden nature.

She is the perspective that comes when you know you are dying, when every day is a gift and the end is staring you in the face. Persephone gives the courage and wisdom of point of view that sees clearly the evanescence of a lifespan. She is the experience of caring for a dying loved one, including a pet, and the unspoken wish to die alongside him.

305

Hades

Many tombstones in Greece bear her name, because the dead person becomes a god once he lives only in images. Many dead were called Another Persephone by their survivors. Persephone washes away the person you were by pouring water over your head, just as her unrelenting glare washes away all self-importance, revealing all secrets, lies and pretense. By taking her point of view, you can live authentically, even if only at the end as in Hemingway's *The Short, Happy Life of Francis Macomber.*

Hekate

The Goddess of Witches lives at the edge of darkness in a cave by the entrance to Hades and wanders at night with the dead. Hekate is the mood of enchantment, whether a mood, an addiction, or an obsession that possesses you like a whammy. She is a god of disinterested action, because this self frankly doesn't care what happens to you and has nothing to lose.

Her magic makes things seem unreal. The Queen of the Dead, *Prytania,* hears Persephone's rape from her cave without judgment or horror, because this dark self is unfazed by terrible events and can't be dragged down by death because she already lives in the neighborhood. She can cause otherwise normal people to commit terrible acts for no reason at all but their disbelief in the reality of consequences, an increasingly common event in this era of virtual experience.

The goddess of ghosts, garbage, and poison—and of everything polluted or shameful--is the terrible secret you keep and the dreaded fate you fear. She is the compulsion to rubberneck on the highway in fascination. She is the strange light shining in the darkness—perhaps a flashlight, a torch, or the headlights of a semi heading straight at you.

Hekate Skylakagetis, the Leader of the Dogs, is the sound of barking dogs in the distance and of howls during fearful nights under dark moons. She is the urge to know the dark truth without judgment, like a dog sniffing feces and urine. She is a god of laughing hyenas, of police at the site of a murder, and of the ruins of 9/11.

The Greek Gods Among Us

In the artwork, she holds a torch to help Demeter look for Persephone after she goes missing. The three are depicted as friends. Sometimes Hekate wears a gorgon face like Persephone that can freeze you in place, watching events instead of participating in them. Or she may have three faces and three bodies: a lion, a dog, and a mare.

Hekate *Selena*, the Far Shooting Moon, is the witch's moon and the realm of magic. Her familiars are the black female dog and the weasel, formerly human friends of hers.

The Friend of the Hopeless is the last minute miracle that saves everything. The only Titan whom the gods allow to retain her ancient powers, Hekate is there when you win the lottery or the terrible MRI reading turns out to be someone else's. Hekate *Propylaia,* the One Before the Gate, watches over literal crossroads and major changes in your life. The Goddess of the Third Way is the unforeseen turn of events and the way life surprises you.

The Greeks prayed to Hekate to *free us from imaginary fears,* like worrying about what others think about you or how you will react to some future event. They asked her to *give us pure desires* so that you can live your life truly instead of trying to impress others or to fulfill someone else's idea of how to live. This ugly face sees through vanity, petulance, and the compulsion to please others.

The World's Key Bearer holds freedom's key, because Hekate allows you to think the unthinkable and to tell the unbearable truth.

Charon

Charon the ferryman escorts dead souls to Hades across the River of Woe, *Acheron,* or the River of Hate, *Styx,* prodding the benumbed travelers along with his wry humor while insulting the obese, who make for tough rowing. His character resembles Hermes the Guide of Souls, only without style and sophistication.

He is the jade. He's the carnival extra with tattoos gazing over the chubby suburbanites. Charon can be darkly entertaining in his crankiness, like an irritable patient who charms the doctors with his

307

Hades

spunkiness and beats the odds amid his constant complaints. Pictured as a skinny old man, Charon is a roughneck who feels at home in the boondocks of those dark waters. His variations include the Ghost of Christmas Past and a living skeleton in a cape, calm and pensive to the extreme as he waits for you to join him.

This famous miser demands a coin from each soul as fare, placed in the mouth of the dead. Souls with no money have to wait by the banks of the river for a hundred years or find the secret path into Hades.

The ritual coin and cookie show that the way out of the natural world and into Hades is not a literal one. It is metaphorical, because Hades is comprised of images. The coin and the cookie are the metaphor, the 'as if' which frees you to speak about the gods without confusing images with reality. This honors Zeus' dictum that *the realms of mankind and the gods are separate.*

Askalaphus

Askalaphus is a son of *Styx*, the River of Hate, which suits him perfectly.

After Hades brings Persephone to his Underworld palace, this gardener seals her fate when he vows to see her eat the food of the dead—the seeds of the pomegranate, the fruit that looks like a graveyard inside.

When Hermes arrives to fetch Persephone in his chariot, Askalaphus cries out, *Having seen the Lady Kore pick a pomegranate from a tree in your orchard and eat seven seeds, I am ready to bear witness that she has tasted the food of the dead.*

Hades grins widely at the news like an underworld boss, for Persephone is now bound forever to his realm. Hades tells Askalaphus to perch on the back of the chariot for the ride up to the world of daylight.

Askalaphus is the lowlife. He is your seedy self and your friend in low places. This *bird of ill omen* is any unlucky sign. He is the loser and the snitch, at least from the point of view of selves like Apollo the Higher Self, Athena the Normal Self, and Hera the Personal Self, who stand for upper world values like character, accomplishment, and reputation.

308

The Greek Gods Among Us

Artwork shows him with wings like a screech owl, *askalaphos,* larger than the common owl of Athena. Demeter becomes so angry with Askalaphus for telling on her daughter that she pushes him down a hole and covers it with a rock, turning him into a spotted lizard, *askalabos,* or *devoid of feelings,* as in 'he's a lizard and a snake'.

Nemesis

Zeus is reality, including your fate. He is the facts and what happens. His female cousin is *Nemesis,* or Ruin, the daughter of the dread goddess, Night.

She is whatever destroys you, especially if you cause it yourself by smoking cigarettes or driving drunk, for instance.

Nemesis visits many successful people, who may have one little fault that catches up with them later, like a strong libido or a love of gambling. She is the crutch which acts like a secret agreement between the gods that says, 'I'll live the way I want and look the other way' until the final downfall or diagnosis. Nemesis brings the long planned revenge of whatever self you have been ignoring or pushing away, like the one who wants you to be an artist, live a healthy life, or follow a budget.

Nemesis comes from *nemo,* or 'to distribute or deal out'—like the image of Zeus scooping out fates arbitrarily from a jug, blindly allotting good and bad luck to each individual. She is your *moira,* your portion in life, and how it ends. *Nemesis* can also mean Indignation or Righteous Anger, because you get to know her when you get what's coming to you for angering or ignoring a self for too long.

She is more final than the Furies, *Erinyes,* who torment you with neuroses, guilt and sleeplessness if you commit bloodshed or forsake your family. Nemesis shapes your *eidelon,* the image of your character, because how you handle your death will be among the things people most remember about you.

The Greeks called her *fair of form* and pictured her as a beautiful woman frowning beneath a veil, sometimes holding a bridle and a measuring rod—beautiful and terrible, because revenge is sweet.

Hades

The Balance of Life punishes anyone who forgets his limitations by acting conceited, flaunting his success, or making others jealous. Philip of Macedon prayed to the gods for some slight misfortune to balance out his great series of victories in war and was relieved when his beloved horse died, hoping that would satisfy the gods and quell the jealousy of others.

Nemesis can reverse even the most fortunate life in a day or even in an hour--through an accident, a diagnosis, or a market crash, which are Zeus' thunderbolts.

Don't ever swear that such and such will never be:
The gods resent it, and the outcome's theirs.

Aidos

Hades means *you hide us* and the variant *Aidos* means *shame, respect,* or *humility. Aidoneus* is his double as the rapist of Persephone. In Hades, all secrets come out because Death cannot be lied to.

The god Shame is the shameful betrayal of the body with old age and illness. This unwanted guest thrusts himself upon you when you suddenly realize that the young people find you old or that you are nowhere near as nice as you think or successful as you hoped.

The Greeks did not value a quiet conscience or good character as much as we do. They were more interested in public esteem, which you get by making the world a better place, perhaps by leaving money to fund a library or to improve the navy, as benefactors in ancient Athens did. Aidoneus wants you to be 'somebody' before it's too late. He is the self who looks back in shame at your fear and hesitation, when it was the ticking clock that you should have been so worried about.

Styx

Hades lies at the center of a giant marsh circled nine times by the River *Styx,* or *Hate,* fed by the rivers *Acheron,* Sorrow and *Lethe,*

310

The Greek Gods Among Us

Forgetfulness. Along its wild coast, Persephone has a grove of ancient poplars and willows that quickly shed their seeds at the edge of the darkness, for she is the darkest part of your soul and the part that knows how short life really is.

Styx is Hatred. To the Greeks, Hatred has a life of its own. It performs an important function in the psyche: it keeps the gods apart in their distinct realms and binds them to their oaths. Your family self 'hates' your sexual self and your athletic self 'hates' your lazy self, because they have separate identities and they strive against each other to affect your behavior. The gods are our multiple selves and each one of them competes to live through our experience.

The very geography of Hades shows that the Greeks didn't imagine a solid self like a rock we do. Instead it was a marsh, with many islands and waterways flowing from different sources. Their image of consciousness is broken up into distinct situations, so that experience is an archipelago of selves more like the map of Greece than the map of Kansas.

In their ethos, Hate is not the opposite of Love. *Styx* is a much younger god than *Eros* and is completely unrelated. Love cannot cure Hate because Hate is permanent and final and doesn't want to be cured. Trying to change it into something else is a recipe for denial, disappointment, or worse, because if you truly love your friends you'll accept them as they are, with all their faults.

Hatred was admired in the Renaissance, a time of great individualism. Enemies were cultivated as carefully as friends because they provide psychological landmarks and contrasts. Enemies are a great motivator.

Styx has strangely hyperactive children named Zeal, *Zellus,* Victory, *Nike,* Force, *Bia,* and Strength, *Cratos*—not exactly what you would expect to discover in Hades. This is Death's call to get things done now, like the depressed artist in Durer's *Melancholia* woodcuts who works frantically at a desk with a skull on it while the clock hangs on the wall in the background.

Beyond Styx lie *Erebus,* Darkness, and the Plains of

311

Hades

Asphodel, a gray region named after the dull white flower that grows there. There the worn out souls of ordinary people twitter around mindlessly, forgetting their unremarkable lives. Further on in the darkness lies the palace of Hades and Persephone, glimmering with jewels in the darkness, just beyond a three-road junction where the judges of the dead await the newly dead and all the secrets come out.

Tartarus

Tartarus, or 'Deep Place', is a pit where most of the Titans are imprisoned--the unshaped forces that the gods defeated in their war ages ago. The Titans are *not fully human in form* because they are drives and blind instincts that have no clear images. They are our current psychology with its gigantic and imprecise, inhuman concepts like Depression, Self, Mid-Life Crisis, Inner Child, and Trickster.

Greek mythology is far more precise and completely human in shape. The Greeks related to mental states as individuals first instead of as concepts or 'parts of myself'.

The region of Hades most like our Hell, Tartarus, is reserved for extraordinary criminals who offend human decency and dignity. There they are tortured forever and usually in a fitting manner.

Tantalus was the former guest of the gods who stole their magic nectar and cooked up his own son for them to eat. Now he suffers perpetual thirst and hunger with a pool of water and luscious grapes ever swaying just out of reach.

Ixion spins on a wheel of fire for trying to seduce Hera. Sisyphus, who revealed one of Zeus' affairs, rolls a boulder up a hill only to see it roll down the other side. Tartarus is for fruitless tasks like weaving a rope while an ass eats the other end or filling a sieve with water. There's room for every kind of neurosis there.

Tartarus is the sense of being stuck. You are in Tartarus when you obsess over your weight or some physical flaw or repeat some destructive behavior. It is addiction and neurosis and anything that makes you feel hopeless, depressed, and unable to change. The images in

312

Tartarus are frozen forever and are a source of anxieties and neuroses for daytime selves.

But they have the right to exist, because selves like the Addict or the Fat Self form part of your *eidelon*. Even if you lose weight, the Fat Self will remain in Tartarus, an unchangeable side of your character.

The Greeks said to *honor all the gods*. We can't pick and choose among them. We only invite disaster and revenge when we try to get rid of them, because that makes them angry. Calling them 'our' problems or hang-ups presumes that we own them and then only in order to destroy them or let them go. In the Greek view, what we can do as humans is to try to shape the selves to conform to an ideal. We can make them into statues. And then we can change how we relate to them and sometimes counter one problematic self with another, opposing self.

Obsessing over obesity only locks you in a battle with a Fat Self, while befriending gods like Artemis the Healthy Self or Hermes the Runner by doing things they like to do and getting into their mindset while you do it counters that self without eliminating it. Only Herakles thinks he has to destroy and conquer everything that stands in his way.

Elysium

A few select people skip Hades altogether and are carried alive up to Olympus directly by some god. There they drink from the pool of Memory and recall the details of their lives forever.

This has nothing to do with personal virtue or goodness. Menelaus gets in because he is the son-in-law of Zeus. Pablo Picasso and Maria Callas get in because they are legends in their own time. The Greeks also said that people who disappear are *taken by a god* and hidden from view.

Elysium is celebrity, like Hollywood stars and famous entrepreneurs whose images are so widespread that they walk like gods among us. Their images are immortal, whatever may happen to the actual person. Indeed, some celebrities like Madonna and Michael Jackson seem to suffer from their celebrity because they identify with it so closely they can

313

Hades

no longer be human and natural. Celebrity thrives in the media, because images are immortal and don't grow old like humans.

In Elysium it is never winter, the meadows are always heavy with the scent of roses and frankincense, and golden fruit hangs from the trees. It is a Greek idea of Paradise, but Elysium is any ideal version of your favorite place in the world. Helen and Achilles party on forever there, reciting Homer with the actual heroes and hanging out with the A-list. The souls in Elysium choose when to be born again.

Individuals who attain Elysium three times move on to the Isles of the Blessed, even farther to the west, where they become a double of a god, like Marilyn Monroe as Venus or Albert Einstein as Apollo. These people are no longer only human because their images now stand for aspects of human nature and universal truths.

But even in Elysium, the dead have no power over the living and never even speak with the gods, except the ones who visit the Underworld like Hermes, Dionysus, and Underworld Zeus. Hades is a one-way street and a dead end, literally, because even if you make it to the Isles of the Blessed and your image is immortalized in hours of film footage, you will never be heard from again and you won't personally be there to enjoy it.

Pluto

Hades is called *Pluto,* the Wealthy One, and *Dis,* the Rich Father. He is shown in the artwork holding the cornucopia, a horn full of fruits and treats.

He is Wealth.

First off, he owns all the metals in the ground. The Un-Sacrificed to God Below doesn't receive gifts because he inherits everything anyway. He has few temples unless you count the graveyards everywhere.

Money brings depth to life, which is why rich people are more interesting than ordinary folks. Observing the rich and famous shows us how humans would act if they could act freely like gods. The wealthy don't need the approval of others, so authenticity comes to the fore. Style is

314

paramount because it shows what metal you are made of and what nobility resides in your soul. Once money is not an issue, class and culture become the overriding issues.

Because Pluto is rich in images he is the Wealthy One, the Nourishing One, the Hospitable One and the Receiver of Many Guests, *Polydegmon.* He is the wealth of the imagination and its depth.

He is also wise. The rich seem to be on to something. Hades *Eubouleus,* the Good Counselor, steers you towards meaningful work or gets you to do things now because death is waiting patiently for your arrival. He would have you keep a few trusted friends rather than play the social butterfly like Hermes or Aphrodite, or worry about other people's opinions like Hera the Social Goddess.

Local Heroes

A local Hero is anyone who makes a difference in his community and deserves to be remembered, like the soldier statues on the town green. The Greeks honored local heroes as weak but supernatural powers, some with yearly festivals including banquets and races. Heroes were prayed to for inspiration and gifts.

The revered dead were a source of local pride and patriotism. White animals were sacrificed to the gods during the daytime with their necks severed facing up, while black animals were sacrificed to the heroes at night with their heads facing down so the blood runs into the ground. The participants did not eat the meat for the heroes as they did at the feasts of the gods.

Heroes' graves were typically hollows in the ground like sunken graves instead of raised tombstones. Some dwelled in caves while others had a stone at the market, a city gate, or some boundary where they protected the city.

Some heroes were said never to have died but to have translated into another dimension at a particular spot. My father was a local politician and when he died, the town named Well Number Two after him—

Hades

as if he turned into a spring like so many Greek heroes.

Often little was known about the hero besides his name and even that was sometimes forgotten like on a worn out tombstone. Many had nicknames like Hero Physician, Hero General, Hero Flower Bearer, Zeus of the Underworld, or just The Local Hero—like a face in an old family album that no one can identify.

People walked quietly past the graves because some of the heroes were malevolent and could send disease, paralysis, or local problems. To keep them quiet, everyone had to be given a funeral without exception. Even a Greek boy who was sold as a prostitute by his father was bound to bury him and give him rites, although he was not obliged to take care of him in his old age.

If there were worries about haunting, the Greeks would chain a statue to the grave to keep the soul in place, but most graves were places of worship and family gatherings. Some families would picnic and set a place for the Departed or the Blessed One or offer gifts at the gravesite like wreaths, ribbons, cakes or favorite foods, as in Mexico. There might be a picture of the dead person on the gravestone posing as Hades or Persephone or some other god, or the dead might be shown in a characteristic moment of pleasure: drinking and feasting with friends, sitting with the spouse, or out hunting.

Some called the dead a Fortunate Fellow because he was no longer in pain, but there was no envying the dead. They craved life so much that *blood for the shades* was spilled on the ground to give them a momentary taste of it, like a drug.

Local heroes were consulted for cures and prophecy, but only at the gravesite. Anyone with a serious question or problem could sleep by the grave hoping for some advice in a dream or upon awakening, a process called incubation. Before going to sleep, the pilgrim would ask a question in an either/or form: 'should I do this or do that?' This lets the psyche articulate a sign during sleep without asking for a broad explanation that would be hard to interpret. You can do this any night when you need advice from the gods by asking an either/or question before going to bed.

Just ask a particular god out loud which of two options you should pursue, rather than a general question, the way the Oracle's had supplicants do.

Nyx

Nyx, or Night, is a primordial goddess of Creation. She is the daughter of Chaos and the sister of Darkness, *Erebus,* and her children include Eros, the twins Sleep and Death, Nemesis, Blame, and Woe.

She is the unconscious and everything you can never know. Nyx is more mysterious than even Artemis and Hekate, who are usually known only indirectly.

Like Hades, Night is mysterious and cannot be explained away. She personifies parts of the brain that can never be accessed and have little to do with your personal history or identity.

Night is the ability to step backwards from identifications and not be any of the things you think you are, like your name or your history or attachments. This can be a spiritual move, like the *neti neti* of the saint, or it can be forgetting or simply not knowing.

But Night is not evil. Her darkness is full of possibilities, which is why she was present at the Greek story of Creation. As Heraklitus said, *when men die there awaits them what none can expect and few can imagine.*

She is the mother of the *keres,* devils that sneak up on a person and devour him or lead him to his doom. Vases show keres stalking up to drag an unwitting fighter on the battlefield towards Hades, but a ker can kill you through illness, age, or accidents as well. They are Imminent Death personified.

Moving On

When you have had enough of images and dreaming and you feel isolated or depressed, it may be time to turn back from images to reality.

The easiest way out of Hades is to follow Hermes the Guide, who moves easily between the Underworld and the world of living. You do

317

Hades

this when you wake up or fall asleep easily and when you can easily get absorbed in a book or a movie. Cultivating Hermes' sense of humor puts Hades' depth in perspective, because it's no good wringing your hands about death all day when there's fun to be had among the living.

Dionysus, who also travels down there, can also lead you up. You can put your feelings to good use with him, like when you turn a dark mood into a poem or you go to the theater or get some culture in his honor, so you can see what people have done with the darkness. A sexual fantasy or a good stiff drink might get you there as well.

Or you can do what you have to do by following Zeus, who also knows the Underworld. Changing the world in some way and being decisive shakes off the dreamy unreality of Hades. Zeus governs your fate and destiny, so he would have you do something worthwhile with the time you have left. Remember: Hades and death are waiting for you.

CONCLUSION

There is no Self. There are only selves. Consciousness evolved with the brain, adding one self or partial self at a time. We are a chorus of competing motivations.

But if there is no single Self, how do we make sense of experience?

The Greek gods provide a framework for these floating, competing selves. They offer a statue for every impulse and they grant the selves the dignity of independence. These selves are not 'parts of me'. They are interpersonal. Greek ritual shows how to relate to these mental states using our highly evolved social skills—and preferably as friends. We can always try to set the stage for friendship, but friendship with a god is ultimately the god's decision, just like people.

The gods want to live through you for their own pleasure, not yours. Each one sets off specific riffs of behavior through individuals, groups, things, and events. The gods are more like the selfish gene than like a concerned parent or Disney animal. The gods are made for this world, the real and dangerous place where we evolved.

Nothing happens without the gods. They are the very shape of experience.

The gods offer a vast repertoire of roles to play and people to be. They are a rich cultural tool-kit that can be tailored by each individual for new life situations. The gods are metaphorical and real at the same time, for they personify the actual world around us: our impulses and attitudes, capacities and inclinations, and the events of our lives.

Aphrodite is sex, love and beauty, personified. She is the actual seashell and the actual orgasm. Above all, she is an individual— someone you can know in your personal experience. Personifying allows us to engage entire personalities and abilities through recursion, the mind's ability to lump things together as a unit. Personifying re-enchants a world emptied out by concepts and its imagined, master Conceptualizer.

Conclusion

The gods can take any shape. The gods can take the shape of anything that can be personified. The gods reside in the meaning of the experience.

They do not offer salvation. The gods are only interested in people through whom they can incarnate as Excellence. They do not ask for your belief and have no interest in your humiliation. The Greek gods do not ask you to deny reality, for Reality is Zeus and he reigns supreme. The gods offer no other, imaginary world where you go when you die but they do offer a way *to know what it is like to be a god* in the world here and now. The gods are knowable within experience, and this knowledge brings joy, help, and meaning.

When a man drinks himself to death, the doctor says he died of cirrhosis of the liver and he is correct, for he speaks as Apollo, who is the medical facts. Yet it is also true that *Dionysus took him,* and to speak that way does not contradict reality for it is meant metaphorically. And it gives his death meaning and dignity, which is pleasing to Zeus, who stands for the dignity of human life.

So let us throw off the rule of the ugly Titans like Self, Unconscious, mid-life crisis, Inner Child, neurosis, and depression—monsters who are *unlike gods and men in shape.* Let them join the long ranks of the many ancient terrors that have ruled over lost civilizations—the hideous artifacts and fetishes of exaggeration and punishment, including monstrosities like the Lamb of God, the bloody crucifixion, and the four horsemen of the Apocalypse. The ugliness grimaces through the ages, its history written in human blood, the destruction of the environment, and the suffering of animals. It's one horror after the next as you flee these galleries in the museum, your mind full of ancient nightmares.

You take the next left turn into the Greek galleries, and suddenly you find yourself by an open colonnade of windows with glorious sunlight streaming through the flowing shears. You gaze around the room in astonishment. It's as if you've stumbled upon a cocktail party of the most beautiful people on Earth. There are the gods walking, standing, lounging with a drink in hand, chatting, gossiping, so elegant and intriguing--and

320

sexy. You recognize some faces and overhear bits of conversation as you begin to mingle freely with the gods, who embody your own uncanny nature.

You don't need a Self to make sense of life. It's the things we do that are interesting, not us per se. The single Self is lonely, by definition. When you lose the Self you gain a world of selves.

The gods are the other people you can be, Dear Psyche. They allow you to meet this complex world with your own startling complexity and variety. The gods are the way to be 'someone else'—to attain Excellence and thereby *know what it is like to be a god for a time.* The greatest joy in life is to see your self as someone else, and the way to be someone else is to let someone else be *me.*

All good things come from the gods.